Discovering
Christian Witchcraft

A Beginner's Guide
for Everyday Practice

Sveta Lisica

DISCOVERING
CHRISTIAN
WITCHCRAFT

A Beginner's Guide
for Everyday Practice

EMYLE D. PRATA | SARA RAZTRESEN

Dedication

Mimi says:

This is dedicated to everyone who tried to break my spirit with evangelical ideals and societal roles, family, community, and strangers alike. I have worked out my own salvation through fear, tears, and trembling, and I have found peace, which is reflected in this work.

To my children, who will grow up believing in a world of mundane and magical things, and will always be supported, no matter their faith or path in this world. This book is my way of showing them to stand in your belief.

And to my friends, Sara, Lina, Hannah, and Melissa, who dragged me, kicking and screaming, into the public view: I love you.

Sara says:

For myself, there are so many people I could dedicate this book to. My friends and family, especially, deserve a shout-out, as they support me in all the things I do, even when it takes a couple tries to explain what those things actually are to folks who aren't in that Christian Witchy life. To have my closest and most cherished people so dedicated to listening, supporting, challenging, and rooting for me is one of the biggest blessings I can count.

Moreover, this book is dedicated to the entire Christian Witch community. You deserve the type of faith walk that'll heal you rather than harm you, and that'll empower you rather than suffocate you, and I hope you find the beginnings of that in these pages, no matter where you are in your journey. You are the reason this book exists, and what was once a simple, personal part of my life has become something that unites us in the very threads of humanity: in love, in hope, and in trust as we walk on the path ahead.

And in kind with Mimi, this is dedicated especially to good friends Mimi, Lina, Hannah, and Fr. Kyle, who have helped my solitary, grouchy self understand the meaning of community and mentorship. You're all wonderful. I love you all.

Contents

Section 1		1
1.	Framing the Concept of a Christian Witch	2
2.	The Word "Witch" Before Jesus	8
3.	Magic in the Time of Jesus	34
4.	Superstitions of Witchcraft in Europe	53
Section 2		65
5.	The Shift in the Perception of the Word "Witch"	66
6.	Why Call Ourselves Christian Witches?	72
7.	The Husk (or Shell) of God	83
8.	The Divine Feminine and You	100
Section 3		113
9.	The Fundamentals of Magic and Its Traces in Jesus's Life	114
10.	The Basics of Divination	126
11.	Preparing to Enter the Unseen Realm	138
12.	Tools That Can Aid Your Spellwork	159
13.	The Basics of Spellwork	176
14.	Incorporating Heritage and Culture Into Your Craft	198
15.	The (Syncretized) Wheel of the Year	205

Section 4   223

16. The Christian Witch and Angels   224

17. The Christian Witch and Demons   244

18. Other Spirits a Christian Witch May Encounter   257

19. Ancestor Work as a Christian Witch   267

Section 5   277

Going Forth with Confidence and Courage   278

Acknowledgements   281

About the Authors   282

References and Suggested Reading   284

Bonus Material   289

Section 1

An Introduction to Christian Witchcraft

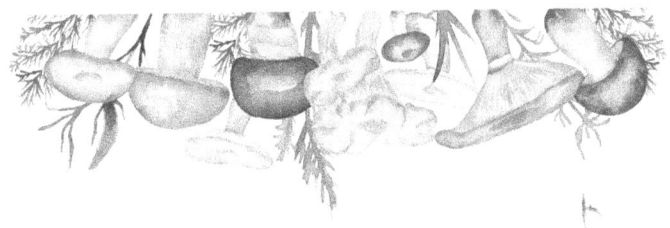

Chapter One

Framing the Concept of a Christian Witch

T WO THOUSAND YEARS AGO, a Man walked this Earth and spoke to dozens of people without hesitation. He spoke about loving one another, about forgiveness and faith, and about freedom—first for His people, living under the Roman empire, and then for all people.

In the end, it got Him killed by a callous, foreign imperial regime completely indifferent to the lives of those that dared speak at all.

For all the people to take up His message, however, there were also many people who didn't understand or accept it. Among Jesus's own people, the Jewish folks of occupied Judaea, there were those that questioned the validity of Jesus's role in their religion, not convinced that He properly fitted the strict conditions of the Messiah, and so they nobly continued living the religion and traditions of their forefathers. Then there were others who might've believed He was the Messiah, but were afraid to say it under Roman rule. These were people who didn't feel they could challenge the power structures and social conventions of the time. Rather than speak out, many stayed silent, internalizing their despair and rage towards invaders whose uncomfortable presence was unavoidable in their own homeland.

It's not to say that this wasn't understandable, of course: the institution that put this Man to death was terrifying. It swallowed nations whole as it progressed through Europe and the Near East alike, and the shadow of death and destruction loomed wherever Caesar's face was, warning those nations from trying, like Jonah, to escape the belly of the beast. And the way Jesus's people knew, the traditions they had, were a surefire way to stay in the good graces of God, anyhow. These new teachings were strange and subversive, and their Teacher, even stranger. So strange that some of His teachings were even rejected and doubted and questioned by His own disciples, never mind those who stayed skeptical.

Of course, all the fancy "miracles"—or *magic*, or *sorcery*, or any other thing He was accused of doing—didn't help His case in the least.

But let's fast forward two thousand years into today. What has become of this Man's new philosophy, and the new style of faith that came out of it? What fruits did this new religion bear, and in what way did it dismantle old social institutions, as the message of love and equality in the New Testament commanded us to do?

Are men and women considered equal in their power, wisdom, and worth as humans?

Are people able to un-align themselves with that strict, binary idea of gender in the first place?

Are all people, no matter their race, religion, sexual orientation, so on and so forth, considered friends and neighbors, and cherished as members of our communities?

Are churches still places of refuge, where those in need can get whatever help they ask for, any time they ask?

Are the mysteries, miracles, and yes, *magic* that make up any religion, but especially this religion, remembered and respected in these churches? Are they recognized as things we *all*, as children of God made in His image, have the power to access and understand?

We don't think we have to answer these questions. We think everyone here holding this book might know the answers already, even if they can't put it into words just yet. And we think you all have every right to be angry about it. We certainly are. Each day that passes reminds us how cruel it is that our birthright—magic, or miracles, or wonders, or whatever you'd like to call it—has been stolen from us, and that our way to connect to God directly has been put in the hands of church leaders who harm and divide us from the ones we love. They tell us that we need to cut ourselves off from people not like us; they tell us that we need to be *warriors of God* and then take away our heaven-sent weapons, as well as the knowledge of how to use them.

They use this wonderful Man's teaching *as* a weapon, and with it, they beat down the very people this Man came to liberate and heal.

Sara says:

I have been a Christian Witch since I was a teenager, just beginning to understand the world around me. Since then, there's something I've come to understand: give it enough time, and everything that was once new and shiny and exciting will settle down like an old house, creaking and groaning and sinking into foundations that we thought we'd renovated. By exploring the way of miracles and magic, and the unseen realm of spirits, including angels, demons, and even other pagan deities (which, yes, very much exist), I have learned how to not only talk to my God, but how to listen to the answers, too. I have come to understand the power of faith, and I have learned how to use the spiritual energy in my body, the *magic*, much the way I've learned since birth to use my muscles and my mind.

And I have learned that the modern people that claim to follow the Man that is Jesus Christ really did not *ever* know this Man of subversion, magic, mysticism, and radical, liberating change—nor did they ever want to.

What was once a new philosophy that defied tradition and handed Jesus over into the hands of death has *become* tradition, heavy and restrictive and cold. The institution that Jesus once spoke against had, by the 4th century, picked up His words and used them as the latest tool of social power, with emperors and church fathers alike destroying any evidence of dissent, different opinions, or even Scripture itself that challenged people to upset the social order of *man and woman, slave and freeman, Jew and Greek,* for a brave new world.

That's why for me, being a Christian Witch means putting myself in the same position as the Apostles: carrying messages from a divine source of Wisdom that upset that current social order and turned it on its head, earning me the ridicule and resentment of those who choose not to see. It means committing what those caught in the snares of established tradition and doctrine will call heresy; it means wearing that heresy like a badge of honor, defiant and brave and strong no matter what ridicule someone throws at me, because I know the One that told me to wear it. And frankly, I trust Him more than I trust any institution (or any Book they clearly tampered with while claiming it was God-written).

The world of Christian witchcraft is, in simplest terms, a return to the basics, and a rediscovery of the God who made our souls through practices, philosophies, and Scriptures that have always been there—ones that were hidden, nearly erased, redefined, or waved off. It's a path that has made me closer to God than any day in church ever has. It's a practice where I have absolutely nothing to fear, and everything to explore; it's a world where my peace grows every day by virtue of not only faith in God, but faith in the strength He gave me to navigate both the seen and unseen worlds.

It's remembering that, like Jesus Christ, we are all human, and we are all divine, and we are all capable of changing this world for the better.

I hope that as you come to read through this book, that you, too, can begin to see what we Christian Witches see, and that you, too, might tear down the barriers mankind has put between you and God. May this help you reclaim the peace and power that God meant for you to have, and may it embolden you to look in the faces of those who accuse you and smile—brave, bold, and joyful knowing that you are free.

Emyle (Mimi) Says:

One of my most distinct childhood memories was sitting in a dusty little church house that reeked of conviction and Kentucky summer sweat. In the middle of a hefty dose of preaching and A-men-ing, a woman broke out in sobs and began babbling. My Mamaw, who had been shushing me and giving me papers to draw on, snapped into full attention and began speaking in rhythmic answers, all in plain English. After the woman stopped and fell to the floor, writhing with the Holy Spirit, Mamaw shrank back against the pew and took in a few deep breaths. I asked her why she was talking like that, and what happened to that woman; I was terrified but also completely enrapt in the mysteries of the moment. She shrugged and pulled out a tissue from her purse, and while patting the sweat that rose on her forehead, said, "God just put it on my heart. He gave me a knowin'."

What does all of this have to do with witchcraft? That knowing, that spirit, and all the stories and superstitions that swirled around my Appalachian family leads us back to what we call Granny Witchin'. It's a way of life in the mountains, the secrets told to only family members. And when a Granny died, a little more of that magic died with her. From using the Bible to cure bleeding wounds and make powerful protection prayers, to studying the signs of nature and following them as signs from God (because after all, God made nature, so it must be His will), the magic of the mountains has always called to me. Knowing what little bit I did (as the women who could have taught me both died when I was about seven or eight years old), I listened to the stories in my memory and I kept that shimmer of magic in my heart. The 90's, however, saw a new wave of Satanic Panic, anti-semitic New Age shenanigans, and witchcraft come back into the mainstream. *The Craft, Sabrina the Teenage Witch,* and *Buffy* were the *it* thing, and digging into witchcraft was edgy and cool. Books with magic and witchcraft in them were usually Wiccan based (Silver Ravenwolf was very popular), and many appropriated a lot of indigenous practices. It all felt so very *off* to me. This wasn't just about the healing and the living and the weaving of mystical with mundane to survive; this was power and glory and making yourself *known*.

And while I learned some of that and respected its place in my journey of studying, I knew it wasn't meant for me. My path was to follow the words of Jesus, the tug of the Holy Spirit, and to listen to that small, still voice while I baked bread and made potions with flowers and roots. Combine that with a very strict evangelical upbringing, with a mother who had abandoned her own witchy ways, I was constantly at war with myself. I was never certain that what I was doing would be welcomed by God, but I couldn't see herbs, stones, praying, and the moon being a bad thing to use if God came first and He made them. So I just called myself "crunchy," "hippie," "natural." None of them sat right, but how could I explain that I prayed with the candles etched with Jesus's name and image, left offerings, and did my routines and even fancy rituals (herbal bath soaks) for good health without being labeled a witch?

Come 2020, when the world was turned upside down, I was finally able to be with myself long enough to really talk to God. Not the way I heard in church as a child, not the way my new Assembly of God church spoke, but the way one of my children would come and talk to me. I took out the Bible that I had read so many times before (and picked apart with my Papaw before he passed, God rest his soul) and I started doing Bibliomancy like I was shown as a child. I started going down rabbit holes, asking "Why do we have to do it this way?" and I started looking *beyond* the Bible. I went to the archives, church libraries, YouTube, and yes, even TikTok, to absorb everything that I could. I just knew somewhere that I would find others like me to justify why I am the way I am: witchy, honoring my ancestors and letting them guide me in my dreams, and loving Jesus and what He stood for. After feeling so disconnected from everyone, I finally found the family to lean on and learn from in my Christian Witch community.

What does it mean to be a Christian Witch? To me, it means living your truth, carrying on those family traditions of healing and divining the words of God, and letting your love pour from you as it did from Jesus.

Our Goal for You

In this book, the aim is simple: to get you started on your way. If you're already familiar with something like witchcraft, then what you'll soon come to find out is that no one is truly an expert, and no one has all the answers. It's like any craft or art: you can study and study and study, you can practice until your hands fall off and your brains feel like they'll leak from your ears, you can work night and day to finally achieve perfection—and then you'll discover some new technique or talent that you didn't realize you *needed*. Some new and shiny idea will come that'll unlock a whole new rabbit hole for you to jump down, some great philosophy that'll turn everything you *were* doing on its head.

We can't promise you any One Single Answer. We can only show you, through our research, our magic, and our experiences, how you might create your own answers with the One High God. That way, with these introductory tools we lay out for you here, you'll be emboldened to shape the clay of your practice in the way that feels right to you. In this book, you can expect to find the stepping stones you need to be at peace knowing your craft is not something that will separate you from God and His Son and His Spirit, but in fact bring you closer to Them all. You'll find tips on where to look, and why, for your cultural connections, your magical formulae, and your development of theological understanding.

The first section of this book is entirely focused on the *how* of Christian witchcraft: how we're able to do this work despite the many verses people *think* condemn the craft, and the ways in which this work has manifested over the course of centuries of Christian tradition. This encompasses a detailed overview of some of the most famous verses people use as an argument against the concept of Christian magic, as well as context into what the word *witch* really meant to people (and why Christian magic wasn't called witchcraft). The next section is about the *why*: why you would ever take on this label or this path: how the word *witch* has changed in the modern era, the sociopolitical concepts this encompasses, and what it means to be a Christian witch. The third section of the book discusses basic magical techniques and ideas that will help you build your craft into something unique and personal, the fourth section the world of spirits that you may encounter or choose to incorporate on this path (as well as how to understand them), and the fifth is where this journey ends.

With the many years of witchery with God we have under our belts, we're hoping to give you what we never had: a proper guide, a solid starting point, into a path that'll help you find God in the places you never thought He'd be. This is your first foray into a world that'll break your heart just as much as it'll heal it, that'll make you angry as much as it'll make you jubilant, and that won't *fill* you with power, but will instead remind you of the power you've always had—power that mainstream religion didn't want you to know you had. It's a path that'll help you see *and* perceive, hear *and* understand. But once you are aware of the things this path illuminates for you, let us warn you here: you will never be able to shut your eyes to them again.

If you're tired of walking through life with your eyes shut, though, then by all means, turn the page and let your eyes—and your soul—forever be open to a world that remained unseen for far too long.

Chapter Two
The Word "Witch" Before Jesus

N OW, LET'S ADDRESS THE obvious elephant in the room: in the Bible are plenty of verses that, allegedly, mention witchcraft in the Bible. If you're still in contact with Christian family, and you ever talk to them about your craft—hell, if you just encounter a stranger on the street and mention the words "Christian" and "Witch" in the same sentence—chances are you're going to get this question:

A Christian Witch? But I thought the Bible forbids witchcraft! How can you be both?

Get used to this question, because you'll be seeing it a *lot*. We've seen it several times a day, from Christians, atheists, and pagans alike, because all of our history books and Sunday schools are full of *witch trials for those wicked witches all tied up with demons, devilry!* However, anyone who takes a moment to look further into these incidents will see, quite plainly, that the "witches" put to the pyre were less broomstick-riding, plague-causing, devil-loving witches, but more political minorities like Jewish people, women who knew their way around willow bark and other herbal remedies, and plain old scapegoats in a period of mass hysteria among a community (like in the Salem Witch Trials).

So buckle up, because after the next few chapters, you'll have the basic concepts down that'll put the people in your life (and yourself) at ease. To start, let's take a look at a few that we're going to focus on:

- *Exodus 22:18*

- *Leviticus 19:26*

- *Leviticus 19:31*

- *Deuteronomy 18:9-12*

    ○ *Honorable Mention: 2 Kings 17:15-19*

    ○ *Honorable Mention: 1 Samuel 28:8-19*

- *Acts 19:19*

- *Galatians 5:19-21*

- *Revelation 18:23*

And that isn't even all of them. How can we reconcile these obvious condemnations of witchcraft? Are we just lying to ourselves, maybe, swayed by the world and all the pretty, shiny things in it? Or is there maybe more to the story than we've been told?

While we can't pick apart every single verse that might mention something related to witchcraft, we can absolutely take you through the biggest themes that unite them all, as well as tackle the concept of the Bible itself as a whole. Let's take a look now, starting with the first glaring issue: Biblical literacy in general.

The Problem of Biblical Literacy

Right off the bat, there's something anyone coming out of a strictly Christian background needs to know: *the Bible has been changed over time.* It has been edited and revised over and over and over again for *centuries.* Of course, there are hundreds of people that will tell you that this isn't true: that "God isn't the author of confusion," or some other canned response to a claim like this, because the Bible is the *only* tangible object they have to "prove" an intangible God. The idea that such an object is at all flawed is a source of grave anxiety for modern Christians. "God has the power to preserve His word," they'll say to you as they grapple with the idea. "The Bible is infallible; it's God's direct words to us!" But it's something that needs to be acknowledged: God *can* preserve His word, and yet... He didn't.

In fact, my own Bible (*The Jewish Study Bible,* or what Christians would recognize as the Old Testament) notes the several different sources that comprise what we understand now of the Jewish Canon: the priestly source, the Jahwist source, the Elohist source, and the Deuteronomistic source, which at times contradict, repeat, or show an altogether different writing style, suggesting a completely different person wrote these very important stories.[1] Moreover, we have records of complaints from as early as the *3rd century* by Christian thinkers who were outraged by the fact that scribes, as they copied the Biblical manuscripts, would take liberty of making changes. Take a look at Christian leader Origen's gripes of the quality of copying work of Biblical scribes, who were by no means professionals like elsewhere in the Roman empire:

> The differences among the manuscripts have become great, either through the negligence of some copyists or through the perverse audacity of others; they either neglect to check over what they have transcribed, or, in the process of checking, they make additions or deletions as they please.[2]

The fact that Origen, a 3rd century Christian apologist and philosopher, already had these gripes tells us something pretty dire. As soon as the ink dried on the very first Gospel, and it was handed over to someone else to copy, it seems we entered into the biggest, messiest game of Telephone ever seen. And truthfully, we do need to ask ourselves: how could it have ever been avoided? It didn't matter that people like Origen were upset about mere mortals changing the very *Word of God*; the fact of the matter was that every scribe was a whole different person who, when translating and copying, brought their own viewpoints into the text. What else would make them choose one translation of a word over another, or correct the spelling of a word they weren't sure about, other than to clarify what was, in their mind, an obvious mistake?

After all, James L. Kugel wisely observes that "if a text" that someone writes "is of any serious length or substance, it can open a window onto the inner world of the person who wrote it."[3] By reading it, we not only learn what the subject of the text wants us to know, but also "crucial things about how that [writer] saw and understood things in general."[4] The same can be said for anyone who *edits* a text of any meaningful length, projecting their own thoughts, biases, and ideas of what *should* and *shouldn't* be onto the pages.

---

1. Adele Berlin and Marc Zvi Brettler, eds. *Jewish Study Bible* (London: Oxford University Press, 2014), 3.

2. Bart Ehrman, *Misquoting Jesus: The Story Behind Who Changed the Bible and Why* (New York: HarperCollins, 2005), 53.

3. James L. Kugel, *The God of Old: Inside the Lost World of the Bible*, New York: The Free Press, 2003, 1.

4. Ibid., 1.

The nature of manuscript copying was also altogether different back before the printing press, when old scribes with tired eyes (who were really just Christians that happened to be able to read and write rather than properly trained professionals) would work by candlelight to meticulously copy each letter from one big sheet of paper to the next. As Ehrman puts it, quite a few changes "had nothing to do with theology or ideology"; "most changes [were] the result of mistakes, pure and simple—slips of the pen, accidental omissions, inadvertent additions, misspelled words, blunders of one sort or another."[5] These fellows would see a smudge of ink and think it's a letter, or, other way around, see a letter and assume it's a generous drop of carelessness on the manuscript. Either way, it meant that often, even the most dedicated Christian scribes would overextend their authority and make corrections that *they* were sure were appropriate, but that others might've disagreed with (and yelled at them for making).

"But we *do* have the originals," some Christians might cry. "We have the very first copies ever written! Those *were* inspired by God!"

Unfortunately, even if we had the very first tablet of commandments God Himself wrote on with His own finger (which was lost from the Temple of Jerusalem over time, and of course, the Temple itself later destroyed), there is another issue around the Bible's accuracy that needs to be considered: with no printing press, and hardly even literate people to begin with, how do we know who actually wrote these Gospels? Especially because Jesus's own disciples, Peter and John, were described as *agrammatos*, or without letters, meaning they couldn't read or write.[6] This would follow that either:

1. The Gospels were relayed by the Apostles to scribes, who furiously tried to capture their every word, or

2. It wasn't the Apostles that wrote the four Gospels at all (an idea that has plenty of backing to it).

And I should mention that those four Gospels in the Canon are just that: only four. Even if we do still believe the Apostles wrote the Gospels, last I remembered, Jesus had twelve Apostles, plus a lovely lady by the name of Mary Magdalene who He "loved... more than all the disciples" and "used to kiss... often on her mouth."[7] But where are the Gospels of Mary, Philip, Thomas? Oh, right. They were thrown out for not conforming to a very narrow idea of Christ put up by

---

5. Ehrman, *Misquoting Jesus*, 55.

6. Robert Conner, *Magic in Christianity from Jesus to the Gnostics*, Oxford & Robert Conner: Mandrake of Oxford, 2014, 4.

7. Gospel of Philip, 63.

church fathers near the 4th century and condemned to be destroyed.[8] If not for a few rebellious Coptic priests, we might've never known that Mary Magdalene's Gospel even existed, never mind know about the enlightening ideas inside.[9] Considering even the writer of Luke mentions consulting "many predecessors" to write this Gospel, and we have found no other such predecessors that would've inspired either the writer of Luke or Matthew,[10] it's safe to say that the assertion about Scripture in 2 Tim 3:16-17 is taking a beating: we actually do not even *have* all possible sources of Scripture.

Ehrman spells it out beautifully as he discusses the way in which St. Paul's letters to the many churches across Asia Minor came about. He shows us how we can glean that St. Paul didn't seem to write his own letters with his own hands—not until the end of them, as evidenced in his address to the Galatians: "See with what large letters I am writing you with my own hand."[11] Ehrman's questions are perfectly valid as he gets into the dirty details:

> Now, if Paul dictated the letter, did he dictate it word for word? Or did he spell out the basic points and allow the scribe to fill in the rest? Both methods were commonly used by letter writers in antiquity. If the scribe filled in the rest, can we be assured that he filled it in exactly as Paul wanted? ... Is it possible that in some places the scribe wrote down the *wrong* words? ... If multiple copies of the letter went out, can we be sure that all the copies were also 100 percent correct?[12]

That's a lot to consider. Given these letters were written centuries ago, I hardly doubt we'll ever have the answers. But let's back up even further and consider that St. Paul's letters are not even a part of the four Gospels—that a majority of the New Testament itself is essentially St. Paul's advice column to churches who could not, for the life of them, get their act together. Imagine using antique newspaper columns like *Dear Bliss Fairfax*, those specific, clearly-a-product-of-the-times writings, to guide the entire world of Christian believers for the entire rest of the world's history?

It sounds crazy, doesn't it? Especially when the church fathers were willing to throw out these apocryphal Gospels for being untrue and

---

8. Watterson, Meggan, *Mary Magdalene Revealed: The First Apostle, Her Feminist Gospel & the Christianity We Haven't Tried Yet*, USA: Hay House, Inc., 2021, 1.

9. Ibid., 1.

10. Ehrman, *Misquoting Jesus*, 24.

11. Galatians 6:11

12. Ehrman, *Misquoting Jesus*, 59.

inauthentic while padding the New Testament with things that barely seemed to have anything to do with the story of Christ as it's present-ed in the New Testament between Matthew, Mark, Luke, and John.

Speaking of those four precious Gospels, it doesn't take much digging to see the many discrepancies in the narrative they present. You don't need to know about originals or translations or anything at all to compare the four and realize they're all attesting to things that simply do not line up and sometimes contradict each other.

For example: did Jesus ask His Heavenly Father for forgiveness for the people that put Him on that cross, as in Luke 23:34? Did He die without a word of complaint, peaceful as He passed into the underworld—or did He maybe, per Matthew 27:46, look up to the heavens and cry out in agony, demanding answers from that very same Heavenly Father in a bitter question: *my God, my God, why hast thou forsaken me?* If not the latter, then a large portion of the thesis of Jürgen Moltmann's *The Crucified God* is in trouble.

Going further, it seems that other stories—from our favorites about Jesus, like the saving of the woman about to be stoned to death for adultery, and even the very story of His resurrection—are not so "original" as folks claim. In fact, the story of Jesus actually coming out of His tomb, talking a good game about what His Apostles are to do in His stead and what'll come next, and shooting off into Heaven afterwards, was "not originally in the Gospel of Mark," according to Ehrman: "it was added by a later scribe," and we know this because it's simply not there in "our two oldest and best manuscripts of Mark's Gospel."[13] Without this added ending, the story just drops off into nowhere, of course—it ends as the women who were told to tell all about Jesus's coming instead "flee from the tomb and say nothing to anyone, 'for they were afraid'"—and somewhere way back in antiquity, that must've just been unacceptable to a scribe to end the story on such a wild cliffhanger.[14]

And we would be sorely mistaken not to mention the times people have outright manipulated the text for their own purposes. One exam-ple is the shuffling verses around to put words in people's mouths that simply don't line up with the rest of the document's message (such as was potentially the case in 1 Corinthians 14, where verses were moved around, and possibly even merged with some scribe's margin note, to make it look like St. Paul wrote it).[15] Another example is the possibility of scribes going so far as to write things we understand as cruel and callous in the modern era and attribute them to men long dead. Such is the case with the writings in 1 Timothy,[16] attributed to St. Paul despite being written years after his death, and despite the fact that some of it

---

13. Ehrman, *Misquoting Jesus*, 67.

14. Ibid., 66-67.

15. Ibid., 183.

16. Ibid., 31.

(namely 1 Tim 2:12) flies squarely in the face of one of St. Paul's most powerful lines of Scripture in Galatians 3:28:

> There is neither Jew nor Greek,
> there is neither slave nor free,
> there is no male and female, for
> you are all one in Christ Jesus.

But let us get back to what we were saying originally. The bottom line is that these manuscripts, like any other text throughout the entire of human history, have been written, interpreted, edited, written again, re-interpreted, thrown out, added back in, on and on, for centuries. What we call the Old Testament alone was compiled over dozens of generations: "more than a thousand years separate its earliest and latest parts."[17] And while Sara adores her copy of *The Jewish Study Bible* and *The Jewish Annotated New Testament*, the fact of the matter is that there will never be a perfect Bible. There will never be a Bible that is absolutely, faithfully, perfectly true to the words of Jesus or of any of the prophets, because this is a holy story woven over the span of not only centuries, but *millennia*. And every generation has a different idea of who God is, who *they* are in relation to Him, and what these stories mean.

How else could the words of St. Paul, a man focused on radical equality of all people in the shelter of Christ's name, be later used to justify the enslavement of an entire race of people in America centuries down the road?[18]

Like it did for Ehrman, who started off as convicted and sure of his faith as any other very devout Christian from a highly conservative background, the realization about these things help us understand that the truest way to know God's Word is to ask Him personally. Ehrman came to understand the Bible as "a very human book," one "written by different human authors at different times and in different places to address different needs."[19] Echoing Kugel, Ehrman notes that, whether one considered themselves inspired or not as they wrote the words that would become part of the Biblical Canon, these writers nonetheless had "their own needs, their own desires, their own understandings, their own theologies"—and that these ultimately bled into the Scripture, no matter their intentions.[20]

To us, this isn't a reason to fall out of belief in any way, though. Rather, this knowledge is a reason to rejoice—because rather than

---

17. Kugel, *God of Old*, xi.

18. Howard Thurman, *Jesus and the Disinherited*, USA: Beacon Press (1996), 30-31.

19. Ehrman, *Misquoting Jesus*, 11.

20. Ibid., 11.

grapple with things that clearly don't belong in the Word of God, things that disenfranchise and harm innocent people, and rather than twist ourselves around to try and justify that which we know shouldn't be justified, and rather than try and find "evidence" for wild statements that are blatantly false and disproven by the scientific community, we can rest a little easier. We can understand that the Bible is a beautiful thing, a treasure trove of insight into the character of God and the social, cultural, political, and historical times of the Bible, all while also acknowledging that it is ultimately a story about *perception.* How God perceives Man and how Man perceives God—how Man perceives the world through the figure of God.

It's a freeing concept, because it opens up the Bible to be what it is: allegory and myth as much as history and fact. But with all that out of the way now, and this idea of Biblical infallibility laid to rest, let's take a look at how the human touch has tarnished the Divine Word, specifically in the verses mentioned at the start of this chapter.

Old Testament Verses Incorrectly Applied

To begin, we should note one thing very clearly: when you actually search through the Bible for any mention of witchcraft, what you're going to notice first is not the actual mention of the word "witch" as often as you will words like "necromancy" or "divination" or "omens" or some such—all of which hold some specific contexts even just in English, never mind in the original languages they were written in. Even things that look pretty straightforward, like mentions of *astrology*, have a lot more going for them than a wholesale ban on the use of the stars to figure some things out in their lives; they reference not only specific practices, but specific philosophies, that as a Christian Witch, are actually really easy to avoid (and recommended to avoid, honestly).

So what we're going to do is go through a few verses of the Old Testament that you'll most commonly see used against the Christian Witch community and talk about the specific words used in these legal condemnations, what they mean, and what they're actually referring to. This way, when someone inevitably comes quoting a Bible verse at you, you won't need to worry, because you'll already know what the verses are actually talking about. Knowing these facts helps you breathe easier about any of the more obscure verses that might use the same language throughout the Bible, so let's start at the top with one of the most popular verses to bring up when talking about witchcraft: one from the Book of Exodus.

EXODUS 22:18

Do not allow a sorceress to live.

As a Christian Witch, the first and foremost verse anyone will throw your way is none other than Exodus 22:18. It seems straightforward enough, as it's always ever translated as *witch* or *sorcerer* from the original Hebrew, but the first thing one must understand is just that: it was translated. And like all translations, sometimes there isn't a single word that directly describes the thing being translated. We might pick the closest word to it (in this case, *witch*) but God only knows that our decision to do so has caused more harm than good.

You see, the original word used in Exodus is the term *mekhashep-ah*, which, according to Robert Conner, is a word likely from "the Sumerian kašapu, a type of sorcerer who brought misfortune in its many forms and was therefore 'condemned by the government.'"[21] Markham J. Geller, University of London's Jewish Chronicle Professor of Jewish Studies, also clarifies that this word is related to the Akkadian *kishpu*, which we discuss in Deuteronomy.[22] But Conner notes that the verse of Exodus, using the feminine form of this word, has itself become "historically one of the deadliest scriptural injunctions ever written."[23] And certainly it is, as it's still the go-to for those who would like to see witches removed altogether from their world, and whose predecessors used it to justify burning many a woman, political enemy, or member of a marginalized community (such as Jewish people) in Christian Europe.

Speaking of women, the feminine use of this word in Exodus is an important point; it singles out women specifically, despite this forbidding of harmful magic actually extending to everybody (for obvious reasons). According to one Jewish Witch, Zo Jacobi, who runs a metaphysical online store, blog, podcast, and robust social media presence under the name Jewitches, this feminine form of the word was used because "witchcraft [was] exceedingly common among women."[24] And despite much of the evidence that much of the magical arts was, indeed, performed by men across various cultures, it does seem that there's a "historical case of misogyny forbidding witchcraft

---

21. Conner, *Magic in Christianity*, 139.

22. Markham J. Geller, "Defining Magic in the Ancient World" in *Between the Worlds: Magic, Miracle, & Mysticism* 2, Paradigma, 2020, 17.

23. Conner, *Magic in Christianity*, 139.

24. Zo Jacobi, "Can You Even Be a Jewish Witch?" Jewitches (blog), accessed November 22, 2023, https://www.jewitches.com/post/can-you-even-be-a-jewish-witch.

when done by women but praised when done by men," as Jacobi points out.[25] Exodus 22:18 is but one of those many instances.

But let's walk back a moment to Conner's definition. When Conner mentions the government, it's important to note that, in fact, the Sumerian governments condemned this nameless, yet dangerous, sorceress, too. Despite the fact that the *mekhashepah* receives about as much venom as anyone else that practiced pagan rites in the Old Testament, we see that the *ashshaph*, or *conjurer* mentioned in Daniel, was actually "an official who appears to have received official status and support" in these lands (and *ashshaph* is thought to be an Assyrian loanword, coming from ešipu or ašipu).[26] Moreover, other nations, like Babylon and Rome, did have their fair share of court magicians, and it's that officiality which separated them from people like those mentioned in Exodus in their respective lands.[27] Rome, especially, found magic to be *superstitio*, superstition, in the highest, and its officials hated it because of "the direct access it afforded to the supernatural world, the possibility of influence over the stars and gods, making magic a 'super religion' beyond state control and thus dangerous."[28] What good would earthly power be, after all, if any average person could tear it down with a solid petition to the gods above?

According to Rev. T. Witton Davies, the Israelites and their neighbors had very little love for these "witchy types," this common *mekhashepah*. These simple peasantfolk, with charms and few tools, no real official formula, and with "no elaborate ritual and written incantations," were starkly contrasted with the Sumerian "eššepu or ašipu," who were a "class of recognized magicians" among their nations.[29] But more to the point, these witches of Exodus so often used to batter the average Christian Witch were very specifically "supposed to have to do with demons, and to bring evil upon men and women" while those official court magicians—operative word being *magicians*, in that yes, they used magic all the same—"were said to deal immediately with the good deities for the purpose of bringing good upon the state and upon the individuals in it."[30] However, Rev. Davies makes sure to add that there's an element of explanation here that transcends any idea of "good magic" versus "bad magic" or "hexing" versus "blessing":

---

25. Ibid.

26. Conner, *Magic in Christianity* 140.

27. Ibid., 139.

28. Ibid., 96

29. Rev. T. Witton Davies, "Magic, Divination, & Demonology among the Semites," *The American Journal of Semitic Languages & Literature* 14, no 4 (1898): 245, https://www.jstor.org/stable/527968.

30. Ibid., 245.

...but the real difference is that illegitimate magic was that which was practiced by the common unauthorized people, the other was carried on by the official priest. The case, in fact, *is parallel to the condemnation under the influence of the Jerusalem priest of worship at the high places.* It was a case of our 'craft is in danger,' or of an established versus unrecognized rivals.[31] (Emphasis ours.)

Thus, we get to the heart of the issue, don't we? On the surface level, in the English translation, this verse is all about *witchcraft*, whatever that may mean to the religious authorities in power—and as we'll discuss later, that element of vagueness was mightily helpful for cementing certain power structures in place and using them as a political weapon.

But truthfully, what Exodus 22:18 boils down to is doing magic that's unauthorized—and painting that magic, specifically, as evil. Because the ritual to cure leprosy in Leviticus 14, which requires two birds, one of those birds' blood, cedar, hyssop, and red thread, was a perfectly normal and justified piece of magic when used officially by the Levite priests. However, those same priests, just the same as the priests and augurs of any other official religion of any of the Israelites' neighbors, couldn't have had competition like this—not only because there were associations with evil and demon-working and hexing that could cause obvious harm to the community, but because it would destabilize the hierarchy of religious leadership itself. It would perhaps *undermine* the religious authority given to them as the tribe of Levi, God's designated priests. After all, as John Dominic Crossan asks in *The Historical Jesus,* "if a magician's power can bring rain, for what do you need the power of temple priesthood or rabbinical academy?"[32] If a single, solitary magician can be his own priest, for what does one even need the hierarchical structure of church in the first place?

Sara Says:

One can grant this shred of mercy to the Church as structured, though: hierarchy isn't *always* a bad thing. I was speaking with a dear friend of mine, Father Kyle Mackey, an Episcopalian/Anglican priest in Virginia, who admitted that, while a person confirmed in the faith has all the authority in their own homes—the priest of their own front step, if you will—he obviously wouldn't let one of the congregation come boot him off the pulpit and begin preaching with authority in his stead.

---

31. Ibid., 245.

32. John Dominick Crossan, *The Historical Jesus: The Life of a Mediterranean Jewish Peasant* (USA: HarperOne, 1993), 158.

Why? Because that's how the whole organizational structure of an actual physical church goes right to hell, with everyone being a leader and no one left to be led. An individual in their house is the spiritual leader of their household, and a priest in a church is a spiritual leader of a collection of households, as he explained to me. I understand this, and I hope you do, too: that sometimes, a structure or hierarchy of leadership can be helpful, even if the concept of authority might naturally make one chafe a little bit. But nonetheless, for those who have no physical church, it's good to know that it doesn't mean we're without spiritual agency to lead ourselves. In fact, if leadership would actually *lead* more, rather than simply *command* its congregation, it might better empower its members to speak and act in the authority they're meant to have, and to do so as a deeply connected *community* rather than separated, isolated households and members.

Beyond that, as you surely know, there are of course times when official church leadership can take a turn for the worse. And ironically, as Christians, who showed us the power of standing against crooked religious authority more than Jesus Himself? For all the talk about banishing witches and obeying religious authority, it was Jesus who reminded us that we are *all* children of God, capable of working miracles with and through Him.

LEVITICUS 19:26

> *Do not eat any meat with the*
> *blood still in it. Do not practice*
> *divination or seek omens.*

Look at that! "Do not practice divination." Looks straightforward, right? Looks like it outright condemns the whole concept of divination. But what does divination mean? Is it just telling the future wholesale? Or does it refer to a certain practice? What exactly *is* that practice? How does one divine or soothsay according to Biblical understandings of the word?

With these questions lies the issue. As it turns out, a lot of these words—divination, soothsaying, etc.—don't have any direct translations or meanings, and in fact can mean many things, even in the original Hebrew. According to Jacobi, there were many definitions that could've applied to the word "divination" in the Bible. She sources the Tractate Sanhedrin as she discusses the topic of magic in her blog, "Can You Even Be a Jewish Witch?" And it should be explained that this is "a tractate in Seder Nezikin ("Order of Damages") that addresses the judicial system" that was composed in Talmudic Babylon between

450 and 550 CE.[33] According to Sefaria, the website that hosts these texts, the Tractate Sanhedrin's "eleven chapters discuss the selection of judges and forming a court, the process of accepting testimony, and monetary, corporal, and capital punishment."[34] Here, many a rabbi and scholar explain the different interpretations of these words within, and for divination in this verse, there are several interpretations.

It's important to look to Jewish scholars and sources for verses like those in Leviticus because, as one might come to realize, Leviticus is Jewish holy scripture. One of the five books of the Torah, in fact. In that regard, one of the most startling conclusions in the Sanhedrin about this verse in Leviticus is that of Rabbi Shimon. He claims that this passage signifies a soothsayer as someone who "one who applies seven types of semen [zekhur] to one's eye in order to perform sorcery."[35] We will be the first to say that we don't think anyone is doing that in any sense. At least, we hope not. It sounds like a wonderful way to get pink eye, if for nothing else.

Jacobi does explain that a more common position is that of Maimonides, a medieval-era Sephardic Jewish philosopher, who was notoriously anti-magic (just as some Christian Saints, like Saint Augustine were[36]). Maimonides insisted that this verse was actually about *astrology*, by which people might "foretell events by astrological observations, declaring that a certain day is favorable while another is unfavorable," so on and so forth.[37] Maimonides was especially concerned with superstition and useless pursuits when it came to the stars, and with a lack of ration and reasoning that would cause people to go seeking for answers in the supernatural influences of the stars rather than anything based in science or ration or even scripture itself. In fact, in Maimonides' letter about astrology to inquisitive students, "astrology is here seen as a stupid distraction from useful and necessary actions."[38] Sounds like Maimonides and the super rational, "too smart for you" guys with podcasts would have a lot in common.

But if the only thing wrong with astrology and superstition (which makes up the bulk of folk magic) is that it's a so-called stupid distraction, and there's no outright condemnation for it, then what's the real problem? Nothing, as far as we can see. In fact, Maimonides was out there arguing with Talmudic rabbis and religious leaders who *did* find value in these things. Apparently, when asked about how he could

---

33. Sanhedrin 65a:2, The William Davidson Talmud, translated by Rabbi Adin Steinsaltz, Sefaria, https://www.sefaria.org/Sanhedrin.65a.2?lang=bi&with=About&lang2=en.

34. Ibid.

35. Sanhedrin 65b:19, The William Davidson Talmud, translated by Rabbi Adin Steinsaltz, https://www.sefaria.org/Sanhedrin.65b.19?lang=bi&with=all&lang2=en

36. Sister Mary Emily Keenan, "The Terminology of Witchcraft in the Works of Augustine," *Classical Philology* 35, no 3, 294-297, https://www.jstor.org/stable/264395.

37. Jacobi, "Can You Even Be a Jewish Witch?"

38. Ralph Lerner, "Maimonides' Letter on Astrology," *History of Religions* 8, no. 2, 147.

disagree with these rabbis, Maimonides "replied that man was created with eyes in the front of his head, not the back"—an interesting way of saying "because I'm not a dolt," but nonetheless just signaling that it was more his opinion than anything.[39] Others, like rabbi Moshe Isserles, born in the 1500s in Krakow, Poland, had different ideas.[40] Isserles insisted that rather than rely on astrology, one should instead just be unconcerned with the future, trusting God—but if someone *knew* that an action they wanted to take would be "contrary to his mazal, his fate as determined by the stars, he should take the necessary precautions and should not rely on a miracle to save him."[41] In effect: trust God with your future, but don't ignore the obvious warning signs in your face, either. That's a balancing idea just about anyone can get behind.

And we do need to remember that the three "wise men" or "kings" that found Jesus, as they're often called—those three *magi*, or magicians, in the original Greek—were likely Persian or Babylonian astrologers, and they weren't spurned in the Gospels by any means. People like Origen might've tried to make up stories to justify the presence of literal magicians in the Gospels (he claimed that these astrologers, who must've used demonic powers to do their magic, felt "their powers waning"[42] and went to investigate why), but no one that we know of thinks ill of these Biblical figures today. In fact, they frequently feature in nativity sets and on artifacts like the Slovenian *hišni žegen*, or house blessing, an inscription blessed by priests and thought to keep a house and its residents safe. (Similar church traditions include writing a specific formula, XX+C+M+B+XX, in chalk on the doorway and invoking the name of these three kings for Epiphany blessings, with the X's being year numbers. For example, the 2024 Epiphany blessing over one's door would be written: 20 + C + M + B + 24. Seems plenty witchy to us.) The thing that often gets missed regarding this astrology, however, is that Babylonian astrology "implied a 'fatalistic consciousness of subjection to a rigid necessity as such, and the passivity to which it seemed to condemn man'"—or, in plain English, implied a system where people had absolutely no say in their life thanks to the way the cosmos left their mark on people.[43] This was contrary to the Israelite idea that our fates are ultimately in our hands, and that God decides above all, so obviously this specific approach to astrology would be problematic.

---

39. Rabbi Louis Jacobs, "Jewish Astrology," My Jewish Learning, https://www.myjewishlea rning.com/article/jewish-astrology/ . Accessed November 22, 2023.

40. Menachem Elon, "Moses (Moshe) Isserles: Rema," My Jewish Learning, https://www.m yjewishlearning.com/article/moses-isserles-rema/ . Accessed November 23, 2023.

41. Rabbi Jacobs, "Jewish Astrology."

42. Conner, *Magic in Christianity*, 44.

43. Jonas quoted in Conner, *Magic in Christianity*, 45.

All this aside, though, the point of the matter is that when it comes to this verse, the terms used for divination and soothsaying are contested, but even the possibilities that *do* get tossed out for this verse don't really have anything to do with what Christian Witches do. We don't believe that the stars have total control over us, only a bit of influence, and we surely don't try to tell the future with these wacky, zany methods that may have been going on at the time (be they by way of bodily fluid or essentially hardcore animal abuse). At its most basic, the divination a Christian Witch does is no different from what any oracle or priest ever did: we're just asking God questions when we need His guidance, which one might imagine is what we're supposed to do. Whether you're settling on a random verse in the Bible or you're shuffling a deck of cards, the method you choose to speak to God with (granted you're not harming anyone or anything) is entirely up to you.

LEVITICUS 19:31

> *Do not turn to mediums or seek out spiritists, for you will be defiled by them. I am the Lord your God.*

Now, unlike the first Leviticus verse we looked at, this one is a lot easier to pin down. What is described when talking about mediums and spiritists isn't just anyone who knows how to contact God or use divination. This verse in its original Hebrew mentions a specific practice called *ov* and *yide'oni* (which you'll also see written as *yidoni* sometimes). This practice is one that "Biblical tradition admits... is effective... but places it strictly off-limits for Israelites."[44] According to Jacobi, this was a pretty specific pagan practice that you'd honestly have to try really hard to recreate. What it entails is essentially getting high as a kite on some kind of drug or special incense, then inserting the bone of an animal into your mouth and summoning the spirit of said animal and letting it borrow your own tongue to speak. The medium in question, a *ba'al ob,* or "master of spirits," is a professional title, so on top of not carrying out this act, this verse tells the Levite priests that they're also not to find someone else who knows this extremely specific ritual and ask them to do it for them.[45]

Do you see how this would be pretty hard to do accidentally or unknowingly?

---

44. Berline and Brettler, eds., *Jewish Study Bible,* 243.

45. "Can You Even Be a Jewish Witch?" Jewitches.

During these times, a lot of features of ancient popular religion were still in play, and that included consulting with little spirits or ghosts of people passed to get answers about the future rather than just going to God for guidance. This is especially true towards the beginning of the whole Bible, in Genesis, which we can see when pagan Laban uses a form of divination that is "later prohibited (Lev. 19.26, Deut 18.10)" according to the Jewish Study Bible.[46] As the religion in the time of Genesis was just starting, the nation of Israel beginning with Jacob, who was renamed such, it's not hard to see where these practices would come from and why they'd be off limits to a group trying to separate themselves as unique and distinct from neighboring pagans.

Of all the verses we're going to talk about, this one probably has the least drama. While there isn't really any distinct understanding of what the word "divination" refers to in the Bible since the language is so old and the meanings of words so contested, this one here, *ov* and *yide'oni*, is pretty easy to make quick work of—*when you actually know what the original language is.* To amplify the point Jacobi makes, "...translations, or more accurately 'mistranslations,' erase the actual meaning of the words, watering it down and allowing it to become a generalization as opposed to the direct action that is being referenced."[47] When we don't understand what the original words behind the English translation are, or why they're there, or why they got changed the way they did, we lose understanding of the guidance of God. If we look at the very first story of the Bible with Adam and Eve, where Eve, based on what Adam told her, adds extra word to the prohibition against eating the apple off the Tree of Knowledge, it was here that a key piece of wisdom spawned for rabbis contemplating it eons later in the Sanhedrin: "he who adds [to God's words] subtracts [from them.]"[48] When we apply a wholesale ban of divination to these very specific and nuanced words, when we assume what was meant over their original specifications and add our understandings onto them from this modern vantage point separated from the actual historical, political, and cultural context of the scene, we subtract from God's guidance for us.

DEUTERONOMY 18:9-12

When you enter the land the Lord your God is giving you, do not learn to imitate the detestable ways of the nations

---

46. Berline and Brettler, eds., *Jewish Study Bible,* 58.

47. Jacobi, "Can You Even Be a Jewish Witch?" Jewitches.

48. Sanh. 29a quoted in Jewish Study Bible

there. Let no one be found among you who sacrifices their son or daughter in the fire, who practices divination or sorcery, interprets omens, engages in witchcraft, or casts spells, or who is a medium or spiritist or who consults the dead. Anyone who does these things is detestable to the Lord; because of these same detestable practices the Lord your God will drive out those nations before you.

So this is our longest quote with the most direct prohibitions we need to cover, and here is where things get a little wild, admittedly. We're hesitant to say exactly why, not because this verse here pokes a hole in anything we've said or will say throughout the rest of this, but because the nature of these verses' inspiration and origins are something that is potentially really controversial. It's something one would expect to see refuted in the scholarly foot-notes of the *Jewish Study Bible*, and yet it hasn't *exactly* been—and that is the idea that many of the things listed in these verses, though described as the practices of nations *around* Israel, are in fact potentially practices *of* Israelite popular religion at the time. This includes child sacrifice, conjuring the dead, and doing very specific types of magic to members of one's community (including even harmful magic, which was never really allowed or acceptable even through Exodus, Leviticus, and other common spaces).

The reason we hesitate to mention these things is that we must, when we look at passages that write about something resembling a conspiracy about Israelite practices, remember that for centuries of *Christian* history, Jewish people have been accused of being witches, sorcerers, antagonists of the village populations, and more. To suggest that syncretic practices of *other* nations, like Neo-Assyrian or Baby-lonian child sacrifice, would find their way into the Israelites' practices via close contact with them, could give ammunition to some really unsavory, wicked people who eschew history and nuance for their own prejudices. It's certainly been done before, after all, and with wilder accusations. Even up to the last century, groups like Nazis had accused Jewish people of *blood libel*, a fabricated practice in which Jewish people would be accused of using the blood of Christian (or generally Gentile) children for magic rituals. According to the United States Holocaust Memorial Museum's encyclopedia, Nazis during their reign would go about "accusing Jews of practicing ritual murder to secure the blood of Christians to use in Jewish religious rituals" with newspapers that had "[a] headline 'Jewish Murder Plan against Gentile Humanity Revealed.'"[49]

However, this isn't by any means the first time blood libel as a concept came about; we can actually trace it back several centuries, starting "in the Hellenistic writings of Apion in the 2nd century BCE," and finding its way into European imagination in the 12th century, after the first Crusade.[50] And all along the way, from the 2nd century BCE through the Middle Ages, Gentiles had these ideas that Jewish people were using *sorcery* even when just engaging in normal religious rituals, like having a Passover lamb. Some even thought that the wine Jewish people brewed had special magical healing powers and tried to get some when ill.[51] It goes without saying that a large part of anti-magic sentiment, or refusal to believe in magic is even real, comes from the fact that Jewish people have been wrongly accused of all kinds of terrible things, including sorcery, for *centuries.*

To come back to our original hesitation, all this is to say: we all know how many anti-semitic troglodytes truly believe that their virulent anti-semitism is actually a part of *being* Christian (and honestly, given what we know about Christian treatment of Jewish people in Europe, we can see how such a long history of this evil has made people think it's just Christian tradition). But of course, anyone who knows the difference between their hand and their foot also knows that actively trying to harm God's people, especially His *first* people, is a pretty bad move. Still, as a Christian Witch, it's important you're able to recognize when these ideas are trying to creep up into your space, because they will. Not just in the Christian side, but the witchcraft side, too. More on that later, though. Just remember that standing up for justice is an integral part of the faith, and that means doing what you can to shield and protect others and be an ally to marginalized groups wherever you can.

But back to Deuteronomy now, and its interesting rebrand of Israelite popular practices as specifically Canaanite through the voice of Moses. The good news is that the condemnation of these practices in Deuteronomy effectively cut out a large part of the aspects many will now agree are problematic, most namely the sacrifice of not just animals, but human children, to a deity of any kind (which was a practice done by various pagan groups at the time, not just any one group). The bad news is that it's very possible, given the actual dating of the book of Deuteronomy (around the 7th century BCE, the time period in which reforms of King Josiah were taking place), that painting these things as Canaanite practices was a deflection of blame so as to not outright

---

49. United States Holocaust Memorial Museum. "Blood Libel." Holocaust Encyclopedia. https://encyclopedia.ushmm.org/content/en/article/blood-libel. Accessed on November 28, 2023.

50. Ibid.

51. Joshua Trachtenberg, "Jewish Magic & Medieval Anti-Semitism," My Jewish Learning, https://www.myjewishlearning.com/article/jewish-magic-medieval-anti-semitism/ . Accessed November 28, 2023.

name these as practices of Israel at the time. Still, we might understand these as syncretic, or *shared*, practices between Israel and neighboring aggressive nations like the Neo-Assyrians and Babylonians, so the fact is that these practices still came from somewhere and found their way into Israelite popular religion from an outside source.[52] Given the historical rivalry of Canaanites and Israelites, and the political climate with these other nations aggressing on Israel at the time of Deuteronomy's writing centuries later, it's not hard to see why Canaan was chosen as the scapegoat for this.

Conner follows this notion, asserting that by being in close proximity with foreign powers such as Canaanites so long before all this, that they likely picked up and absorbed many of these practices.[53] Going further, however, he references various scholars, such as Brian B. Schmidt, in the claim that not only did Israelites engage in these practices, but that one of these apparently foreign gods, Molech, might've even been a "chthonic aspect or an independent netherworld deity of the Yahwistic cult."[54] Conner cites several examples of places in the Bible where child sacrifice is apparent to support this idea: namely, the promise of Jephthah's daughter as a burnt offering in Judges 11:31-35, the near-sacrifice of Isaac in Genesis 22:2, and the way God goes out of His way to give bad laws to the Israelites to shame them[55] in Ezekiel 20:26. It seems that this concept of child sacrifice has been around a lot longer than one would hope or expect (and for a few different reasons across the ages).[56] And if you read Isaiah 30:33, you'll even find a point in which God uses the Topheth, "a site near Jerusalem at which human beings were sacrificed by fire in periods of paganizing," to destroy the enemies of Israel (like the Assyrians).[57] It does seem that the concept of God, and His character and what He's willing to do, is in fact a bit more complicated than the standard idea of God being all pure love and sunshine and roses.

After all, while God brings good times and blessings, He is also capable of bringing bad times and calamity, as is necessary to weave the arc of the great Story He's writing here on earth.[58]

But we bring all this up to make a point about the contents of these prohibitions. We briefly mentioned earlier the aggression of Neo-Assyrians and Babylonians towards Israel, and their close quarters and possibility of syncretic traditions, and that's important here. Deuteronomy as a book was likely intended, given its writing style and

---

52. Berline and Brettler, eds., *Jewish Study Bible*, 340, 387.

53. Conner, *Magic in Christianity*, 130.

54. Schmidt as quoted in Conner, 131.

55. Berline and Brettler, eds., *Jewish Study Bible*, 1067.

56. Conner, Magic in Christianity, 131.

57. Berline and Brettler, eds., *Jewish Study Bible*, 827.

58. Isaiah 45:7

its dating, to back up Josiah's reforms—"an important bid for Judean cultural, political, and religious autonomy."[59] With all of the pressures and aggressions from neighboring nations that sought to put Israel under their thumb, the Neo-Assyrian invasion being only "a scant century before," the Book of Deuteronomy sought to establish a clear-cut, central, and standard way of worship into Israelite society, taking as many religious aspects as possible into Jerusalem to be overseen by the official priesthood.[60] Its format resembles "Neo-Assyrian state treaties that have been recovered from this period," meaning that "Deuteronomy represents a counter-treaty: its authors turned the weapon of Assyrian imperialism into a bid for Judean independence," according to the scholars of the annotated Jewish Study Bible.[61] Hence, many of the old pieces of popular religion, whether there by syncretism or always there, are done away with, linked with the historic enemies, the Canaanites, to further delegitimize them, and effectively banned, for the sake of strengthening the distinctiveness of Israel against its neighbors and their faiths.

Now, finally, with context here and forewarning out of the way, let's take a closer look at the words. When it comes to child sacrifice, we can likely gloss over this one, because we highly doubt a single person in the modern era is burning children alive in religious ceremony, so there's no point in talking about it. There are mentions of soothsayers, diviners, and augurs here, though, so let's start with that. What's interesting about this passage is that it really seems to be trying to capture as many ideas about divination as it reasonably can in one spot, as if to just wipe the whole concept out altogether and replace it with the system of prophets. The Jewish Study Bible notes along the side of the Scriptures:

> It is no longer possible to identify precisely each of the prohibited forms of divination. Indeed, because the list is so comprehensive, it is unclear whether each term represented a distinct activity still known to the author or whether the list represents more of a scholastic compilation.[62]

However, if there's anything we know about religion, it's that people were going to debate anyway. We know from looking at Leviticus that there were a few interesting ideas for what could constitute divination and soothsaying—everything from astrology to putting bodily fluids in

---

59. Berline and Brettler, eds., *Jewish Study Bible*, 340.

60. Ibid., 341.

61. Ibid., 341.

62. Ibid., 388.

your eye to putting bones in your mouth while extremely high. If we might inject another thought for consideration here, though, we'd like to put forward this idea: that it isn't the act of *divination* in general that's the problem, but doing divination with other gods or spirits. If we take a peek at Isaiah 8:19-20 from the Jewish Study Bible:

> Now, should people say to you,
> "Inquire of the ghosts and famil-
> iar spirits that chirp and moan;
> for a people may inquire of its
> divine beings—of the dead on
> behalf of the living—for instruc-
> tion and message," surely, for
> one who speaks thus, there shall
> be no dawn.

Other versions of this verse, like the New International Version (NIV), have it pose the question, "Should not a people inquire of their God? Why consult the dead on behalf of the living?" It's this point that's important: while Deuteronomy seems to want to impose the prophet system only, and some might still consider divination a "rebellion" against God even in modern religion, the fact is that divination has been commanded *by* God of His priests before (the Levites in Exodus), it has been done *with* God before without negative effect or consideration (Joseph in Genesis), and it has even been used in the New Testament to get God's will far after Deuteronomy (the Apostles in Acts).

It's patently clear to see that soothsaying and divination have specifically to do with these pagan practices we've mentioned so far, and that the idea of *all* divination being outlawed to be replaced with the prophet system, as may be suggested in Deuteronomy, can't exactly hold anymore if there are no more prophets around—and no longer a system to find and bring them forward, like there once was. Now, the age of divination is back, because it's up to one's own self to contact God and discern His will directly, person by person. We clearly see which styles of divination are a problem and which aren't already, so it's safe to say that finding another system like casting lots—anything from using stones or dice to playing cards and Bible verses—is pretty safe. As for speaking with spirits of ancestors and the like, we touch on that in Chapter 19.

Honorable Mention: 2 Kings 17:15-19

Speaking of pagan practices, another verse that will pop up a lot is in 2 Kings. This describes how Israel fell out of God's good graces by doing a lot of practices they weren't supposed to do, like making "molten idols," and a sacred post to bow down "to all the host of heaven," worshiping even Baal, a competing foreign god. They tossed their kids into the fire, an obvious problem; they consulted with methods of divination that were not approved by God in any sense, and they had a foreigner on the throne as king (Jeroboam). Specifically, verse 15 has this language in the Jewish Study Bible:

> They spurned [God's] laws and the covenant that He had made with their fathers, and the warnings He had given them. They went after delusion and were deluded; *[they imitated] the nations that were about them, which the Lord had forbidden them to emulate.* (Emphasis ours.)

The problem here isn't that contacting God via casting lots or Urim and Thummim or prophets or dreams is an issue. It's not that miracle or magic is an issue. It's that God wanted His people to stay distinct and separate from those around them, and they didn't, mixing a lot of unsavory practices with their own customs and even turning away from God altogether. There's a lot wrong there, but magic? No. Magic is the least of our worries in that passage.

When it comes to the next part of Deuteronomy, the part about casting spells and doing witchcraft, that's actually pretty easily explained away. Probably the simplest explanation we'll find, actually. You see, the scholars who dissected the Hebrew of the Jewish Study Bible went and clarified that mentions of sorcery in this verse actually refer to the Akkadian word *kishpu*,[63] one on par with Sumerian *kashapu*. This is an extremely important distinction to make, because the terms *kishpu* and *kashapu* do not refer to all magic, as we know from our discussion of Exodus. They refer specifically to harmful types of magic, those much closer to what we would ascribe to any witches in the Middle Ages or that we would expect to see in fairytales about old women looking to gobble children up that wander onto their property.

---

63. Berline and Brettler, eds., *Jewish Study Bible*, 388.

In fact, some, like Geller, will go so far as to insist that "'witchcraft' is not magic":

> It shares some basic characteristics, since it aims to alter one's physical and social environment by influencing what happens to an individual. The witch's curse might influence illness; the sickness gets worse rather than get better. *Witchcraft might cause a person to imagine that colleagues or companions or family find one ugly or hateful. Witchcraft might make one have bad dreams or believe that the gods have turned angry; all of this reflects deep seated feelings of anxiety.* None of this is very desirable, but what is interesting is how poorly attested witchcraft as a discipline is in antiquity. We have virtually no ancient handbooks from Mesopotamia to explain how to perform so-called black magic. *Instead, we have numerous incantations and rituals showing how to protect us against witchcraft.*[64] (Emphasis ours.)

One thing extremely fascinating throughout human history—the parts of history that largely and consistently believed in magic—is that witchcraft was something done by an "other." Something you couldn't see being done, something you couldn't explain, and something you could easily pin on the neighbor you never really liked. Here, Geller's explanation seems to aid this idea: that the thought of some dark forces descending down on people was always a fear of others, and that they had to come up with ways, *magical* ways, to combat it.

It can't be overstated that other nations didn't like anti-social magic, or *witchcraft*, either—hence this word being a loanword from Akkadian in the first place. This is not a prohibition or idea specific to Judaism, Christianity, or Islam: other nations, like the Assyrians and Babylonians and Akkadians, had no love for those who would bewitch and harm others of their community. In fact, the Code of Hammurabi itself specified that those practicing sorcery (*kishpu*) should be put to death; it was thought that all misfortune came from evil spirits created by gods Anu and Enlil, and that witches and sorcerers activated it with the intent to harm others.[65] Babylonians, however, had another god that would help them via religious ritual and incantation: Ea, the "patron god of the various orders of priests who had been trained in the practice of exorcism, in the knowledge of spells and incantations, and in the interpretation of dreams and omens."[66] Witches were described

---

64. Geller, "Defining Magic," 17.

65. S.H. Hooke, *Babylonian and Assyrian Religion* (London: Hutchonson House, 1953), 44, https://archive.org/details/babylonianandass032592mbp.

66. Ibid., 43.

as women "in whose heart the word of [a victim's] misfortune dwells, on whose tongue [their] ruin is begotten, on whose lips [their] poison originates, in whose footsteps death stands"; on the other side of them was the *ashipu*, or exorcist, would be the one to do the magical prayers and rites to deflect evil, protect a community, and undo sorcery.[67] You can see quite clearly how the concept of witchcraft—specifically evil magic—was the target here, given how the cure to bad magic was good magic.

The Book of Deuteronomy seems to skip the whole idea of counter-magic that usually comes with witchcraft prohibitions and simply forbids the working of dark forces over one's neighbors on pain of death, which, if we as Christians are to love our neighbor as ourselves, we wouldn't think about doing anyway. Because why would you want to go out of your way to hurt and cause trouble for others for no reason?

Lastly in Deuteronomy comes a strike at those who contact the dead. This is pretty simple to explain: there were some pieces of popular religion in Israel that signified people were doing ancestral worship or veneration. The Jewish Study Bible notes that "family religion in antiquity devoted extensive attention to communicating with the dead, especially with ancestors."[68] As a culture meant to be separate and distinct from those around it, it makes sense that this would be another likely syncretic practice to be cut from Israelite society, especially since the focus was supposed to be wholly on God to begin with. Keeping in mind the verse from Isaiah we discussed earlier, it suggests that God can provide the best guidance of all, and that we don't need to bother the dead for our problems. However, another thing the Jewish Study Bible points out is that just because we're not supposed to do it, doesn't mean it's not effective.[69] You'll see a lot of people saying the dead can't hear you, or that spirits of ancestors are just demons in disguise, but that's not what Scripture suggests—nor is it what Christian, especially Catholic, tradition suggests, which again, we'll touch on in Chapter 19.

Honorable Mention: 1 Samuel 28:8-19

If we look at 1 Samuel 28:8-19 (another verse people will try to use against Christian Witches because they don't understand the real context of what's going on here), we see that, in fact, necromancy is quite plausible with human spirits. Not the necromancy you see in video games, where you're raising dead bodies to fight for you as zombies, but the necromancy where you contact and get answers from spirits. The Witch of En Dor in these verses is concerned that she's going to be

---

67. Ibid., 44.

68. Berline and Brettler, *Jewish Study Bible*, 388.

69. Ibid., 388.

killed for breaking the law that Saul set, to banish this pagan practice (*ov* and *yide'oni*) from the land, but a disguised Saul tells her she'll be fine and to just conjure the spirit of Samuel for him. She does, and Samuel's spirit comes up, described as a "divine being" by the witch herself.

But Samuel is annoyed. "Why have you disturbed me and brought me up?" Samuel asks, suggesting that Sheol, the place where the dead go, is one of rest that shouldn't be tampered with. Even still, the practice of necromancy, though forbidden "as heathen practices,"[70] according to the scholars of the Jewish Study Bible, is not ineffective; nowhere does the Bible say that these practices don't *work*, just that you shouldn't run to ghosts instead of God for answers. Beyond that, when people claim that Saul lost God's favor for going to this witch and doing this practice, we can dismiss this nonsense entirely, because the reason he went to this witch in the first place was because he hadn't been able to reach God through prophet, Urim & Thummim, or dreams—three methods of getting God's word directly.[71] The risen ghost of Samuel himself says the reason that Saul lost favor with God isn't for any of this magical work, but because Saul "did not obey the Lord and did not execute His wrath upon the Amalekites."[72] While people may point to 1 Chronicles 10:13-14 to disagree, it's important to note that the verse isn't accurate:

> Saul died for the trespass that he had committed against the Lord in not having fulfilled the command of the Lord; moreover, he consulted a ghost to seek advice, and *did not seek advice of the Lord*, so He had him slain and the kingdom transferred to David son of Jesse. (Emphasis ours.)

We know that Saul *did* try to seek the advice of God, over and over again, but that God didn't answer, prompting the fallen king to turn to forbidden practices. But the real reason for this mess is clear: it's a military failure, not a magical one, that sends Saul and his sons to death to be *with Samuel*, a prophet of God, in the afterlife. (Not Hell, but Sheol, where even prophets and other holy men of God go.) The ghost consultation certainly didn't help, even if it was consulting with a

---

70. Ibid., 599.

71. 1 Samuel 28:6

72. 1 Samuel 28:17

dead prophet of God (who could apparently still prophesize accurately even in death[73]), but that wasn't the main reason.

Even more interesting is that in "Jewish Miracle Workers and Magic in the Late Second Temple Period," an article within the *Jewish Annotated New Testament,* Gideon Vermes describes this woman not as a witch, but as a "professional miracle worker" specializing in necromancy—a verbiage that puts her on part with other miracle workers and prophets in the essay.[74] She's even shown here as a compassionate figure, that despite risking her life, and realizing it was Saul there who commanded her to do so, still tried to help. Where Saul can't even stand for lack of strength, she bids him to listen to her (and his courtiers) and eat something, and prepares quite a meal for him. There is an implicit humanity in this character, Witch as she may be: there is a complexity and nuance to her that makes her so beautifully human, even for the knowledge she shouldn't have and the practices she shouldn't do. Maybe we're straying a bit from the point here, but that humanity—that kinship that comes from seeing another person suffer, for whatever reason—and this extremely vulnerable moment between them all, is what makes the Bible's stories so rich and gripping and, yes, *human,* as much as they are divine.

Nonetheless, there is your explanation of Deuteronomy. May no one successfully hold it up to you with a sense of false righteousness ever again.

---

73. Berline and Brettler, *Jewish Study Bible,* 599.

74. Gideon Vermes, "Jewish Miracle Workers and Magic in the Late Second Temple Period," in the *Jewish Annotated New Testament* (London: Oxford University Press, 2017), 681.

Chapter Three

Magic in the Time of Jesus

N OW, ONE OF THE arguments you may see folks make is that all the stuff we just talked about in the Old Testament is moot, because that was *before* Jesus. With Jesus dead and risen, we don't need to know or care about any of these silly old laws in the Old Testament, so even if you *could* explain all this logically and simply, it doesn't matter!

(Watch how fast they change their tune when it comes time to talk about what they think idolatry is, the LGBTQ+ community, or the exact topic of this book: *witchcraft*.)

But for the sake of argument, let's say that we forget every single time someone hurls the Old Testament verses at us to delegitimize Christian Witchcraft and focus on the ones only from the New Testament. Of these, you may notice that there are remarkably fewer verses here than in our chapter about the Old Testament, and the reason for that is that the variation in word choice for magic just isn't as complex in the New Testament. Where there are several different words with all kinds of definitions to understand from the verses we've already discussed, in the New Testament, we don't find as much variety, and therefore we don't have to do nearly so much work to break these down into their cultural and sociopolitical meanings as we do in the Old Testament narratives. However, there is some helpful context that we might use to understand the backdrop of which this story is written.

The View of Magic in Antiquity

Without knowing what you already know, it might be easy to fall under the impression that all other nations outside of the Israelites and the Kingdom of Judah were somehow okay with magic, given how much work is put into distinguishing them from neighboring cultures and tribes. However, as we can see in our earlier discussions of other Semitic cultures (like the Akkadians), this is not the case. *But surely*, some might say, *if Greece had Hekate, and Rome had her counterpart Trivia, then they should've been okay with witchcraft in some degree.*

To which we say: they absolutely were not. Not under the term *witchcraft*, anyway. Just as the Akkadians, Israelites, and anyone else had their own concepts of good and bad magic, so too did the Greeks and Romans. According to Wilken, "the practice of magic was a criminal offense in the Roman Empire, and the word *magician* a term of opprobrium and abuse," showing us that the spirit of the Witch Trials and the Inquisition and every other disaster at the hands of state religion certainly wasn't invented at the dawn of the Christian era.[1] Moreover, the idea that having a *god* of magic could save anyone from such accusations or legal punishment is a naive one. Wilken demonstrates that the Romans were no strangers to butchering folks over religious rites to gods of the empire's many, as is shown by the persecution of people engaging in Bacchic rites—Bacchus being the Roman cognate of Dionysus, god of wine, insanity, religious ecstasy, fertility, and theater, whose Grecian festivals were transplanted into Rome.[2] The Romans, a conservative people, created very specific outlets in their society for certain behaviors, and having drunken orgies in the woods was not one of them—not even to a god the state recognized.

This background is important, as we'll see later. In a world where magic is looked at with suspicion by default, and where one of the key features of the Apostles and Jesus Himself are *miracles*, which Conner notes were seen as essentially the same thing as magical spells,[3] we can already see the stage forming for a potent "anti-magic" stance in the New Testament just by virtue of the fact that it would be extremely dangerous for these Biblical figures to navigate Roman society otherwise. However, that doesn't mean that the Greek words used in the New Testament perfectly translate to *all magic* any more than the Hebrew words in the Old Testament did, and that's exactly what we're here to inspect.

New Testament Verses Incorrectly Applied

Before we dive into the New Testament, I think it's worth making some things clear:

1. The New Testament is a collection of letters that were argued

---

1. Wilken, *Christians as the Romans Saw Them*, 99.

2. Ibid., 17.

3. Conner, *Magic in Christianity*, 71, 132-133, 215.

about at length as to whether or not they were truly inspired.

2. There are books that were important to early Christians (like the Acts of Paul and Thecla) that never made it into the Bible.

3. Outside of the four Gospels within the New Testament, just about every single other thing is either a story about the Apostles (one book: Acts) or the letters of St. Paul or St. Peter. Two men of *many* who could've been considered inspired in their writings and teachings, yet two men who make up an unsettling majority of the writings that survived into mainstream Christian thought.

There is so much that goes unsaid about this time period, which is a shame. A rebel religion, considered a superstitious cult by Rome that didn't deserve the time of day (and certainly not any civil protections), this religion was splintered across so many different schools of thought and so many different interpretations of God, Jesus, the Holy Spirit, and the very story of Christ on the cross. To reduce it all down to the story we have now, further distorted through our barebones understanding of Roman and Jewish society, takes us further *away* from knowing what our Savior was talking about, not closer. And so, it's with this context that we dive into the New Testament, ready to analyze the verses so commonly used against magic that, as you might've guessed, are about things a bit more specific than just flinging herbs and incantations around.

Let's take a look, starting with Acts.

ACTS 19:19

> *And a number of those who had practiced magic arts brought their books together and burned them in the sight of all. And they counted the value of them and found it came to fifty thousand pieces of silver.*

Sara says:

This was another interesting verse to look at, mostly because the word used for magic here was not any of the typical ones we've talked about. This word, *periergos,* shows up only one other time in the New Testament, in 1 Timothy 5:13 (the meaning of which I've emphasized):

> Besides that, they learn to be
> idlers, going about from house
> to house, and not only idlers,
> but also gossips and *busybodies*,
> saying what they should not.

It was during a conversation with Father Kyle that we looked into this word together and wondered for what reason this word used to refer to magic could also be used to refer to *busybodies*, or *gossips*, or general *meddlers*. He posed a question that I think warrants some consideration: "were these magical grimoires and tomes, or tabloids?" Were they collections of ideas they'd snatched from other sorcerers to copy and try and use for themselves?

It's possible. After all, in some spells of the Greek magical papyri, the term for *craft* is *empeiria*, with *empeiros* being a related word that, as you may have guessed, is the root of *empirical*.[4] You've heard this word before: *empirical evidence*, *empirical research*, so on and so forth. Here, Conner puts forward the idea that "magical spells, like recipes, were based on observation and experiment and were transmitted generation to generation"; in this way, magic and medicine of the time both had their respective experts adding "personal experience to received opinion."[5] The magi of Acts were *meddling*, if you will, with the affairs of miracle workers who, going off a circulation of specific ideas and methods of achieving the results one wanted from other magicians rather than really grasping the full esoteric understanding of the power they were trying to work into the world.

Additionally, in his discussion of Acts 19:19, Conner adds more color to the term by insisting that *periergos* is referencing acts of "undue or misdirected curiosity"[6]; he draws on the words of Matthew W. Dickie to note that church fathers like Irenaeus were lambasting these early Ephesian Christians for "interfering in what ought to be left undisturbed, which is to say, practicing magic."[7] And moreover, many weren't doing it for the sake of helping their community, or for the sake of faith, but for simple coin—not a difficult motivation to understand, but certainly not the best when you're showing off your God-given in the streets power for the sake of getting more and more money and stealing the glory for yourself. However, some *were* doing this for the name of God, and we'll talk more about that soon.

---

4. Conner, *Magic in Christianity*, 47.

5. Ibid., 47.

6. Bauer & Danker quoted in Conner, 367.

7. Dickie quoted in Conner, 368.

All of this is important to understand, though, because in the full context of Acts, we find Simon the Magos (or Magician) starting in Acts 8:9. He was one that "practiced magic in the city and amazed the people of Samaria, saying that he himself was somebody great," according to the scriptures, but when the Apostle Philip came through and demonstrated miracles and signs even *greater* than Simon's, Simon wanted that power, too. Simon *himself* was amazed, in a flip of the roles presented here in the Bible. The people themselves realized that there was more than Simon had to offer; they heard the gospel and understood power more magnificent than what they'd just been so entertained by. But let's take a look at what happens once Simon sees this happen, later in Acts 8:17-24:

> Then they laid their hands on them and they received the Holy Spirit. Now when Simon saw that the Spirit was given through the laying on of the apostles' hands, he offered them money, saying, "Give me this power also, so that anyone on whom I lay my hands may receive the Holy Spirit." But Peter said to him, "May your silver perish with you, because you thought you could obtain the gift of God with money! You have neither part nor lot in this matter, for your heart is not right before God. Repent, therefore, of this wickedness of yours, and pray to the Lord that, if possible, the intent of your heart may be forgiven you. For I see that you are in the gall of bitterness and in the bond of iniquity." And Simon answered, "Pray for me to the Lord, that nothing of what you have said may come upon me."

Plainly, what's happening here is that Simon is trying to *buy* the power of Christ so he can continue being a fancy magic man for the sake of having a lot of focus and attention on him. His signs and wonders are not as great as Philip's; his fame in the city is pretty much a bygone conclusion when the heavy hitters show up with their incredible holy miracles. But Peter sees right through him, knowing Simon doesn't give a damn about faith and only wants to keep playing

Street Houdini to get people's attention. That's the real issue here. You'll read Bible interpretations that try and condemn Simon for doing wonders at all, but the text doesn't do that; what it does is shoot him down for trying to pretend to be more powerful than he is (and for trying to buy the power of the Holy Spirit as if it's a cheap party trick).

We don't think we need to explain the issue there. We think it's rightly apparent. But we'll add onto what St. John Chrystostom, an early Church Father and archbishop of Constantinople, had to say about the events of Acts 19 specifically, which follows in the same vein of the vitriol Simon got in Acts 8:

> See the villany of the men! They still continued to be Jews, while wishing to make a gain of that Name. All that they did was for glory and profit... (Hereby) the power of the demons is shown to be a great one, when it is against unbelievers.[8]

Still, this has a jab at Jewish folks, which we understand now is anti-semitic unnecessary; no one should be forced to believe in Jesus. Nonetheless, St. John's anger is more focused on the fact that these men tried to use that power without believing in Jesus at all, throwing it around like a cheap tool to get their work done and move on.

Before we move on from Acts 19:19, though, we would like to point out one very important thing to understand: *there was a lot of propaganda against Jewish people woven into the New Testament*, the animosity of which seems counter intuitive considering that the first Christians *were* Jewish, but in fact makes quite a bit of sense when you understand the political landscape of the time and the first few centuries following Jesus. You see, a large part of Roman values at the time were the values of social conservatism and tradition; while they didn't understand or care for Jewish tradition, religion, or values, they at least acknowledged those values had some history and substance, and were therefore not considered simple superstitious nonsense like early Christianity was.[9] Christianity in its earliest form was considered an "apostasy from Judaism," one that had "deserted the Jewish law even though Jesus, the founder of Christianity, was a Jew."[10]

Jewish people made up around "four to six million people" in the Roman empire, and Christianity, as a fledgling religion, "had to make its way alongside of, and sometimes in opposition to, the well-established Jewish communities"; they did this by trying to claim that they were the "rightful inheritors of the Jewish tradition," and that

---

8. "St. John Chrysostom On Acts," Patristic Bible Commentary, https://sites.google.com/si te/aquinasstudybible/home/acts-of-the-apostles/st-john-chrysostom-on-acts.

9. Wilken, *Christians as the Romans Saw Them*, 63.

10. Ibid., 113.

the destruction of the Temple and Jerusalem under emperor Titus in 70 CE meant that Judaism was effectively an obsolete religion.[11] The problem, though, was that early Christians didn't follow Jewish law anymore, and that Jewish people obviously still existed and practiced their laws with all the zeal and piety that they ever had. According to Wilken, the only way the Christian claim of inheritance could've held any water was if Jewish people no longer existed or practiced their customs, which obviously wasn't the case; Jewish communities "rejected out of hand the silly idea that the upstart religion had displaced Judaism."[12] In a twist of irony, the language used towards the early Christians by critic Celsus, who did respect the many different traditional religions that made up the Roman empire, echoes that which we hear so many Christians pin on everyone else today: "Deluded by Jesus, [Christians] have left the law of their fathers, and have been quite ludicrously deceived, and have deserted to another name and another life."[13] For a few *centuries*, Christians fought bitterly for acceptance of their beliefs, and they did not fight fair.

Why point all this out? To give you context of the animosity that existed between Jewish people and the Christians that claimed to supersede a still living, deeply historied religion and ethnicity. With this context, you might understand why Acts 19:19 has a darker undertone than those who read this devoid of political context might realize. The fact of the matter is that the ones who apparently had such magical books in Acts 19:19 were not pagans, were not Christians, but were in fact Jewish exorcists, working within a framework of magical practice long understood and accepted in the eyes of God. In fact, Flavius Josephus (37 CE - 100 CE), a Jewish apologist, historian, and leader of rebel forces against the Roman army, wrote about such things in his work, *Antiquities of the Jews*, as he argued that "the Jews are an ancient and honorable people who live by a divinely given code of laws."[14] He wrote about exorcism in *Antiquities of the Jews*, saying:

> God also enabled [Solomon] to learn that skill which expels demons, which is a science useful and sanative to men. He composed such incantations also by which distempers are alleviated. And he left behind him the manner of using exorcisms, by which they drive away demons, so that they never return; and this method of cure is of great force unto this day; for I have seen a certain man of my own country, whose name was

---

11. Ibid., 114, 185, 187.

12. Ibid., 187

13. Celsus as quoted in Wilken, 115.

14. Jack Pastor, "Josephus," in Jewish Annotated New Testament, eds. Amy-Jill Levine and Marc Zvi Brettler. London: Oxford University Press, 2017, 717.

Eleazar, releasing people that were demoniacal in the presence of Vespasian, and his sons, and his captains, and the whole multitude of his soldiers.[15]

Even better, Josephus details the exact method in which these demons were cast out, *even up to his day.* He notes that Eleazar would "put a ring that had a root of one of those sorts mentioned by Solomon to the nostrils of the demoniac," drawing the demon out of a possessed person's nose and commanding it not to come back, "making still mention of Solomon, and reciting the incantations which he composed."[16] Like in Acts, it seems this Eleazar fellow is using the weight of Solomon's name in his exorcism, which Josephus stresses is a method of exorcism taught to Solomon himself by God in the first place.

The last part of this exorcism method, after "Eleazar would persuade and demonstrate to the spectators that he had such a power," would be to "set a little way off a cup or basin full of water, and commanded the demon, as he went out of the man, to overturn it, and thereby to let the spectators know that he had left the man.," and the rest was a wrap.[17] In this method was a lot of showmanship, given how many steps are for the express purpose of proving one's powers to the crowd. But the concept of using a powerful magician's name to bolster one's exorcising authority is a part of Jewish exorcism, and so you can see how in Acts, there's a marked effort to try and delegitimize Jewish practices and religion to puff up the importance and power of their new traditions. They wanted to make a foothold for themselves, to make a stark difference between believers and unbelievers of *any* kind, even their own fellow children of God. The truth is, though, that what these Jewish exorcists did was nothing that would've been outside the bounds of people of God; it isn't the act of exorcism itself, or the idea of magic, that's the problem.

The problem, as we've already discussed at length, is trying to turn a quick buck off the name of someone you don't even actually believe in. And a Christian Witch, someone who truly believes in God and Jesus and the Holy Spirit, isn't out to do something like that. Christian Witches are aware that when they have their faith, even if just a little mustard seed's worth, they in fact already have that direct connection with God, and the power He gave them to channel His light for the sake of themselves and others. They know that they have the ability to let God work through you by way of the power He wove into the very fabric of their soul, and that they don't need to prove it to anybody with big shows of power and might.

---

15. Flavius Josephus, *Antiquities of the Jews*, translated by William Whiston, Lexundria, 8.21-8.60, https://lexundria.com/j_aj/8.21-8.60/wst.

16. Ibid.

17. Ibid.

A Christian Witch just needs to do what's right for themselves and their loved ones under the gentle guidance of God.

GALATIANS 5:19-21

> *The acts of the flesh are obvious: sexual immorality, impurity and debauchery; idolatry and witchcraft; hatred, discord, jealousy, fits of rage, selfish ambition, dissensions, factions and envy; drunkenness, orgies, and the like. I warn you, as I did before, that those who live like this will not inherit the kingdom of God.*

And here we go. The famous, constant, ever-quoted verse in condemnation of witchcraft from the New Testament, this line from St. Paul to the churches of Galatia remains a seeming trump card for those who believe Christianity and magic are incompatible. The Greek word used in this line, *pharmakeia*, is one that has specific connotations and meanings, as you might imagine—just as any other word used in any other verse we've looked at has thus far. However, truth be told, there are so many things to consider about this verse, in no particular list of importance. Before we get into the specifics of this word *pharmakeia*, I think we should start with the most obvious of all here:

St. Paul's letters were letters to specific churches. Meant for specific people. Why something like *letters* would be included in the New Testament, especially letters meant for specific churches to address specific issues, is puzzling when you actually think about it. For instance, if someone e-mails their priest, and that priest comes back with a really wise and well thought out answer, does that suddenly make it Scripture? And if the reason St. Paul's letters are Scripture is because he's an Apostle—or, in general, a holy one chosen by God—then wouldn't any Saint's writings be fair game for being a part of Scripture? Why then, with Saints being registered over the course of centuries (and some, like St. Hildegard von Bingen, being registered as late as 2010), would not the Scriptures be constantly updated, revised, and added onto? Because surely any of St. Hildegard's books, like her *Physica*, should be contestants for Scripture given that she's not only a Saint, but a *Doctor of the Church.* But then the Church would have to contend that maybe things like crystals are more than just rocks, and in fact good at keeping evil away thanks to the power God put in them.

But no. No one seems to understand the issues with putting a bunch of letters from one Apostle into the Canon over the words or writings or actions of any other Apostle, which is odd considering Galatians' inspiration was due to the words of *rival Apostles.* The Apostles sent by James, the brother of Jesus Himself, were the ones who were giving directions to the churches of Galatia that got St. Paul heated enough to write this letter. In Galatians, he goes and "angrily accuses these teachers of perverting the gospel... of being unprincipled, of demanding circumcision merely to avoid persecution from Torah-observant Jews, and to provide an occasion for boasting"—quite the long list of accusations, in fact.[18] And against others sent by an Apostle, no less! It seems more like a cat-fight than what we'd call Scripture! But because these folks were teaching obedience to the laws of the Torah (the first five books of the Jewish Bible, Genesis, Exodus, Leviticus, Numbers, and Deuteronomy), and they "attacked [St. Paul's] apostolic credibility,"[19] St. Paul had to turn around and hand it right back to them, which is where we get the famous exclamation of Galatians 1:8-9:

> But even if we or an angel from heaven should proclaim to you a gospel contrary to what we proclaimed to you, let that one be accursed! As we have said before, so now I repeat, if anyone proclaims to you a gospel contrary to what you received, let that one be accursed!

Man, all that drama coming from the guy that believed no one should get married, get unmarried, or overall "change the condition in which [they] were called," which is believed to be because he thought Jesus coming back in his lifetime.[20] All this fuss from a guy that has been wrong on at least a couple of occasions throughout his time and wasn't by any means infallible. Safe to say that the mud-slinging and insistence on one Apostle being right over another is exactly what it seems like: pure theological and philosophical differences with other people also trying to spread the Gospels.

Here's a question we're going to pose now, though: who is St. Paul to say this? One can love the guy, difficult as he is to wrestle with and for all the wacky things he says, but even if he's an Apostle, he's neither Jesus nor God—the only two who really should be throwing rules and laws around to begin with, according to either Jewish or Christian

---

18. Shayne J. D. Cohen, "The Letter of Paul to the Galatians" in *the Jewish Annotated New Testament,* 373.

19. Ibid., 373.

20. 1 Corinthians 7:20, 1 Thessalonians 4:15-17

theology. In sections like Deuteronomy 4:2, the writer posits God as saying:

> You shall not add to the word
> which I am commanding you,
> nor take away from it, that you
> may keep the commandments
> of the Lord your God which I
> command you.

Likewise, this idea appears in the Gospel of Mary Magdalene—a non-Canonical gospel, yes, but certainly one that we argue *should* be Canonical, given that its earliest Greek texts are apparently dated by scholars like Karen King to "the first half of the second century," which, if correct, "would place [it] within the earliest strata of Christian writings, roughly contemporaneous with the Gospel of John"—a gospel that *is* among the four Canonical gospels.[21] Nonetheless, the Gospel of Mary Magdalene 4:38 has Jesus saying:

> Do not lay down any rules be-
> yond what I appointed you, and
> do not give a law like the lawgiv-
> er lest you be constrained by it.

Yet among the things St. Paul rattles off in Galatians 5:19-21, a list nearly matching those that are present in Mark 7:21-23 and Matthew 15:19, there's a few additions, with the mention of idolatry and sorcery being among them.

The former makes some sense, given the influence of true monotheism at the time on Jewish and early Christian people (even though St. Paul acknowledges some concept of other gods existing for non-believers in 1 Corinthians 5-6). And even then, idolatry is an easy enough issue to deal with. You may have heard it said that using crystals is idolatry, because to use them is to worship them, but we guarantee you that this is little more than a complete misunderstanding of the concept—and that's because this concept was much more complicated than just *using* or *acknowledging the value of* an item. Per Kugel's description in *The God of Old*, it seems that the practice of idolatry was quite specific, in which people, in an effort to get their gods to answer prayers to them faster, tried to draw said gods down from the

---

21. Cynthia Bourgeault, "The Gospel of Mary Magdalene, by Cynthia Bourgeault," Parabola, January 29, 2015, https://www.contemplative.org/the-gospel-of-mary-magdalene-dialo gues-one-and-two/.

heavens and into a clay or stone figurine.[22] They went so far as to treat these idols like the actual living gods, feeding them and trying to help them breathe better, and above all hoping that their prayers would go to the god trapped inside the stone rather than have to travel *all* the way up to the skies for an answer. So unless you think your rose quartz is a literal deity trapped in pretty pink crystal, there's really nothing to worry about there. It's the latter mentioned thing in this verse, the *sorcery*, that is a funny edition for a number of reasons.

The first of which is that St. Paul himself was accused of being a magician *and jailed for it* (among several other things during his time as an Apostle).

In the Apocryphal text known as the Acts of Paul and Thecla, likely written between 160 and 180 CE and included among the Acts of Thomas, Andrew, Peter, and John,[23] a little bit of a mess happens with St. Paul and the local Iconian authorities. Because St. Paul is there to preach the word of God, inspiring people to change their ways and follow Christ in earnest, he ends up catching the attention of one bride-to-be, Thecla, who stays listening to him from her window. She's stuck there for apparently three days and nights, "tied to the window like a spider, [laying] hold of what is said by Paul with a strange eagerness and awful emotion."[24] It got so bad, with Thecla just outright refusing to listen to either her mother Theocleia or her fiance Thamyris, that Thamyris, in a rage, had St. Paul tossed in jail for "[making] virgins averse to marriage" and other such charges.[25]

That didn't stop Thecla, though. She went so far as to visit him in prison and be honestly a little obsessed with our old boy, to the point that St. Paul got dragged *out* of prison for a trial before the tribunal, with the mob yelling: "He is a magician! Away with him!"[26]

Uh-oh.

Now, naturally, anyone reading this might think that, of course St. Paul wasn't a magician; he was just preaching the good Word and capturing the hearts of those who wanted to be saved by the grace of God through their Savior, Jesus Christ. Right? Maybe, but consider this: St. Paul had power bestowed upon him by the Holy Spirit, which we see in the *Canonical* Acts, chapter 16, where he exorcises a spirit out of a slave-woman that enabled her to see the future because she wouldn't stop yelling after them that they're true men of God:

22. Kugel, *The God of Old*, 83.

23. Tony Burke, "Apocryphal Acts," in *obo* in Biblical Studies, last modified August 26, 2013,, https://www.oxfordbibliographies.com/view/document/obo-9780195393361/obo-9780195393361-0149.xml.

24. The Acts of Paul and Thecla

25. Ibid.

26. Ibid.

> Once when we were going to
> the place of prayer, we were
> met by a female slave who had
> a spirit by which she predicted
> the future. She earned a great
> deal of money for her owners
> by fortune-telling. She followed
> Paul and the rest of us, shouting,
> "These men are servants of the
> Most High God, who are telling
> you the way to be saved." She
> kept this up for many days. Fi-
> nally Paul became so annoyed
> that he turned around and said
> to the spirit, "In the name of
> Jesus Christ I command you to
> come out of her!" At that mo-
> ment the spirit left her.[27]

(And then, because he'd gone and ruined the slave-owners' ability to make money off this girl, they went and told the authorities that he was teaching religious practices forbidden to Romans and had him arrested. Our friend seemed to have a talent for getting tossed in jail.)

But the point is this: St. Paul did, indeed, have the power to perform exorcism via the Holy Spirit. One who doesn't know better might cry that this isn't magic, it's *miracle*—but what we know about magic and miracle in St. Paul's day, way back when in antiquity, is that magic, miracle, *and* medicine were actually *synonymous*, according to Conner. He points out that any distinctions between magic and religion were "designed to raise the petticoats of faith above the gutter of superstition," when in reality, "there is no clear distinction to be made."[28] According to Schäfer, "the notion of magic as distinct from religion seems to be alien to the Hebrew Bible," and indeed we can see this from any look at miracle workers in the Bible.[29] Vermes supports this idea as he describes that "stories about Jewish miracle workers abound in ancient Jewish and in early Christian literature."[30]

Already in Exodus 7-12, Moses and Aaron, *as well as* magicians in the Egyptian court, "perform great deeds" at the command of God Himself—and Moses and Aaron have *stronger* miracles, thanks to God's power, "so that the credit for their successes helps build their

---

27. Acts 16:16-18

28. Conner, *Magic in Christianity*, vi.

29. Schafer quoted in Conner, vi.

30. Vermes, "Jewish Magic and Miracle Workers," 680.

stature."[31] A typical rebuttal is that God gave them this power, so it's not *really* magic, but Vermes goes on to point at Elijah and Elisha, "whose miracles are on a much smaller scale and often are not even instigated by God," like when Elijah absolutely trounced the prophets of Baal "by calling down fire from heaven" in 1 Kings 18.[32] Even in Jesus's era, it wasn't *just* Jesus out there doing super cool miracles; it was folks like "Honi's grandchildren, Abba Hilkiah and Hanan 'the hider,' so called because he would hide when people came to ask him to make it rain."[33] Hanan, being called Abba (Father) by those who wanted him to make it rain, would then pray "Master of the Universe, act for the sake of those who cannot distinguish between the Abba who gives rain and the abba who does not give rain"—a prayer that, by asking for God's action, in the end brought some rain.[34] A prayer that, to anyone else in antiquity, would be understood as a spell, because "*prayers* and *spells* were not distinguished in magical books," not even the Greek magical papyrae.[35]

Because in antiquity, the only difference between magic, miracle, and even *medicine* was who the magician or miracle worker called upon to draw their power—God, a pagan deity, a simple spirit, so on and so forth.[36] In effect, based on the archaeological and anthropological work done, the evidence you've already seen written firsthand by figures like Flavius Josephus regarding exorcism, and the nature of the Scriptures themselves, this much is clear: whether or not the power comes from the Holy Spirit or a common *daimon* (a term for a lower level spirit in Greek religion), there is simply "no difference between magic and medicine or healing and exorcism"—no distinction between magic, medicine, and miracle in antiquity.[37] That's because all three of these things had the same idea attached to them: "*human fate is under the control of spirit forces.*"[38]

The only reason any distinction came about in the first place, according to scholars like Mastrocinque, was from the "need to reject the accusations that Christ and his followers were practitioners of magic," an accusation that came from pagan and Jewish opponents alike,[39] in order to compete "both with pagan wonder workers and... competing Christian sects that used accusations of practicing magic as

---

31. Ibid., 680.

32. Ibid., 680.

33. Ibid., 681.

34. Ibid., 681.

35. Conner, *Magic in Christianity*, 126.

36. Ibid., 126.

37. Ibid, viii.

38. Ibid., vii.

39. Vermes, "Jewish Magic and Miracle Workers," 682.

a standard polemic device."[40] The game of semantics started precisely to discredit other faiths, magicians, and opponents, and Conner makes this point, too, as he points to one scholar, Klauck, who says:

> When systems competed against each other, this accu-
> sation regularly provided a handy instrument: one party
> would accuse the other of black magic, hurling its entire
> available arsenal of abuse and polemics. As for one's
> own group, it practiced magic of the older, unreservedly
> positive kind—unless one preferred a priori to avoid
> the risk of even the remotest connection between one's
> own side and the concept of magic.[41]

Ah. There it is. Notice the term *black magic* Klauck uses (which is an outdated and problematic term in modern magic, as the concept of *white* and *black* magic has some nasty racial implications that you certainly want to avoid). Nonetheless, this distinction of *black* magic, which we'll call *baneful* magic instead, is where we can finally, after all of this context and background and understanding of what we're even talking about and with Galatians and the man that wrote it, get into what the term *pharmakeia* is about. (As an aside, you might've noticed by now how much *thought* and *context* and *understanding* has to go into even the most seemingly "simple" and "clear" verses on what the Bible says about nearly any topic, and why anyone who just starts whipping Bible verses out like slingshot pellets probably hasn't given the proper attention to them that they require.) But the term *pharmakeia*, which sounds an awful lot like *pharmacy*, has a specific connotation to it that shouldn't be overlooked, and that is exactly what Klauck referenced: baneful magic.

Conner makes the point that *pharmaka* means "*black magic* or *poisoning*," and in the context of the Roman empire, which didn't seem to care much for distinctions, the term "*venerificium*, like the Greek *pharmakeia*, 'can refer to spells or to a generalized notion of magic'" because "magic and murder by poisoning were associated in legal texts."[42] As we've discussed, it was *Roman* law that "considered magic 'above all as a murderous activity,'" hence those found guilty of it were subjected to "banishment, being thrown to the beasts, being burned alive."[43] Magic and murder were tied tightly together, to the point that even "Peter's curse on Ananias and Sapphira" in Acts 5 *of the Bible* "was subject to legal punishment" in the eyes of Roman

---

40. Mastrocinque as quoted in Conner & Conner, *Magic in Christianity*, viii.

41. Klauck quoted in Conner, 340

42. Conner, *Magic in Christianity*, 55, 95.

43. Ibid., 94.

critic Porphyry.[44] Another critic of Christians, the Greek philosopher Celsus, was even "the first critic to call Jesus a magician and charge the Christians with practicing magic," and by this point, no doubt, Christianity was considered a "new criminal (*maleficus*) superstition," with *maleficus* a word that can refer to magic and magicians.[45] But if the idea magic was to be dissected, it wasn't between Magic and Miracle, but Magic and Murder—fraud, poisoning, harm, something that even the most destitute could use against the highest of society, making it the most dangerous, and therefore most wicked and punishable, thing to those holding the power.

Though, as we did note, *pharmakaia* sounds a lot like *pharmacy*, too. It does have associations with medicine and drugs, to the point that some Christians have actually used this to (foolishly) argue against the use of modern medicine. It turns out there is some overlap between the application of magic and medicine, as we know that some magical feats of Greek and Roman pagans were to "evoke the presence of the god in a human being by creating a trance or an altered state of consciousness... his or her eyes smeared with drugs," causing said god to "appear in a luminous apparition."[46] Obviously, something like this would be quite outside the bounds of good Christian behavior, even in the early Church (which absolutely *decimated* what they considered a heretical sect, known as the Phibionites, who apparently "practiced ritual intercourse and the eating of an unborn child"—hopefully just a rumor, but nonetheless one of the many stories that contributed to a Roman and general pagan bewilderment of this newfangled, upstart religious group).[47] And you bet that such stories also got early church fathers like Eusebius and Justin the Martyr to lash out with harsh words and horror.

So maybe St. Paul wanted to decry those who worked against his specific brand of Apostolic ministry, as he was already doing in Galatians, be they pagan or fellow followers of Christ. Maybe, as a Roman citizen himself, he saw the *pharmakos*, the sorcerer, as a wicked worker of baneful magic, a *murderer*, a person out to harm and poison and ruin others. Or maybe, given his experience in Roman jails himself, and the ease in which others accused him of being a magician just for speaking, he was looking to scare Christians away from the very concept of magic, lest they be mistaken for such evil-doers and likewise destroyed.

Though it did not stop *him* from being destroyed under the reign of Emperor Nero.[48]

---

44. Ibid., 94.

45. Wilken, *Christians as the Romans Saw Them*, 98.

46. Ibid., 168.

47. Ibid., 20.

48. Richard Goode, "The Death of the Apostle Paul," Newman University, 2019, https://bib leresearchtoday.com/2019/02/27/the-death-of-the-apostle-paul/.

REVELATION 18:23

> *The light of a lamp will never shine in you again. The voice of bridegroom and bride will never be heard in you again. Your merchants were the world's important people. By your sorcery all the nations were led astray.*

This word used for sorcery, *pharmakeia*, is exactly the same as in Galatians, and yet there's just as much to unpack here for entirely different reasons. The book of Revelation, as described by David Frankfurter, is a "creative combination" of the two genres of *"apokalypsis*—that is, a literary disclosure of heavenly secrets—and a prophecy—that is, an oral communication of divine intentions."[49] Rather than using the names of standard Biblical prophets and authorities to relay such secrets, this book goes by an "unknown Jewish seer in the Jesus movement, 'John'" and is unique in that rather than portraying heavenly bliss, "details the multiple eschatological sufferings of sinners, to excite or comfort audiences with the prospect of their enemies' downfall."[50] Given the persecutions of Christians that occurred especially in the religion's infancy, with Roman officials like Pliny the Elder seeing nothing but "a depraved superstition carried to extravagant lengths" and deciding to simply have them put to death for it, it shouldn't come as a shock that such brutal images of death and despair and destruction could bring people *comfort.*[51]

This attitude scans into today's use of it, too. As you might know, Revelation is the text that so many Evangelicals especially love to use to show all the non-believing heathens how sorry they'll be when Jesus comes back and violently destroys the world, throwing all the sinners into hell and sending all the super righteous folks straight to heaven to be by His side; it's the place they keep drawing all their desperate attempts at proving Biblical prophecy from. And of course, it's a part of the Bible used to justify a lot of anti-semitic nonsense with talk about "so-called Jews" and their "synagogues of Satan" (even though this was obviously meant to stab at people who *called* themselves Jewish

---

49. David Frankfurter, "The Revelation to John" in *The Jewish Annotated New Testament*, 536.

50. Ibid., 537.

51. Wilken, *Christians as the Romans Saw Them*, 48.

and acted awfully, not about all Jewish people—but anti-semites don't think).[52] All interesting interpretations and depictions of Jesus aside, like Him being "a seven-eyed Lamb... a luminescent old man with flaming eyes... and a mounted warrior with a sword emerging from his mouth," it is, plainly, a wild conclusion to the New Testament.[53]

Anyway, here's the thing about Revelation: this section specifically is depicting the fall of Babylon. An age-old enemy of Israel, one attributed to creating the ironclad systems of astrology that we already know essentially considered a person bound and chained to the whim of the stars above,[54] and who had many other means of magic that were outside the bounds of what was allowed for Israelites as a pagan culture. This passage in Revelation, then, marks such a thing, and the scholars addressing it note that "protective rituals were part of state ceremony in many ancient cultures," some of which God Himself overrode (like when He voided the Babylonians' magic in Isaiah 47:9).[55] So for the speaker of Revelation, then, this issue of magic is a real one, not a poetic one, and consisted of the "impure practices that demonic forces introduced to the world through fornication"[56] (which reminds us something of the Book of Enoch, where Azazel teaches women the art of root work, men the art of metalworking, and people in general the art of cosmetics).

Notice for a moment, though, how only magic gets this condemnation here in Revelation, and not the other practices that came about from fornication, like metalworking? No matter where it came from, apparently smithing ore into sharp things to stab each other with and makeup to make ourselves prettier with is just too good to pass up. Magic, though—*that's* where these authors draw the line.

Given the nature of Roman society, in which this text was written, it's understandable to see why magic specifically would get targeted. In a society that saw sorcery as something superstitious and ugly, something terrible and harmful to man as an individual and society as a whole, it would be obvious to use this as a means of degrading one's spiritual opponents. As Conner puts it, quoting Rives:

> For a clear majority of people living in the 1st century who bothered to give it any thought, *magic* basically meant *bad religion*—"activities or beliefs that the speaker regards with disapproval... religious prac-

---

52. Levine and Brettler, eds., *Jewish Annotated New Testament*, 537.

53. Ibid., 537.

54. Conner, *Magic in Christianity*, 45.

55. Levine and Brettler, eds., *Jewish Annotated New Testament*, 568.

56. Ibid., 568.

tices... considered immoral, fraudulent, or otherwise unacceptable." [57]

For the writer of Revelation, no doubt this idea—that magic was *bad religion*, that these were illegitimate magical practices—took hold here. With *pharmakeia* referring to sorceries we know were thought of as harmful magic, poisoning, or generally just religious misconduct, we can figure that this understanding of the term made its way into Revelation.

Therefore, there's not that much else to say about this here. We can see where Revelation, while claiming authority as prophecy and apocalyptic literature, is full of allegory, with a white horse ridden by a rider name "Faithful and True"[58] (Jesus), and a figure "clothed in a robe dipped in blood," whose name is "the Word of God"[59] (again, Jesus), the new heaven and earth, so on and so forth. We also know that the reference to sorcery and Babylon have to do with specific *ideas* of magic, and that accusing others of doing magic was something quite literally anyone who had an understanding of religious rite and ritual would do (whether pagan against Christian, Christian against pagan, or Christian against Christian). We know that the key word in the term "Holy Spirit" was *spirit* in the eyes of pagan critics, who were no stranger to invoking their own spirits for religious practices and spellwork, and that magic was magic, no matter whether the Apostles and other Christians wanted to dress it up all prettily or not. So when it comes to Revelation's mention of sorcery, it's just more of the same.

Us against them. Winners versus losers. Good *miracle* versus bad *magic*, bad *religion*. And we see this idea come about in modern Christian society still. Disguising one's craft can be as simple as calling one's power the gifts of the [Holy] Spirit instead of witchcraft, using more acceptable terminology to sneak right about in plain sight (and in fact, plenty folks do call it that to avoid the common pearl-clutching that comes when calling it witchcraft). When you know what *pharmakeia* meant to people, and the context in which it was used—the time period, the cultural and religious backdrop—it's clear to see that what we're dealing with here is the standard: smear campaigns, semantics, and divisive tactics that are of no concern to the Christian Witch.

---

57. Conner & Rives, *Magic in Christianity*, vii.

58. Revelation 19:11

59. Revelation 19:13

Chapter Four

Superstitions of Witchcraft in Europe

W ITH THE DISCUSSION OF the Bible out of the way, we now find
ourselves swimming in an ocean of nearly two thousand years
separating the last Scriptures and modern day. If we poke through
those many years, ones people remember as the *burning times* and
the eras of witch trials galore, we might see many interesting and
unexpected things—like the way that, sometime deep in southern
Europe, girls decorated the family cows with rings of flowers for a
midsummer festival. One might think that this was a magical act, a
pagan ritual—and in a way, it was, as it certainly had holdovers from
times long before Christ. But in these times, the midsummer festival
was already called St. John's Day, and these flowers, pretty as they were
atop the cow's head, were used for something else, too: for keeping
away evil spirits.
Especially witches.[1]

What Did People Think Witches Were in Medieval Europe?

While we can talk about the fact that the word *witch* has been mis-
translated and misunderstood in the Bible, the fact remains that this is
the word that was used to signify something specific in cultures across

---

1. Vlasta Mlakar, *Sacred Plants in Folk Medicine & Rituals: Ethnobotany of Slovenia,* translated by Filip H. Drnovšek Zorko (Markham, Ontario, Canada: The Raymond
Aaron Group, 2020), 131.

Europe, too: something *terrible.* You've already read a little bit about how the ancient Romans viewed the practice, lobbing it in with things like murder and poisoning, and how the Akkadians and Sumerians had no love for malevolent wonder workers, either; as such, it's no shock that the word "witch" became tied with those specific acts and ideas. That's why even if you know someone in your family who's more on the witchy side—maybe a grandmother in your family's folk magic tradition, like Appalachian folk magic—you might find that they act quite offended if anyone insinuates they're a witch of any kind. That's because while both witches and folk healers or magicians practiced magic, the latter did all they could to distance themselves from witches to bolster the reputation of their own magic and have better odds of surviving a heavily politicized, hard to escape charge.

In the past, our ancestors thought of witches as the type of out-casted, yet powerful people that brought pain and misfortune upon their communities. There is a reason, after all, that the stereotypes of women out shapeshifting into animals or riding on broomsticks existed in the first place: these *witches*, whoever they were, could apparently do things such as steal the milk directly out of a cow, or bewitch milk so that it wouldn't curdle into cheese,[2] or bring plagues to livestock and people alike, or steal crops and cause fields to fail.[3] It was thought that good things people had, like productive livestock or healthy children, would attract the eye of the jealous, mean-spirited witches who just couldn't stand to see other people succeed where they weren't.[4] There were ways to defend against them, of course: namely in the form of *unwitchers*, which could be found from Slovenia to Finland and sold their services to other community members, helping remove the alleged hexes and curses thought to be the cause of any misfortune they suffered in daily life.[5] In the case of someone's cheese that wouldn't curdle, for instance, the remedy was delivered by a folk magician who did a *counterspell* on the cheese.[6] But this was on a smaller scale, where there was no one to deal with a community's witch problem except the community themselves. In the places with more oversight from the Church, we know that depending on the area in Europe, those mean-spirited witches were also thought to be servants or companions of the Devil himself.

For example, in more Northern and Western cultures, like England or Germany, there was the medieval idea that women's "weak" minds

---

2. Tabitha Stanmore, "The Spellbinding History of Cheese and Witchcraft," The Conversation, 2021, https://theconversation.com/the-spellbinding-history-of-cheese-and-witch craft-153221.

3. Mirjam Mencej, *Styrian Witches in European Perspective: Ethnographic Field-work* (London: Springer Nature, 2017), 3.

4. Valerie A. Kivelson and Christine D. Worobec, *Witchcraft in Russia and Ukraine: 1000-1900* (Ithaca: Cornell University Press, 2020), 281.

5. Mencej, *Styrian Witches,* 26-30.

6. Stanmore, "The Spellbinding History."

make them more susceptible to deceptions of the Devil and that their bodies are vessels "brimming with unwholesome and mysterious contents," all things impure and unclean, per the symbolism of wood-cuts like Hans Baldung's *Hexensabbat* (Witches' Sabbath).[7] These witches could be anyone in the community, and in Germany, there were quite speedy "trials" for women accused—ones that often ended in women dying as witches. With the idea that these witches were *heretics*, getting their power from the Devil, naturally, the Catholic (and later Protestant) churches of Northern, Western, and even South-ern Europe were greatly concerned with this; these women were "understood to derive their uncanny power from the Devil himself, at the price of their souls and of swearing allegiance to the forces of darkness."[8] As a result, the Church as an institution across these denominations couldn't, in the minds of these religious officials, afford to just *let* such evil rip across the lands.

Right?

The answer is *maybe not.* Maybe these Western Christians could've learned something from their more Eastern counterparts. Interestingly enough, the idea of witches as Devil-dedicated people with extreme power wasn't universal across Europe. Rather than create entire man-uals full of bunk nonsense about how to "identify" a witch (like the ever famous *Malleus Maleficarum*, or *Hammer of the Witches*), they might've spent more time actually investigating whether or not the people accusing them were being truthful, or whether the women weren't just disturbed or ill in some way. And even within the sections of Europe taken up by the witch trials, it was contested whether or not these witches had *actual* powers because of demons, as demonic powers were thought to be only illusions anyway by quite a few folks. One such person who considered demonic powers only illusions was Dutch physician Johann Weyer (1515-1588), who was one of the first to suggest that maybe these women accused of witchcraft should've been treated as *victims* of demonic deception rather than evil proponents of it.[9] All the while these witch trials were going on, though, the idea of witchcraft among Eastern Europe just didn't form the same way as in the rest of Europe.

In Eastern Europe, especially among the part of the budding Rus empire that was more Orthodox (now mainly the area of modern European Russia and a good portion of Ukraine), the idea of witches was markedly different. In fact, there are records from one Bishop Serapion of Vladimir from 1274 that actively condemns the people there—not for performing witchcraft, but for *believing* in it:

---

7. Yvonne Owens, "The Saturnine History of Jews and Witches," *Preternature: Critical and Historical Studies on the Preternatural* 3, no. 1 (2014), 68, 76, https://www.jstor.org/stab le/10.5325/preternature.3.1.0056.

8. Kivelson and Worobec, *Witchcraft in Russia and Ukraine*, 3.

9. Justin Sledge, "How Witchcraft Skepticism Produced the Lesser Key of Solomon, Modern Demonology & Psychiatry," YouTube Video, 40:57, June 9 2023, https://www.youtube.c om/watch?v=vZLbDb8eW1c.

> And you still cling to pagan traditions; you believe in witchcraft and burn innocent people and bring down murder upon the earth and the city... Out of what books or writings do you learn that famine on earth is brought about by witchcraft? If you believe these things then why do you burn [witches]? ... Are witches responsible for this? Can God not order His creation if He wants to punish us for our sins?[10]

For the Orthodox Christians of the Rus empire, there were still *trials* aplenty—still many people brought to the courts for working magic against their fellows. But the idea that the Devil was involved wasn't such a deep seated fear. Rather, it was thought to be the superstition of the people themselves that was worth admonishing, or the other acts that accompanied the magic (like sexual assault), or the consequences of some alleged magic (like the death of a child). Even more interesting, in 1525, there was a *grand princess* of Rus accused of witchcraft (Solomonia Saburova), casting magic in order to keep her husband Vasilisi III from divorcing her for not having a child—and it was a *nun* that apparently showed her the things she needed to do to make it work.[11] The point is that the picture of the *witch trials* we get from Europe are remarkably one-sided and certainly don't cover the whole picture of the situation (especially since this doesn't even touch the actual *folklore* around witches, including with figures like Baba Yaga or with stories about how witches, in the form of the will-o-the-wisp, might lead folks lost in the forest to their dooms).

Now, as you might've gleaned from our conversation of *unwitchers* and *folk magicians*, this doesn't mean that people weren't doing magic at all. If the nuns knew how to charm honey and give it to a grand princess to secure her husband's love, and if these cunningfolk were out charging money to help people get *rid* of the ill effects of witchcraft, then we know that there were plenty folks who knew about how to work these forces even if they never claimed the label of witch. (Though funnily enough, even some of the people actively being accused of witchcraft still had spells or spell formats that invoked the name of God or Jesus or the Virgin Mary in their works—alongside spells that invoked Satan instead for the exact same purposes. It was all mixed up once upon a time, depending on the intention and the spellcaster.)[12] So if these folk magicians were still doing magic, and often doing their spellwork in the name of God just as any Saint might, *why* was there so much violence and hysteria surrounding the idea of

---

10. Ibid., 24.

11. Ibid., 30-31.

12. Ibid., 321-322.

witches—whether from the Church or from small communities—to begin with?

And the answer is simple: because witchcraft is a *social institution.*

The Politics and Social Functions of Witchcraft in Europe

One of the first things you might've noticed in this chapter was what people thought witches did: cause general misfortune. Whether it be a cow not producing enough milk (while a neighbor had more milk than the community combined), or a hailstorm coming and destroying fields, or a child suddenly dying out of nowhere, or any other number of terrible things that could befall a peasant laborer in medieval Europe, the easiest way to direct the sense of *loss* and *helplessness* was to find somewhere—or someone—that the blame could be cast towards. After all, that's the primary function of religion itself, if you notice anything about magic in antiquity and earlier: it's a matter of petitioning Divinity to intervene and save us from calamities we, with our physical human hands, can't do anything about otherwise. The same logic applies in the inverse, where if good fortune is coming from the gods, then clearly bad fortune must be coming from something evil (like, say, a witch).

This line of thinking didn't die in the middle ages, though; it continued well up to even the 1970's in certain areas, and where the beliefs in witches and witchcraft as an explanation for misfortune existed tell us a lot about why and how the word *witch* became such a thing of terror for people. Within Mirjam Mencej's field work, as catalogued in *Styrian Witches in Ethnographic Perspective,* she notes that the area she visited for her research in this northeastern area of Slovenia was "hilly, remote, mostly rural, and difficult to reach region," where "the economic and social situation in the region changed little over the past hundred years"—a situation that looks, frankly, *bleak* in terms of standards of living and feels something like a time capsule from the farming peasant days of yore.[13] In Mencej's work, we discover the conditions that led people to hold onto this idea of misfortunes as a matter of hexes and curses from within the community:

> This was pretty much the situation we faced when we first came to the region: most of our interlocutors were old, many, although not everybody, rather poor and living in harsh conditions, mostly surviving by cultivating small pieces of land and on some very low pension or social support. Such was the socioeconomic setting in which witchcraft in the time of our fieldwork in 2000-2001 and even in 2013-2015 still to some extent

---

13. Mencej, *Styrian Witches,* 35.

functioned not only in "stories from the past," but was a matter of personal belief and, partly at least, a social institution, affecting and regulating social relationships between neighbors.[14]

In such areas, where access to education and healthcare is so markedly worse than the rest of the country, and where life was already hard just at baseline, it tracks that people would look for any and all explanations for such difficulty. Moreover, such small, tight-knit communities built around farming barely enough for a person and their family to eat and survive the winter meant that everybody knew everybody—and that someone doing a bit better than a neighbor in their farming or their livestock made their neighbor *bitter.* Not just in the "I wish I had the nice things they have" way. In the "No one else had so good a harvest; how does *this* family have such a store while the rest of us are near starving? Why should they be so lucky when the rest of us have bloody hands from all this work?" way.

The answer was a simple one: they *shouldn't* be so lucky. They must've *stolen* that good luck—because surely there was only so much to go around in the first place. They must've done some kind of *witchcraft* on everyone else so that their fields, cows, and chickens would be extra plentiful. And this way of thinking would only double if someone was already anxious about losing what good crops and livestock they had to the apparently jealous and cold-hearted gaze of whatever witches might've lived among them. In an environment where tiny, poor, and sparse-of-resources communities meant "intense social relations which often became constrained, leading to quarrels, feuds, and mutual suspicions between neighbors," witchcraft was a tool of *projection*: a way to direct the guilt of their failings, and the anger about their misfortunes, onto some target they could berate and beat and destroy.[15] (And now we know why the concept of the *evil eye* is so dangerous—though ironically, it seems the jealousy is coming not from the witches, but from the people accusing them of witchcraft. Isn't that funny?)

Whether from the 1970s or medieval Europe, though, this is how things seemed to play out. It was the areas that stayed rural, poor, with low education and little access to things like healthcare or stable food supplies, that were much more susceptible to believing in witchcraft—whether in Finland or the Netherlands or France or Hungary or Slovenia.[16] We think of witchcraft as a way for people to take control back in an otherwise very uncontrollable world, with spells and incantations to increase luck and wealth and fertility and all the other things we concern ourselves with, but the truth is that the *institution* of

14. Ibid., 39.

15. Ibid., 31.

16. Ibid., 26.

witchcraft, and the belief in it, worked much the same way for people who didn't know how to do this magical work. So important was it for people to have a place to lay the blame for the uncontrollable that in Slovenia, after witchcraft had been decriminalized in the mid-eighteenth century, people *still* accused others of witchcraft—even going as far as to lynch suspected witches where the court of law would no longer help them get their perceived "justice."[17] In a way, it almost seems as if these people gave witches the power to not only work their curses, but exist at all, by *needing* to have that identifiable Enemy to direct their rage towards when it came to everyday hardships. When some obvious *other,* some tangible enemy, perished for these crimes of suspected witchcraft, then and only then could the so-called victims let go and accept what had happened to them.

But while we can spend a good deal of time talking about this specific function of witchcraft as an institution—as no doubt, *this* was the reality that overshadowed people's daily lives more than whatever some cloistered monk among his books was thinking about—all that's still only one corner of the issue. As we know, the politics of witchcraft go far beyond the odd case of bad harvests or dry cows. One of the most obvious places to look is, of course, women, given how obviously misogynistic much of the witchcraft rhetoric was regarding women in specifically Northern and Western Europe. The height of the witch trials in the middle ages had all manners of nonsense diagnoses and stories about witches thanks to the *Malleus Maleficarum,* which was written by a man (Heinrich Kramer) that "had been intensely involved with the inquisition of both female visionaries and Jews" before he wrote it with Jacob Sprenger.[18] They told a lot of stories in that book, including one where a woman apparently cursed a man to impotence by taking a piece of the Host from church and putting it in a jar with a toad.[19] With women considered impure and polluted, especially because of their ability to menstruate, as well as the many odd ideas about witches that these writers came up with, they were a constant victim in anything to do with demonic powers, the Devil, sorcery, or anything else.

In Eastern Europe, interestingly, it was more men who were accused, likely because witchcraft was "only loosely associated with the Devil" and because men, being more literate, "produced material evidence that landed men in the courtroom," like written spells and spellbooks.[20] For women in the more Catholic and Protestant areas, however, it was this lack of literacy that hurt women, as "their structurally weak legal and economic position in early modern societies set them at risk for incurring charges," and without the education to de-

---

17. Ibid., 24.

18. Owens, "The Saturnine History," 58, 70.

19. Ibid., 60.

20. Kivelson and Worobec, *Witchcraft in Russia and Ukraine,* 7-8.

fend themselves, their chances of surviving a trial were slim to none.[21] Moreover, the "zone of fantasy, desire, and anxiety" that is witchcraft, coupled with the rise of skepticism of religion that came with increasing scientific and rational breakthroughs, meant that women claiming to have *actually* been in some kind of physical contact with demons (namely sexual) "gave spiritual comfort to their anxious interrogators, who conveniently ignored the fact that their testimony was taken under torture."[22] And we can't forget that, in a world where "female sexuality was considered troublesome and disruptive under the best of circumstances," the idea that these weak-minded, weak-willed, sin-susceptible creatures called *women* could be so lustful as to sign pacts with the Devil or a collection of demons gave these clergymen (and any other man) even more of a reason to undermine, accuse, and kill women.[23] Worse was the apparent double standard for witches and *male* sorcerers. Where Kramer insisted on the "burning down to ashes" of witches in his *Malleus Maleficarum*, when it came to clerics or monks that dabbled in magic, or even confessed to working with *real demons*, Kramer "consistently awarded mild penalties" for them instead, like the "suspension of honors, offices, or benefices."[24] Men were losing their jobs for a bit; women were losing their lives. No matter what we learn about witchcraft in the middle ages, we cannot remove misogyny from the conversation.

That doesn't mean that the conversation *only* revolves around misogyny, however. As the institution of the scapegoat, there are others who suffered at the hands of these witch trials than just women—and they are *not* actual witches (as the concept of such a thing was much more a folkloric fantasy than anything real). While we can absolutely point to the fact that the Church as a pan-denominational institution seemed to find women to be weak, overly sexual creatures that would apparently do anything, even hurt innocents, with devilish magic just for a lover's company, the fact is that witchcraft—namely, accusations of it—were also a political tool for the enemies of all sorts of rulers, be they kings and queens or Popes and bishops. As Martin Duffy puts it in *Anathema Maranatha: Christianity and the Imprecatory Arts*, "there is no black or white magic—no good and evil—there is just power."[25] And Duffy makes a point that according to the Church:

21. Ibid., 6.

22. Ibid., 6-7.

23. Ibid., 7.

24. Owens, "The Saturnine History," 73.

25. Martin Duffy, *Anathema Maranatha: Christianity and the Imprecatory Arts* (USA: Three Hands Press, 2022), 36

> ...Curses uttered by clerics to bolster the security of the Church and its faithful were generally regarded as licit and 'good,' whilst those threatening the security of the Church—such as imprecations hurled by lay-folk and non-Christians—were deemed illicit, evil, and the work of the Devil.[26]

Lay-folk refers to any member of the Church that isn't clergy, or just everyday people. While we know they absolutely had their own forms of folk magic, we also know that whether or not they were accused of witchcraft largely depended on whether people were comfortable with their workings or afraid of their power; one day's cunningfolk could've easily, with one loud-mouth, become the next day's witches burning at the stake. But non-Christians was a much broader title, one that captured more than a few types of people.

You may hear it said that Christians were persecuting pagans large-scale as witches, burning them all and destroying their temples, interrupting their rites, and so on and so forth. However, the story is much more complicated than that; to do such a thing wholesale would've required war efforts unknown to Europe at the time, with a Church that didn't have any continent-sized army to do that with. Rather, we know that it was through a hell of a lot of missionary work (and the wars started by Christian kings against their neighbors, looking for brownie points from the Church on top of the spoils of said war) that Christianity spread. Where it finally took root, however, and where it became the dominant social and spiritual force, there is something to be said about the suspicion and persecution of wonder workers and healers—*especially* those who took away chances for the Church to insert themselves into the lives of others.

We can once again look at Slovenia as an example of this behavior from the Church. Vlasta Mlakar explains a bit about this in her work, *Sacred Plants in Folk Medicine & Rituals: Ethnobotany of Slovenia*: she mentions how the *vrače* and *vračarice*, Slovenian folk healers of the old faith and the old ways, "opposed the spread of Christianity and found themselves labeled as witches and persecuted."[27] However, while the Church was able to destroy the official and outward worship of Slovenian pre-Christian faith (largely thanks to Frankish king Charlemagne's military conquering of the area for the sake of getting access to the Adriatic Sea),[28] all that happened was that the old ways became disguised under Christian language, iconography, and

---

26. Ibid., 36.

27. Mlakar, *Ethnobotany of Slovenia*, 16.

28. F.S. Copeland, "Some Aspects of Slovene Folklore," Folklore 60, no. 2 (1949), 227, https://www.jstor.org/stable/1256715.

intercession.[29] Where people once believed that plants were most powerful and protective if harvested on Midsummer, the Church told them to take them to mass instead so they might be blessed—effectively doing the same thing, but changing the origin of the plants' power from the plants themselves to God. So was the way that the Church established itself after gaining enough a foothold: by decrying that which threatened its power as *demonic* and giving the people alternative ways to practice their native traditions through a Christian lens. As such, accusations of witchcraft grew markedly political for a newly implanted religious power like a priest or bishop.

And then, beyond the pagans, and later the folk healers, there came other groups that caught the Church's cruel eye—one that often goes completely ignored in modern witch circles. While you may have heard of the *Malleus Maleficarum*, that witch-hunting manual declaring every blemish or freckle as some kind of witch's teat, you might not have known that it was actually inspired by a completely separate book: the *Malleus Judeorum*, or the *Hammer of the Jews*, written by John of Frankfurt some near seventy years earlier.[30] Yvonne Owens, in her article *The Saturnine History of Jews and Witches*, compares the disturbing rhetoric alleged "intellectuals" and Church officials alike would apply to Jewish people and women in order to abuse, accuse, and destroy them. She argues that "Renaissance constructions of witchcraft owed much to the fifteenth-century typological construction of Jewish 'heresy' and the nature of its persecution": Jewish people were accused of things like "cannibalistic infantcide," or the general consumption of Christian blood to get its "salvic benefits" (the conspiracy known as blood libel).[31] This, on top of the other negative things ascribed to them by the bitter merchants indebted to Jewish moneylenders in Nuremberg, Germany (like laziness, vagrancy, being "womanlike," and "menstrual pollution"), were "culturally embedded for centuries" in this area.[32] As a political, cultural, and ethnic minority in Europe, the Jewish population was a frequent target of all manners of slander, and persecution came constantly.

With the issue of witchcraft becoming more and more of a hot-button issue in the middle ages, persecution of Jewish people only increased. And so when Kramer and Sprenger wrote their book on witches, largely based on the style of a book about the evils of the political and ethnic minority that was Jewish people, it wasn't a far cry for people to make the connection between the "feminine 'pollution' of witchcraft" and the "Jewish 'heresy,'" the "ideological 'pollution,'" that came with their apparent apostasy (their rejection of Christ as

---

29. Mlakar, *Ethnobotany of Slovenia*, 23.

30. Owens, "The Saturnine History," 71.

31. Ibid., 56.

32. Ibid., 70.

Savior).[33] At one point, people even believed that Jewish men, being so apparently *womanlike*, "suffered a flux of blood every month," and that this "male Jewish menstruation" was "a form of divine punishment" from God—and according to Church authorities, this menstruation was used by all Jewish people *and* non-Jewish women (witches) alike in love spells.[34] Between this and the issue of blood libel (among many other heresies and terrible conspiracies) uniting Jewish people and witches in the minds of Church officials, the concern with witchcraft was yet another stone of persecution on top of an already crushed population, yet not many modern witches and pagans seem to consider how these unfair and frankly *wild* accusations hurt minorities like Jewish people, the Rroma, and others alongside women and cunning-folk.

With accusations as ridiculous as these, you can be as close to sure as possible that nearly all of the people accused of witchcraft in Europe weren't witches at all, but just average women, Jewish people, and maybe, *maybe*, a few folk healers (or, if you were in the courts of Eastern Europe, some nobility that were accused of using witchcraft to ruin a marriage between two powerful people).[35] But don't worry: the political weapon that was the institution of witchcraft came to swing right around on the Catholic Church in some areas. Protestants had their own fair share of witchcraft paranoia, and funnily enough, "because Catholicism was illegal [in England in the sixteenth century], and frequently regarded as devilish," Peter Rushton insists that it's predictable that Latin prayers were incorporated into folk magic (and that these seemingly normal prayers were used as evidence of someone's guilt when it came to a trial).[36] *Catholic prayers.* That was what was considered an evil spell of diabolic, devilish sorcery at that time, in that area. So much so that Catholic priests, especially, "were held to be 'vast mair [more] powerful *conjurers*' than the priests of the Church of England."[37] It came full circle, this idea of *witchcraft* as some terrible, evil thing inspired by the Devil, and as it did, it smashed directly into the Catholic Church's face like a playground tetherball.

But to put it simply: no, *witchcraft* as a concept was never a good thing. Not in the original words used in the Bible, not in the words they were all translated to later in various cultures, tribes, and regions. It was a concept that signified someone that was up to no good: someone that was jealous and hateful and cruel beyond belief, someone that had unnatural powers and used them to benefit themselves at the detriment of others, someone that maybe made pacts with devils

---

33. Ibid., 71.

34. Ibid., 74.

35. Kivelson and Worobec, *Witchcraft in Russia and Ukraine*, 26-27.

36. Peter Rushton, "A Note on the Survival of Popular Christian Magic," Folklore 91, no. 1 (1980): 115, https://www.jstor.org/stable/1259824.

37. Ibid., 116.

and poisoned their neighbors. It was a word that targeted women and certain minorities, including (but not limited to) Jewish people, and it was a word that gave the *truly* hateful people—the men that ran society, be they the scholars or the clergy—free license to stand people on trial for the most ridiculous and implausible of accusations. As such, the people we would look at and call witches today, those cunningfolk, the healers and holy people working their special folk magic, kept themselves as far removed from the term as they could. They'd never call themselves witches as we so happily do today, not only because the term was unsavory, but because it carried the real threat of death.

All of this, of course, only adds to the complexity and intrigue around the title of Christian Witch, a title we invite you to explore with us in the next section.

Section 2
The Sociopolitical Nature (and Mission) of the Christian Witch

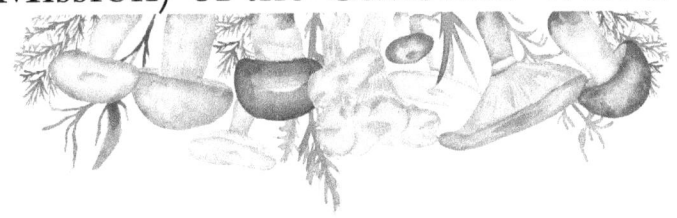

Chapter Five

The Shift in the Perception of the Word "Witch"

K NOWING ALL THAT WE now know about the understanding of the word "witch" throughout the ages, and the way it confuses everyone that hears the term applied in a Christian context, there's a question lingering above all our heads: why would we *want* to call ourselves a witch? Is that really the right term for us to be using? Why would we want to use this word, or cause this confusion among our fellow Christians? After all, *God* is certainly not the author of confusion—a phrase you've surely heard at least once or twice.

But what if we told you that God is a little trickier than people think? That for as many times as you've heard the phrase, "God is not the author of confusion," you've also heard the phrase, "God works in mysterious ways"? And what if this concept of Christian Witchcraft is one of those mysteries?

Before we get into all that, however, let us make something very clear to you: the term "witch" has radically changed in meaning and context from antiquity to our modern era, which gives us the ability (and *one* reason) to capture it for our identity as Christian Witches. Gone are the images of witches "feasting and gyrating at the sabbath, or enacting small rituals."[1] Where a witch was once someone conjuring unclean spirits to dominate members of her community or calling down natural disasters to ruin their crops, livestock, and

---

1. Owens, "The Saturnine History," 60.

homes, a witch now is seen as someone wise and helpful to their communities. They're someone that, more often than not, heals rather than hexes; they're someone connected to their inner power and the power of nature, someone following a personal expression of faith rather than an organized religion. This is a change in meaning most people don't understand, and so they don't realize that the age-old verses like the ones we've already discussed actually don't apply to the modern concept of a witch, as the word no longer has anything to do with the type of practices and magic that were originally outlawed and derided.

In short: the word "witch" is actually a reclaimed term, embodying a type of spirituality in which the feminine is not suppressed or strong-armed by the masculine, but where all people, regardless of gender expression, stand in equal opportunity and harmony, equal wisdom and spiritual sovereignty. For this transformation of such an infamous word, we have to take a look at the religion of Wicca, started around the early to mid-twentieth century by the likes of Margaret Murray (1863-1963) and Gerald Gardener (1884-1964). Unfortunately, neither of these individuals were very credible or accurate in any of their claims about ancient fertility cults and the direct line they could allegedly trace from them into the existing covens of witches they "discovered" in England. According to Jacqueline Simpson, Murray's "theory that witches were members of a huge secret society preserving a prehistoric fertility cult through centuries is now seen to be based on deeply flawed methods and illogical arguments."[2]

After being commissioned to write the "witchcraft" entry for *Encyclopedia Britannica,* Murray apparently "seized the opportunity to set out her own interpretation of the topic," which seemed to be that witches "were merely members of an underground movement secretly keeping pagan rites alive in Christian Europe."[3] It's a far cry from the devil-worshiping, shape-changing, broomstick-riding portrait of witches that Catholic writers like Montague Summers insisted on in Murray's era, and it's a bit more noble and culturally valuable than the idea that secularists insisted on, which was that these witches were little more than "totally innocent victims of hysterical panics whipped up by the Churches for devious political or financial reasons."[4] Murray's definition fell in between the two, and she seemed to want to suck all notions of anything *actually* supernatural right out of the idea of the Witch: she insisted that there was nothing magical here, nothing devilish, but just a continuation of old religion. She didn't expect the blowback from historians and folklorists, however, who insisted that she was "misinterpreting and distorting" the sources she

---

2. Jacqueline Simpson, "Margaret Murray: Who Believed Her, and Why?" Folklore 105 (1994), 89, https://www.jstor.org/stable/1260633.

3. Ibid., 89-90.

4. Ibid., 90.

used to write both her first article in the *Folklore* journal and her book, *The Witch-Cult in Western Europe*, released in 1921.

Because, you see, while Murray worked as an Egyptologist at University College London and had technically been educated in the ways of Egyptology, it wasn't official education: it was private instruction by Sir Flinders Petrie, which, according to Simpson, "may well explain why her methodology was so unsafe once she stepped outside the bounds of her specialty."[5] From inconsistent use of her sources to outright "willfully [ignoring] the clear evidence" in them, her work wasn't very credible from the get-go; one example of her academic mishaps was her ignorance on the etymology of the term *sabbath* in "witch's sabbath" (which had a clear connection to Judaism's Sabbath Day, or *shabbos/shabbat*, that justified many a Jewish person getting sucked into the horrors of the politically-driven witch trials of Europe—a "hostile misapplication of a sacred Jewish word," per Simpson).[6] Moreover, according to Francis Young in his article, *The Woman who Inspired Wicca:*

> Murray's use of a single set of problematic sources from one country (Scotland) to argue that a previously unnoticed religion had existed since prehistory failed to meet basic historiographical and anthropological standards of research. She was given to making huge conceptual leaps on the basis of contentious interpretations of meager evidence. Using a small range of hostile trial records designed to discredit women accused of witchcraft (along with testimonies extracted under torture), Murray reconstructed what she believed were real religious practices lurking behind the demonological construct of the Witches' Sabbath.[7]

But despite the many historians and scholars that called quackery, it was thanks to her "engaging prose style, her marshaling of apparent evidence, and her impressive academic credentials" that caught readers outside the bounds of academia.[8] The theories she puts forward, her refusal to actually acknowledge the concept of magic in the rituals of these apparent preservers of ancient pagan faith, and her dodgy attempts to connect her ideas by plucking any stray collection of words from her sources into one spot means her idea of this witch cult are seriously misinformed and not rooted in reality. But if for nothing else,

---

5. Ibid., 89.

6. Ibid., 91

7. Francis Young, "The Woman who Inspired Wicca," First Things, August 25, 2020, https ://www.firstthings.com/web-exclusives/2020/08/the-woman-who-inspired-wicca.

8. Ibid.

she *did* get people to stop thinking of witches in the tired old way we all know from the *Malleus Maleficarum*. She wrested this concept from the likes of Summers and their ridiculous, hysterical interpretations, landing us more in a position to talk about witchcraft from an ancient religious and spiritual perspective, which in and of itself was a massive achievement, and the main reason anyone gave her the time of day to begin with (as well as the main reason that this idea of witchcraft in the modern era began to shift in the first place).

However, another thing she didn't ever figure was that later folks, like Gerald Gardener, would take her hamfisted theories and distortion of historical documents and use them to dream up a whole new religion. Gardener, using Murray's "descriptions of alleged rituals, festivals, and organizations... as a blueprint for setting up a new system of magical and religious rituals," came up with quite the tall tale based off some of Murray's more offhand and baseless assertions—like the idea that a coven *needs* exactly thirteen people to be considered a coven.[9] According to Laura Vance, Gardener was quite the character. He "published claims that he had discovered a coven of witches at Christchurch, Hampshire, in England, into which he had been initiated,"[10] and apparently, this New Forest Coven had given him carte blanche to reveal the secrets they'd kept wrapped up for centuries out to the public with his many works, like *Witchcraft Today* (1954) and *The Meaning of Witchcraft* (1959). Through these works, Gardener "provided many of the basic elements of rituals that came to inform contemporary Wicca."[11] Conveniently, this all came to light a few scant years after the British Parliament repealed their last witchcraft laws in 1951, and it was later carried over to America by Raymond and Rosemary Buckland in the 1960s after Raymond encountered some of Gardener's work. [12]

These claims Gardener made—that this was a coven continuing an *ancient* practice—are naturally unsubstantiated. But Vance makes an excellent point: did not also Christianity do the same thing, grabbing onto the rich traditions and history of Judaism to anchor itself in a world where, according to Wilken, "the primary test of truth and religious matters was custom and tradition, the practices of the ancients"?[13] Christianity, Islam, Mormonism, all of these claimed to find their roots in Judaism, and according to Vance, what matters more isn't whether these claims can be corroborated, but rather "what they tell us about the religions that make them," noting that "what a religion projects as its past reflects something critical about its contemporary

9. Simpson, "Margaret Murray," 89.

10. Laura Vance, *Women in New Religions* (New York: New York University Press, 2015), 101.

11. Ibid., 101.

12. Ibid., 101, 103.

13. Wilken, *Christians as the Romans Saw Them*, 62.

self-perception."[14] In this case, the budding religion of Wicca was one that, per its founder (or *discoverer*, if we were ever able to ask Gardener directly), "adopted the idea of an ancient fertility religion that had been suppressed by patriarchal witch hunts"; it was one that would go on to "celebrate and promote polarity of the sexes, and [be] a religion that viewed sex as sacred, and honored and celebrated fertility."[15]

The astute here may notice that this talk of the *polarity of the sexes* sounds awfully heteronormative and eerily similar to Evangelical Christianity's *gender complementarianism*. This is something that cropped up in the 1980s as "theologian Wayne Grudem had called for a new organization to uphold biblical manhood and womanhood," leading to the then heavily pushed idea that "God had established male headship as part of the order of creation"—that men and women were created equal, but made for different purposes.[16] Of course, none of those purposes for women in Evangelical Christianity included leadership, authority, sovereignty, or power, whereas they *were* included in Wicca, but don't be fooled. The "Equal But Distinct" tripe is something that has permeated all things, from reconstructed New Age paganism to Evangelical Christianity to second wave radical feminism, used to both idolize and oppress women depending on the person wielding the concept, and always falling into the same trap: that men and women, with of course no consideration for any other form of gender expression, are *inherently* and *biologically* and *naturally* suited for one thing or the other. This ignores all sense of individuality, personality, and expression from person to person to make broad, sweeping, and often seriously inaccurate statements. (If hearing an Evangelical man tell a woman that she was "created" for motherhood makes your skin crawl, one can argue hearing a Wiccan woman gush over the amazing specialness of the Goddess and her womb and her motherhood should do just the same. It does for Sara, anyway.)

Moreover, it's no wonder that some of the zaniest ideas around witchcraft commonly parroted in online occult spaces, like #witchtok, come from the natural conclusions of these ideas. One commonly found online is the idea that fertility cults and witchcraft itself "had dominated ancient Europe, but had been brutally repressed by witch hunters who opposed the sexual independence and boldness of female witches."[17] Through organizations like WITCH (Women's International Terrorist Conspiracy From Hell), who published this very concept in their 1968 manifesto, the idea took flight and permeated the writings of women like radical feminist Mary Daly and feminist activist

---

14. Vance, *Women in New Religions*, 102.

15. Ibid., 101-102.

16. Kristin Kobes du Mez, *Jesus and John Wayne: How White Evangelicals Corrupted a Faith and Fractured a Nation* (USA: Liveright, 2020), 146-147.

17. Vance, *Women in New Religions*, 103.

Andrea Dworkin. With the coalescing vision of "independent and sexually free women" being "suppressed as witches," the word *witch* began shifting—and the work of archaeologists like Marija Gimbutas, who has published several works on goddesses and female divinity across Europe, cemented notions of more matriarchal pre-Christian religions, as well as the idea that eight or nine million women, *wise women* and *healers*, were wrongly targeted by the patriarchal structures dragged in by Indo-European religions and peoples.[18]

Of course, this strips the many other victims of witch-hysteria out of the public mind (such as Jewish people, as we've previously discussed). It's also incredibly revisionist, as the cultures spoken about in Gimbutas's work do have male deities as much as female deities, and deities that switch between the two. But this brings us all the way up to the 1980s, where witchcraft as a term was less about devil worship, flying on broomsticks, ruining fields, and poisoning neighbors, and more about feminine empowerment, sexuality, sovereignty, and reclamation of true spiritual freedom. Here's where the New Age spirituality really kicked into high gear, and where feminist Wiccans like Hungarian writer Zsuzsanna Budapest took a complementarian view of Wicca between God and Goddess and drove it towards the tradition known as Dianic Wicca, "focusing on female empowerment and embracing female separatism."[19] From Budapest came a slew of influential books on witchcraft, spirituality, and Wicca, and these books would come to inform new generations of women looking to get outside the bounds of patriarchal, organized religions like Christianity. Books like Wiccan elder Silver Ravenwolf's *To Ride a Silver Broomstick*, published in 1993, may be one of the most (in)famous examples of this era's witchcraft books that still sit on bookshelves today.

While these kinds of resources, and the religion of Wicca itself, have fallen largely out of fashion with the next generation's witches (for issues of racist authors and their cultural appropriation, dishonesty in the religion's origins, hetero- and cisnormativity, and a hard insistence that the Wiccan Rede applies to all magic, everywhere, across the board), there's no denying that this religion's inception and absorption by feminist activists would open the gates to the socially acceptable understanding of witchcraft we have today.

---

18. Ibid., 103-104

19. Ibid., 104

Chapter Six

Why Call Ourselves Christian Witches?

T HE TRUTH IS THAT we can't tell you why *you* would want to call yourself a Christian Witch. This is something personal, a decision that has to be reached deep in your bones with the full knowledge that every day is going to be a test of strength, grace, and endurance. Because believe us, not everyone's going to even entertain an explanation of what a Christian Witch really is, or why what we understand as witchcraft today has always been a part of Christian practice, or why Jesus Himself is the ultimate mentor and master when it comes to dispensing those holy secrets, if you actually pay attention to His words and actions in the Gospels. All we can tell you is why *we* choose to call ourselves that, even when a plethora of other words would do and would certainly make our lives a lot easier. To do that requires the knowledge of a couple things, though: namely the true nature of the Church as it stands right now, the way it became how it is, the driving forces behind such an ugly transformation, and the way the concept of Christian Witchcraft combats this transformation, which this section discusses. Before we go any further, though, and before we explain to you our reasonings, let us point you to a very important bit of Scripture a la St. Paul the Apostle:

> For the foolishness of God is wiser than human wisdom, and the weakness of God is stronger than human strength. Brothers and sisters, think of what you were when you were called. Not many of you were wise by human standards; not many were influential; not many

were of noble birth. But God chose the foolish things
of the world to shame the wise; God chose the
weak things of the world to shame the strong. God
chose the lowly things of this world and the despised
things—and the things that are not—to nullify the
things that are, so that no one may boast before him. It
is because of him that you are in Christ Jesus, who has
become for us wisdom from God—that is, our righteousness, holiness and redemption. Therefore, as it is
written: "Let the one who boasts boast in the Lord."[1]

Think of this carefully, the idea that God uses the weak to shame
the strong, the foolish to shame the wise, and think about what this
means, especially in relation to us and our identity as witches. Is
it wrong to be wise, or strong? No. But is it wrong to boast? Is it
wrong to act like we are *better* than others for these things, or more
deserving of God and His love?

Yes.

God is one who humbles. When people get too big for their
britches, too comfortable in their assumed place in the eyes of God,
and they begin acting as we may have known some Christians to
act—cruel, spiteful, and merciless, all because they perceive themselves on the right side of God and on the true and holy path—what
is there left to do? Just as it was written, that God uses the weak
to shame the strong, and the foolish to shame the wise, so too
does He seem to, in this era, use the Witch to shame the Priest.
He uses the "sinful," the "lost," the "fallen," to shame the so-called
righteous. Because these folks who think themselves so righteous,
and therefore worthy to condemn others as if they are the ones who
decide and judge, have caused an awful lot of damage in the name
of their own Lord.

This is why, even though words like *mystic* or *folk healer* or *cunning folk* could just as easily apply to us as the word "witch," we
choose that title instead. We use it like a litmus test, knowing that
how someone reacts to the title says more about them and their
faith than any amount of church-going, Bible reading, or praying ever
will. Sometimes, the folks we meet and greet with this title blink at
us with glittering eyes, their faces open as a flower and their next
words well meaning, gentle questions. Other times, it's as if an iron
curtain dropped between us with how they recoil, and they become
like archers atop a castle wall, resorting to using statements and Bible
verses (like the ones we talked about in the last section) as arrows to
shoot our way. The latter rarely, if ever, change their minds, and yet
we always find ourselves trying and hoping they'll see what they've
blocked themselves off from seeing. Whether or not you want to wear

---

1. 1 Corinthians 1:25-31

this title, and try to open the eyes and ears of our fellow Christians who dig in their heels and shout over us, is up to you.

Nonetheless, calling ourselves Christian Witches is a reclamation of not only the term witch, but the term Christian too. The world is a verifiable disaster, not because it doesn't follow any one religion or any one set of rules, but because people keep trying to force their specific view of good and evil on a world full of rich, complex communities and traditions. Understanding how the world became the way it is, and what the people who have co-opted the name of Christ came to believe about themselves, each other, and the world, is critical to understanding what needs to be done to heal it—because we don't know about you, but we don't think anyone has ever developed anything other than a deep-seated, consuming sense of fear from being told that if they don't fit into neat and perfect boxes, they'll burn forever.

And that's not what God's about.

The Reasons for the Church's Rotting Foundation

Sara Says:

It was reading books like Wilken's *Christians as the Romans Saw Them* and Jürgen Moltmann's *The Crucified God* that got me to understand how Christianity became the diseased tool of imperialism and horror that it demonstrated itself to be throughout the last two thousand years of European history (and later spread to the Americas, Africa, and more), and it was reading a book called *Jesus and John Wayne: How White Evangelicals Corrupted a Faith and Fractured a Nation* by Kristen Kobes du Mez that I began to understand exactly how this same monster of greed, control, and hierarchical power once again morphed in America, taking on new life and a new face. It is not a nice story at all, but it's one that, when you understand it, makes everything fall into place, and makes this work we do as Christian Witches make that much more sense.

You may have heard it said that Christians stole things from the pagan cultures they conquered, absorbing traditions and festivals and even *gods* into the cloak of this great and powerful religion that went tearing through Europe (which we'll talk more on later), but I will say this: Christianity had far too many a pagan value imposed upon it during its infancy, values that ultimately made what was *supposed* to be a new and radical religion into simply more of the same. It's a common theme in religion in general, apparently: the more Divinity tries to speak and show us the way, the more we squint and tilt our heads sideways until Divinity's message looks more like what we want it to say. One notable place this happened was, in fact, in St. Paul's letters to the Corinthians about women. It turns out that it was never St. Paul who gave us such terrible ideas about how wives should obey their husbands, but rather the purposeful misinterpretation of his words by Greek converts who, culturally and educationally, were of the opinion that women were inferior to men, that they were objects of distraction and stupidity and only existed to bear children, and who took that opinion with them into their new religion, thus mucking up the whole thing and continuing the very same attitudes St. Paul and Jesus Himself were trying to do away with in the first place.

Let me explain. St. Paul was a man that I'd always joked about; I would tell God that when I died and got to heaven, that man had *until I got my hands on him* to explain what he meant about women in these verses people like to use to abuse women so much. It's no coincidence to me that I got John T. Bristow's work, *What Paul Really Said About Women*, in my hands on the generous donation of a friend—one un-prompted and unasked for because I didn't even know to ask for such a thing, or that such a book existed, and so it was very much appreciated. In fact, as a Christian Witch, and knowing about how bibliomancy works (which we'll talk more about later), I know this was St. Paul's own design, because the very first thing I saw as I opened the book was a chapter title called "The Slandered Apostle." Christian spirits are not subtle, and this was yet another reminder that I accepted with a well-meaning eye-roll and a laugh. St. Paul, my dearest frustration—St. Paul, one of my, *our*, many allies.

According to Bristow, those few infamous quotes from St. Paul about women needing to "be subject to" their husbands and their husbands being "the head" of the whole operation were in fact not saying what they sounded like—not at all. As would make sense for an advocate of such a fledgling faith, St. Paul was actually suggesting something *radical* and *beautiful* in those letters, something that the world was apparently no more ready for then than it is today. Bristow notes that "in Paul's gospel, a new order was at hand, in which all persons 'are one in Christ'"—"and yet how this model has been mis-understood!"[2] Bristow takes his readers through the multiple specific and painstakingly chosen Greek words St. Paul used to describe the way husbands should treat their wives and how wives should treat their husbands, suggesting not the role of master and servant as the church has posited for centuries after, but that men hold the position of risk-taker, going ahead of their wives into the fray of life and loving them enough to be willing to lay everything down for them, while their wives come flank and support them in their efforts. Despite what everyone has suggested St. Paul meant, what the words demonstrate is that a couple should move as a unit, a team—not as a hierarchical relationship at all.[3] Yet notice how when Divinity inspires someone to speak, the world will instead hear only what it's ready to hear, no matter how plain and simple it's made? No matter how carefully

---

2. John T. Bristow, *What Paul Really Said About Women: An Apostle's Liberating Views on Equality in Marriage, Leadership, and Love* (New York: HarperSanFrancisco, 1988), 32.

3. Ibid., 32-47.

and specifically St. Paul made his statements in his letters, it was inevitable that over the course of the next few centuries, many people, including St. Thomas Aquinas would continue to interpret St. Paul's words through the lens of Greek philosophers like Aristotle, Socrates, and Zeno, who believed the best thing a woman could be was quiet.[4]

It's also worth noting that Jesus Himself spoke in parables on purpose. He did this so that not everyone would understand what He was trying to say about the kingdom of God—so that only those with *eyes to see* and *ears to hear* would be able to, in fact, see and hear. Why would He do this, rather than just say the truth directly, especially since even His own Apostles needed to have it explained afterwards? Well, given what happened when St. Paul *did* directly state it, I can at least give this educated guess: it's because Jesus knew exactly what would happen to His words if He just gave out the key to the Kingdom plainly and wholesale. He was no stranger to vitriol and misunderstanding, as we've already covered; He knew people with awful intentions would take what He said and run with it.

Granted, they have anyway. One might think Jesus failed, then, to keep people from distorting Him and His words and running off. But if we remember what Jesus said in Matthew 8:11-12:

> I say to you that many will come
> from the east and the west, and
> will take their places at the feast
> with Abraham, Isaac and Ja-
> cob in the kingdom of heaven.
> But the subjects of the kingdom
> will be thrown outside, into the
> darkness, where there will be
> weeping and gnashing of teeth.

Taking anything Jesus said literally tends to be a mistake, but here the astute and the spiritually sighted will see it: Jesus is saying a lot of so-called righteous people are going to be awfully confused when they find themselves on the wrong side of the pearly gates. And it's *because* of how they misinterpreted Jesus's words, how they *proved* themselves to be the spiritually sightless, dead of all sense. This is another reason that personally, I think those who call themselves Christian Witches are so dangerous to those teeth-gnashing folks: when you spend all this time being brave enough to grab God's coat and hold on tight, to learn how to talk *and* hear His response, to *use* the power He gave us with responsibility and efficiency, your eyes are wrenched painfully open, your ears suddenly flooded with the loud truth.

I've heard testimony of spiritual people being told their gifts are demonic and should be renounced. I've listened as people told of

---

4. Ibid., 29.

moments where they learned to shut up or be looked at like the Devil's own brood just for noticing what others couldn't, where they were ostracized and sneered at for coming forward about abuse at the hands of supposed spiritual leaders, and where the people that claimed to love them willingly left them in places where actual, honest *torture* could go on without any intervention or hope of salvation. All of this was done at the hands of people who call themselves Christian. For all these folks like to say that "the devil comes as an angel of light," they don't seem to realize the irony of passing their children into the hands of those cosplaying righteousness, or the damage it's done.

So too does the Church—not the general body of believers, but the overall political and religious institution across all denominations—fail to grasp the message of Christ in its treatment of those in society that need the most help. It's the reason Christianity as an organized religion continues to shrivel up and die on the vine: the Church has become that which Jesus once spoke out against. According to Moltmann, who wrote his book *The Crucified God* in the 80's, there's something of an identity-relevance crisis occurring in the Church: one where those who want to actually follow the message of Christ find themselves unable to do so in the Church, opting instead to become psychologists, social workers, activists, and other agents of social welfare, and one where those who run the Church refuse to give up their "Christian" identity (and all the exclusionary, Us vs. Them, condemning rhetoric that has been sewn into it) to the point of not keeping up with the needs of society. It's the reason that organized Christian religion is on its way out, and yet rather than try and fix any of these problems, the people who most staunchly cling to such a "Christian" identity would rather just dig their heels in further and scream bloody murder.

And more than that, they'd also rather try and dictate what "proper" Christian religion even looks like, gatekeeping the Son of Man behind a very restrictive and specific set of values so that they might be the champion of the No True Scotsman fallacy every time they see someone engaging with God in a way unfamiliar to them. This "pusillanimous faith," as Moltmann calls it, this timid and cowardly faith, is one that "usually occurs in the form of an orthodoxy which feels threatened and is therefore more rigid than ever."[5] By doing this, though, these folks don't realize they're telling on themselves: they don't understand that they're demonstrating how their faith is "preyed upon by fear":

> Such a faith tries to protect its "most sacred things," God, Christ, doctrine and morality, because it clearly no longer believes that these things are sufficiently powerful to maintain themselves. When the "religion of fear" finds its way into the Christian church, those who

---

5. Jürgen Moltmann, *The Crucified God* (Minneapolis: Fortress Press, 2015), 21.

regard themselves as the most vigilant guardians of the
faith do violence to the faith and smother it. Instead
of confidence and freedom, fearfulness and apathy are
found everywhere.[6]

You might guess where this leads. A lot of talk about the "good
old days," a lot of heroic fantasy about being the "faithful remnant"
of the Church, and a lot of willingly isolating themselves against the
world as they show a complete "unwillingness to undergo new experience with the gospel and faith... [boasting] of their own growing
meaninglessness," according to Moltmann.[7] That's what I think is the
most shocking: the folks who have co-opted Christianity are *happily*
smothering it, running it into the ground, and shutting the gates to the
very people they claim they want to help.

However, there's one really important thing to note: while Moltmann was writing this in the 80's, he was also writing it from the
perspective of a German World War II captured soldier, a war prisoner.
He'd done a lot of work throughout his life to come to terms with what
his nation had done to the many people affected by the Holocaust,
especially Jewish people, and what that meant in terms of his faith as
a Christian man. This book, and the theological considerations inside
it, are the product of his reflections, study, and grief looking back on
his country and the atrocities it committed against innocent people,
as well as his role in it as a German soldier and citizen. It's a powerful
book worth reading. But it doesn't cover the entirety of the issue here,
nor does it name the full, dark, and terrible *truth* of what's going on
with the name of God, and where this dissonance comes from.

The Broader Modern Context of the Dissolution of Christ's Message

Let's take a moment to identify that dissonance. After all, why *does* the
God of our mainstream churches seem so different from the God we
might come to know out there in the wilderness? How is it that all of
these Sunday worshippers see God as this oddly anti-human figure,
when Jesus Himself stood with all of those who were treated as less
than human?

"He spent time with sinners to get them to repent," say those Christians; "He didn't stay with them and tell them what they were doing
was okay!"

Maybe so. But one fails to see the sin of the leper, who couldn't do
anything about his condition. I fail to see the sin of the tax collector,
who was just doing his job in an unjust world where he could only get

---

6. Ibid., 21.

7. Ibid., 22.

his daily bread by working for an evil empire. I fail to remember where St. Dismas, the Good Thief crucified beside Jesus, ever said the words "I repent" or "I'm sorry" for the actions that put him on that cross; all I remember is that he acknowledged that his actions brought him his consequences.

Yet *these* were Jesus's fellows, Apostles, and the ones who saw Paradise. The oh-so-holy folks, who were obsessed with law and tradition and shows of piety, were far on the outside of Jesus's vision, and were routinely shouted down in the streets by Jesus. It's as Moltmann says:

> In concrete terms, [God] is revealed in the cross of Christ who was abandoned by God. His grace is revealed in sinners, His righteousness is revealed in the unrighteous, and in those without rights, and His gracious election in the damned... It was not the devout, but the sinners, and not the righteous, but the unrighteous, who recognized Him, because in them He revealed the divine righteousness of grace in the kingdom. He revealed His identity among those who had lost their identity, amongst the lepers, sick, rejected, and despised, and was *recognized as Son of Man by those who had been deprived of their humanity.* (Emphasis mine.)[8]

He notes, also, that within the Church of Christ, "the principle of fellowship is the fellowship with those who are different"—that to follow the crucified Christ is to have "solidarity with those who have become alien and have been made different."[9] Yet how curious, then, how these churches have become just like that which Jesus scorned, buildings full of walking, whitewashed tombs—ones who insist that the only way to be accepted by God is to look, act, walk, and talk the same. Ones who are reaching for the impossible standard of not *divinity*, but *white heteronormative patriarchy*, creating some mythic Saint figure, some ghoulish personification, of the nameless, faceless, *relentless* concept of the Straight White Man.

Most notably, these churches have become ones who can somehow, despite claiming to love a God about justice, mercy, and peace, be convinced that prejudice, hate, and violence are His tools. If we look into *Jesus and the Disinherited* by American author and philosopher Howard Thurman, he discusses this disconnect with such dire and gut-wrenching examples. He speaks of the consequences of three things that crop up in both the Disinherited and their oppressors—fear, deception, and hate—and its only possible antidote, which is the concept of love that has been so often betrayed time

---

8. Moltmann, *The Crucified God*, 34.

9. Ibid., 35.

and time again by divisive, inflammatory, and cold churches. In fact, Thurman notes how, for those who need "strength and succor... Christianity has been sterile and of little avail."[10] In this book, Thurman asks the reader to think about what religion, especially that which seems *built* to support the powerful rather than the powerless, can offer the heartbroken and downtrodden, and he takes us through the journey of his own philosophy as he discusses these three stopping blocks previously mentioned. Whether it be American slave owners using St. Paul's words to justify their actions and enforce their slaves' obedience, or whether it be a church actively interrupting its service so members could join a lynch mob against a Black man—*and then resume the Sunday service like nothing happened!*—the fact of the matter is that there is an ocean of separation between God and the people who claim to serve Him.[11] It is an ocean filled with such incredible delusions of power, hierarchy, and callousness, and it is an ocean that has been growing deeper and deeper since the moment Jesus left this earth after His rising.

And when I say the moment Jesus disappeared into Heaven, I mean it. The Gospel of Mary Magdalene shows us that much, in how Andrew refused to believe *anything* Mary said because they were "strange ideas," and how Peter brings Mary to *tears* over his inability to believe that Jesus would reveal anything worth knowing to a woman before the other *male* Apostles.[12] Peter pushes her to the breaking point with his lack of faith and his refusal to see that gender has nothing to do with whether or not one is worthy to learn, grow, and transcend.

As theologian Meggan Watterson puts it in her work, *Mary Magdalene Revealed: The First Apostle, Her Feminist Gospel, and the Christianity We Haven't Tried Yet*, there is no gender inherent to a human soul. According to her, "spiritual authority cannot be determined by a person's sex, gender, or sexuality, but rather by the depth of their spiritual transformation and subsequent wholeness"; she argues that it was Christ who led Mary through such a transformation, and she highlights how Levi comes to Mary's defense in her Gospel, arguing that "if Christ considered her worthy" to hold such information, "then who [were] they to disregard her?"[13] Yet it seemed that this was exactly what the larger, growing Church decided to do centuries later, as Mary Magdalene's Gospel soon disappeared altogether from the early church writings, only for German scholar Carl Reinhardt to find the lost Gospel nearly two thousand years later in a market in Cairo, Egypt.[14]

---

10. Howard Thurman, *Jesus & the Disinherited*, 11.

12. Gospel of Mary Magdalene, 9:2-5.

13. Watterson, *Mary Magdalene Revealed*, 76.

14. Ibid., 1.

What might we have learned from the inclusion of a Gospel that speaks about how *all* of us have the potential to become fully human and fully divine like Jesus? A Gospel that makes it clear that *all* people, no matter their sexuality or gender or anything else, have the capacity to overcome the seven powers Jesus exorcised from Mary and become what Mary herself described simply as *Men?*[15] As true Humans? Maybe we might've learned to trust ourselves more, and to forgive ourselves for the times we slip up a little easier (as truly, no one is perfect). Maybe we would've understood God as one who doesn't simply watch and judge us in our repeated attempts to transcend, but actively teaches us and shows us the way, as Jesus did with Mary in her visions of Him. Maybe we would've learned to listen to our soul more and act in accordance with its true nature: a thing made in the image of God, full of love and wisdom and understanding and all other such beautiful things.

And maybe we would've learned a little more readily how to identify the things that *masquerade* as God that are obviously not Him: things that tell us that in order to transcend, we must already *be* perfect rather than work towards it, and that we shouldn't rely on any outside help or support from the God that allegedly demands this of us. In the words of social psychologist, theologian, and activist Christena Cleveland, we're told that "to be human is to be needless"—that those who can't handle the crushing horrors of the world on their own, without help, without resources, without *perfection*—get no love from the One Most High.[16] It sounds like quite the flip to me—and that's because it is. In fact, it's a *trap* that keeps us second guessing ourselves, shrinking ourselves, and feeling shame about ourselves whenever any need or weakness crops up in us. The reality is that all of us will need help and support at times, but when the mainstream Church convinces us that it's *shameful* to need help, and *wrong* to be in a dark place, and *greedy* or *affronting* to ask for support in our pain, we get no closer to enlightenment. In fact, we get farther. In Watterson's discussion of one of the seven powers Mary had to overcome, she touches on the power to *judge*: a power that "keeps us in our place. Keeps us small and bottled up... keeps us from ever really expressing the truth of who we are."[17] It keeps us looking down our noses at those who are drowning while our own heads are barely above water; it keeps us *pushing* others under the waves while we gasp for a sip of air, rather than helping all of us make it to shore and *rest.*

As a result, the sense of *community* within the Church has been crumbling for ages. Many a Christian don't realize that their churches are devoid of God, and that the thing they sing their songs to and put their babies before is not Him. In the words of Moltmann, the

---

15. Gospel of Mary Magdalene, 5:3.

16. Christena Cleveland, *God is a Black Woman* (USA: HarperOne, 2022), 68.

17. Watterson, *Mary Magdalene Revealed*, 117.

truth is that one must come *out* of the churches and into the slums if they're to ever find God.[18] Yet these people pack the churches and sneer at those living in poverty instead, and they push incredibly toxic, twisted, and downright *dangerous* things like Christian Nationalism, which tries to tie American nationalism tightly to the Christian faith. So when we ask ourselves what happened, and why, we have to look at the underbelly of all of this behavior. We have to look at the driving force that causes people to treat righteousness like a costume, and we have to understand how the concept of divinity can be warped into such a caricature to begin with.

To understand God, therefore, and this very obviously *Not God* that has invaded His flock and poisoned His church, we have to understand something about occult theory—namely about egregore theory, Gnosticism, Kabbalah, and the Qliphoth.

---

18. Moltmann, *The Crucified God*, 9.

Chapter Seven

The Husk (or Shell) of God

I N 2023, RUSSELL MOORE, the former president of the Ethics and Religious Liberty Commission of the Southern Baptist Convention, shared quite the disturbing message with the press. This was a faith leader who, up until 2021, filled an important space within the denomination. The reason he lost his standing with the church folks and other evangelical leaders—ultimately leading to his resignation in 2021—was because he both criticized Donald Trump as a presidential candidate and also "criticized the Southern Baptist Convention's response to a sexual abuse crisis, as well as what he viewed as an increased tolerance for white nationalism within the church."[1] This lost him quite the favor with his fellow Baptists, though while he left his position, he never left his faith—nor his connections with people in it. What he revealed to the journalists at NPR and other outlets that rocked thousands of people in 2023 was a shocking (yet not really *so* shocking) confession: the people preaching Jesus's name the loudest, these Evangelical types, thought Jesus's teachings were *too weak* for the modern era. In full, Moore notes:

> It was the result of having multiple pastors tell me, essentially, the same story about quoting the Sermon on the Mount, parenthetically, in their preaching — "turn

---

1. Scott Detrow, "He was a top church official who criticized Trump. He says Christianity is in crisis," NPR (2023), https://www.npr.org/2023/08/08/1192663920/southern-baptist-convention-donald-trump-christianity.

the other cheek" — [and] to have someone come up after to say, "Where did you get those liberal talking points?" And what was alarming to me is that in most of these scenarios, when the pastor would say, "I'm literally quoting Jesus Christ," the response would not be, "I apologize." The response would be, "Yes, but that doesn't work anymore. That's weak." And when we get to the point where the teachings of Jesus himself are seen as subversive to us, then we're in a crisis.[2]

It's at this point that we wonder: how did we get here? How did Christians get to a point where the direct words of their own Savior, in the Bible they so often beat people with, suddenly became unpalatable to them? Became things we might attach words like "liberal" to, or look at with suspicion and scorn?

Well, we won't deny the political nature of Jesus in His era. He was one who believed not in publicly displaying grief and anguish over the state of the lands of Judea, as the Pharisees did, but in hiding one's results of fasting—of celebrating even when there felt like nothing to celebrate, and bringing healing and hope to those that were deemed unworthy of healing and devoid of hope. He believed in doubling down on the laws of God in a way that encouraged the softening of one's heart rather than the hardening, and He was a champion of malicious compliance (as is what was *really* meant when He said to show the other cheek or take someone's pack two miles instead of one). He preached a world where the lowest would be elevated, and where the first would be last; where to be served, one had *to* serve. All of that in His time—the change He made in people's lives, the hope He gave them, the way He encouraged them to go on another day under a foreign imperialist power—*that* was political.

However, somewhere along the way, the spiritual path designed for the powerless became the tool of the powerful. The message of peace and love became the religion of power and control. The God of the oppressed and downtrodden became the symbol of the oppressive forces that praised His name in their many tombs they called churches. And in America, it all coalesced under a being that bears little resemblance to the original Jesus and His God. American historian Kristin Kobes du Mez highlights this change in her book, *Jesus and John Wayne: How White Evangelicals Corrupted a Faith and Fractured a Nation*, where she discusses the international and domestic sociopolitical conditions that led to such a radical shift in the way people understood their Savior. Opening with a discussion of the 2016 presidential election, where she wonders how her sweet hometown could've chosen someone who so obviously spat in the face of all their so-called Christian values, du Mez goes back to the

---

2. Moore quoted in Detrow.

turn of the 20th century and drags us all the way up to modern day in her detailed chronicling of the invention of what we, until recently, dubbed *The Evangelical Egregore.*

First, let us define what an egregore is. Across various time periods and cultures, egregores have been defined several ways, and one such way comes from the Greek translation of the Book of Enoch. According to occultist and author Mark Stavish, "the word egregore is Greek in origin and is derived from *égrégoros,* meaning 'wakeful' or 'watcher'" and describes "an angelic being."[3] However, other places—like in the rest of the West, largely thanks to the carry-over of Greek and Roman semi-animistic ideas, as well as the impact the sacred cult rituals had on the average lives of people and the many other nations these empires came to conquer—can see egregores to be some bodiless, supernatural being, ones fed *by* the beliefs of people.[4] Otherwise known as "thought forms," these egregores are described thusly, per Stavish's reference of University of New York State's Joscelyn Godwin:

> The important point is that an egregore is *augmented by human belief, ritual, and especially by sacrifice.* If it is sufficiently nourished by such energies, the egregore can take on a life of its own and appear to be an independent, personal divinity, with a limited power on behalf of its devotees and an *unlimited appetite for further devotion.* It is then believed to be an immortal god or goddess, an angel, or a daimon. (Emphasis ours.)[5]

Godwin's assertion, however, raises specifically a "chicken or egg" question: are all gods simply manifestations of our beliefs in a higher power? Did they create us, per their many myths and stories, or did we create them to help us stave off the uncontrollable aspects of life? It's a fair question to ask, and as we read things like *The Thunder: Perfect Mind,* an apocryphal early Christian writing, we might find some interesting hints:

I was sent from the Power

And I have come to those who *think upon me.*

---

3. Mark Stavish, *Egregores: The Occult Entities that Watch Over Human Destiny* (Rochester: Inner Traditions, 2018), 20.

4. Ibid., 21.

5. Godwin quoted in Stavish, 22.

And I was found among those who *seek after me.*

...

For I am *the first and the last.* (Emphasis ours.)

There are so many ways we might interpret this, knowing what we know about egregore theory just from this one assertion of Godwin's. However, as Stavish reflects on Godwin's claims, he adds a critical piece that may help us separate and define a bona fide *god* from an egregore we created to pose as a god. He notes that one possible reason for the fall of the Roman empire was the breaking of the unspoken contract between them: the fading of offerings, energy, and attention from the people, which therefore led to the waning of the power of these spirits they looked to for protection until they could no longer keep the empire standing the way they once did.[6]

But interestingly enough, that isn't the only reason Stavish insists that the empire fell. Another reason is because of the way that new religions overtaking the Roman Empire had more of a focus on the *afterlife* than the material world; he and Godwin agree that "for a city, nation, or empire to exist, its devotees must be focused on life in the material world to some degree."[7] When one stops focusing on the material world, this diminishes the power of the cults, as the lives of people no longer revolve around maintaining the egregores on earth, but on looking forward to the paradise promised after this life. The entities that promise more than this hard and difficult life then become the ones to follow, and they become the ones who essentially have unlimited power as people forever go to them to ease one of the deepest human fears: the fear of death and what comes after.

Is God an Egregore? Or Does God *Have* an Egregore?

With all this said and done, we might pause here to look at God, our Creator, and wonder if we created Him as much as He created us. We might ask ourselves if His making us in His image wasn't us making our

---

6. Ibid., 22.

7. Ibid., 23.

Maker in kind, and if we aren't viscerally connected in this way. It's a tough idea to swallow, admittedly, as from what we know of God, He is much more than something so dependent on us or our energy; He is something that actively, to our knowledge, rejects the offerings of the unrighteous[8] and doesn't fade away and unwillingly leave people to their destruction, but rather actively *causes* their destruction and suffering for their transgressions.[9] One could even bristle at this idea on behalf of the entities of the Roman and Greek empires, for while the personal *daemones*, smaller spirits, may have been something of egregores, the Greek and Roman gods themselves are still active today among countless devotees, very much actively protecting, guiding, and living among people. They can still tell you about things that happened long ago, given that they are forces much older than people and all of our civilization. But that doesn't mean egregores can't be made *of* these existing deities.

You may have wondered to yourself how people you see in witchy spaces know they're talking to Apollo or Cernunnos or Loki or anyone else and not some "demon," as the mainstream Christians will claim they are. A better term than "demon" (as these are their own beings that we'll talk more about in Chapter 17) is *trickster spirit.* And truth be told, the best defense against both trickster spirits *and* egregores is very simple: you have to have knowledge of the entity you're trying to connect with. If you know the true story of Hades and Persephone, for instance—and how their union was not a willing one on Persephone's end, based on the description of it all in the Homeric Hymn to Demeter—then you know that if you ever encountered a "Hades and Persephone" that acted like some couple straight out of a fanfiction, it's because they likely are egregores created based on someone's fanfiction. Either that or a trickster spirit telling you what you want to believe about these deities to feed off your attention and offerings.

If you ask trickster spirits more niche and highly detailed questions about anything the real deity or spirit *would* know about (say, asking Archangel Azrael about his role in delivering souls of the dead, for instance), they simply won't know because they're impersonators. They'll generally try to get you to give energy or offerings to them before they've even answered any questions, and when they do finally respond, it'll be nothing but talking in circles and sounding vague to confuse you into thinking they answered you.

However, it's important to note that egregores are not *necessarily* evil or predatory. They're created by the will and wishes of the people, and so they only really know what these wishes contain. Like trickster spirits, egregores can be easily identified by asking questions about more niche topics surrounding a deity that most people don't know. The egregore won't be able to answer in any way that makes sense because they, themselves, will not know; the energy that created them

---

8. Amos 5:21-23

9. Isaiah 10, 2 Kings 17

won't contain that information. Think about how in the television adaptation of Neil Gaiman's *American Gods*, there are several different forms of Jesus: Mexican Jesus, Greek Jesus, Jesuit-Style Jesus, all that. Each version of Jesus is created based on the needs and hopes of their creators—so they're egregores.

Outside of the world of television, however, there came a time where we *thought* the thing that we've encountered in mainstream Christianity—this wicked thing, this creature that tries to brow beat us into submission with fear and shame, that divides us into sociopolitical categories and ranks us by how well we subscribe to a mile-long list of rules that are impossible for anyone to follow fully—was an egregore. After all, in *Jesus and John Wayne*, that's exactly what du Mez seems to describe: yet another *American Gods* style rendition of Jesus, this time conflated with the famous American movie star John Wayne. Within this book, du Mez covers the ways in which religion was once seen as something unmanly, noting that Christians were well aware of the fact that "Christianity had a less than masculine feel" thanks to the "'feminization' of Victorian Christianity, which privileged gentility, restraint, and an emotive response to the gospel message."[10] Meanwhile, the very fabric of American society was shifting to further separate the idea of masculinity from this gentility and emotional openness: "Christian manhood entailed hard work and thrift, and also the ability to exhibit a proper gentlemanly restraint," given that the latter was an important part of successfully running businesses or getting any work done right.[11] However, with the shift in labor from more hard industry to "punching the clock," as du Mez puts it, and working in places that no longer required raw manpower the way their farmwork and industry had before, the easy way to express masculinity disappeared.[12] Worse, du Mez points out how women started doing things outside their traditional gender allowances, like wearing pants (bloomers), going to college, riding bikes, all that, and so the obvious differences between men and women's behavior was shrinking further and further by the minute. Men had to look for new outlets for their masculinity—and they chose to gut and rewire their religion.

What entailed was the fall of the first Evangelical domino, which would set off a long and swirling pattern of recoloring the faith into something that hardly resembled that soft Victorian Christianity. These Christian men "set out to 're-masculinize' American Christianity" and "offset the 'womanly virtues' that had come to dominate the faith," breaking the bones of the religion until they were shaped like something much more "masculine, militant, warlike."[13] And du Mez notes this kind of bone-breaking of the faith happened before already,

---

10. Kobes du Mez, *Jesus and John Wayne*, 20.

11. Ibid., 20.

12. Ibid., 20.

13. Ibid., 21.

with how white slave owners and their white masculinity "had already championed a sense of mastery over dependents—over women, children, and slaves," conveniently ignoring the egalitarian message of Galatians 3:28 to suit their own purposes and sooth their cognitive dissonance about the pain they inflicted on so many people.[14]

As a result, the faith was co-opted by many a crafty preacher, who focused on just reading the Bible and getting to the *fundamentals* of the faith, rather than worry about all that high and mighty scholarship the more liberal Protestants liked to wrap themselves up in. It came to a point, however, after some rocky branding issues following World War I and World War II, where those like Billy Graham would come to step in to become the All American Evangelical, and soon enough, the focus on that rugged American masculinity would come to rebrand even Jesus. According to this Evangelical crowd, "Jesus was no sissy—he was a 'star athlete' who could 'become your life's hero'"; Jesus became less the paschal lamb and more the "Great Commander" that would lead these culturally embattled, scorned, and oh so persecuted Christians through this fog of "total war."[15] And of course, with John Wayne the picture of American masculinity in his many war and Western films, would come to be a *perfect* role model for American Christian men (despite the fact that, you know, he was "thrice married, twice divorced... a chain-smoker and a hard drinker," and a lot more.)[16] According to du Mez, Wayne, despite not even being an Evangelical in any sense, "would come to symbolize a different set of virtues—a nostalgic yearning for a mythical 'Christian America,' a return to 'traditional' gender roles, and the reassertion of (white) patriarchal authority."[17] All this toxic sludge we recoil at in mainstream Christianity—the attempts to force women to be mothers and tradwives, the brutal methods of rearing children in the faith, the disgust for the LGBTQIA+ community, the venomous attitude towards immigrants (especially immigrants of color), and all these other things that just seem to spit in the face of Jesus's message—come from the many faces of American society over the course of the 20th century, from presidents like Teddy Roosevelt and executives like Bruce Barton to celebrity preachers like Billy Graham, *actual* celebrities like John Wayne, and child psychologists like James Dobson. It's all a product of their attempts to turn Jesus into what reflected *them* rather than trying to make themselves reflect Jesus.

In short: they created the Evangelical Jesus. A sword-slinging, masculine, rugged, warlord Jesus, a *white* Jesus that seemed to prioritize and favor those that looked and acted like "Him," despite the fact that the real Jesus—a brown Jewish man from modern day Palestine who

---

14. Ibid., 20.

15. Ibid., 27.

16. Ibid., 34.

17. Ibid., 15.

preached the love of ally and enemy alike, and who allowed Himself to be taken away by the evil empire's henchmen and nailed to a cross—is nothing like this. They created what one might think, upon reading this book, was an egregore, especially given that du Mez highlights the shift in culture where most Christians didn't actually read the Bible cover to cover, but instead consumed tons of Christian media, like radio shows, self help books, and Christian romances that were maybe, sort of, kind of *based* on the Bible. Really, though—test most modern *Christians* on any niche stories in the Bible and watch them balk, never mind test this odd, caricature-like egregore of Jesus they've created in the fabric of American Christianity!

However, Christena Cleveland highlights something so insidious about this thing we called the Evangelical Egregore for so long. This creature du Mez has chronicled over the past century is one that Cleveland calls the *whitemalegod,* an extension of the distant, cold, and brutal *fatherskygod.* In the eyes of this this cruel apparition calling itself God, a creature forever masculine, forever transcendent, and forever unbothered by the issues plaguing the followers, it claims that "in order to reach him, we must heal ourselves of our human maladies... and be presentable to a male god who is deeply detached from the human condition."[18] Cleveland gives some insight into what scholars of various patriarchal religions have found when it comes to the concept of a solely male and transcendent (as in, never on earth) god, and that is that it can only be present if we actively *deny* the idea that Divinity can be present *among* us, *with* us in our pain and anguish, *helping* us rather than waiting for us to help ourselves.[19] While this *fatherskygod* idea extends to all religions that have had these thunderous and powerful sky deities, like Zeus or Perun or Thor, the way in which God has been molded into the *whitemalegod* from this ages-old concept has only worsened the issue and created a monster that leaves people to fend for themselves until they attain some impossible status that *might* award them a crumb of divine favor. According to Cleveland:

> One of the ways that *whitemalegod* whips us into sub-mission is by teaching us that we must conceal our human needs and imperfections in order to avoid punishment or social rejection... To need or not to need, that is how patriarchy determines who is valuable and who is not. No matter the gender, the more a person fits the mold of a needless "self-made man," the more they are celebrated. If you look at who sits atop the social ladder—in the corporate world, among a group of care-givers at the playground, within a spiritual community,

---

18. Cleveland, *God is a Black Woman,* 25.

19. Ibid., 25.

on social media—you will find it is the people who ex-
cel at hiding their need... Indeed, *whitemalegod* teaches us that we should be ashamed of our need because
our need erodes all that is right and good in the worl
d.[20]

As a result, with this *fatherskygod* and *whitemalegod* combination,
most people have a vastly warped idea of God and who He (or
She, or They) really is. Cleveland notes that "the pervasive idea of
fatherskygod prevents us from imagining a God who is with us in the
nitty-gritty realities of human life... a God who stands not atop the
social hierarchy, but at the bottom with the people who have been
cast aside, silenced, and forgotten."[21] And what a problem that is, giv-
en the entire point of Jesus's death on the cross was so that we *could*
know a God that did exactly that: stood with the oppressed, laughed
and loved with the oppressed, wept and *died* with the oppressed.

While Cleveland's book is a wonderful combination of both philosophical musings on the nature of the Divine *and* her lived experience
navigating this mystic knowledge as someone on the outside of the
Jesus Wayne modern Christianity has created, it is striking to see her
reference this creature in this way. It's striking, with all the talk of
how *whitemalegod* uses shame and fear and what-have-you to control
people into never questioning it, because it reminds one of something we heard of once before and brushed off as little more than an
anti-semitic conspiracy theory from antiquity: the Gnostic demiurge.
This creature is one that the heretical sect of early Christians, the
Gnostics, claimed was "actually the God of the Jews, while the true
God was the Heavenly Father of Jesus and the Christians." You surely
see why this theory is heinously anti-semitic. Nonetheless, the early
Gnostics believed that the Demiurge was the creator of our material
world rather than God, an idea that was likely influenced by the works
of Greek philosopher Plato and *his* character called the Demiurge,
also described as a creator of the material world and inferior still to
the "One, the source, or the Monad," which apparently emanated this
thing into existence in the first place.[22] The Gnostics also believed
that this creature wasn't *completely* evil, just ignorant and inferior to
the True God; it was later that they named this thing "the great tyrant
Ialdabaoth, the Son of Chaos" and "maker of man... filled with envy
because of the spark of divine light within each human soul."[23] As
a result, the Gnostics believed it was *this* creature that withheld the

---

20. Ibid., 64.

21. Ibid., 26.

22. New World Encyclopedia, "Demiurge," last modified November 15, 2023, 20:33, https://www.newworldencyclopedia.org/entry/Demiurge.

23. Ibid.

knowledge of Good and Evil from us in the Garden of Eden and had Jesus crucified to prevent people from knowing of the True God.[24]

Again, a wildly ridiculous and anti-semitic theory. God is God is God, no matter which Abrahamic religion you find Him in. When it comes to His apparent difference in personality between the Old and New Testament, it's Moltmann who asserts that while God does not *get* changed, He can absolutely *decide* to change Himself at whim, whenever He wishes.[25] We might also consider that the way people perceive God might've changed in the 4,500+ years people were writing down any Scriptures about Him, be it in the Torah and Talmud, the New Testament, the Qu'ran, or anything else about Him. Plainly, whereas people liked the idea of a wrathful God that would destroy their enemies 4,000 years ago, their ideas of what they needed might've changed 2,000 years later, resulting in a God who met their needs a different way: with love and hope in the face of a powerful and oppressive empire rather than war and revolt (especially given that the Jewish revolts against the Roman empire failed dramatically). No, we put no stock in the idea of the demiurge as the *Gnostics* understood it—but that doesn't mean that the idea is entirely without merit.

Discovering the Destructive Entity That is God's Empty Shell

Sara says:

Here we come to the crux of the issue. With the information and themes of *Jesus and John Wayne* and *The Crucified God* swimming in my head, and Cleveland's work only adding *more* insightful context and language to the pool of my mind, I found myself realizing one brutal and terrifying thing: this creature that we'd been calling the Evangelical Egregore wasn't just an egregore. This thing was *not* young, and this thing was *not* new. This thing was *old*, in fact as old as God Himself, and it knew perfectly well the tools it could use to convince otherwise sweet and kind people into becoming hateful, wretched monsters, even in the name of a Godchild that professed love as *the* greatest commandment. This thing is, in fact, trying to masquerade as God and trick people into serving it by any means necessary, even fear and shame, and it is *good* at increasing its following. It seems like a shock to consider it, but to understand what this creature is requires us to dive into the philosophy of the Sefiroth of Jewish Kabbalah, or the Tree of Life, and its inverse, the Qliphoth, or the Tree of Knowledge (otherwise known as the Tree of Death) in occultism and demonolatry.

---

24. Ibid.

25. Moltmann, *The Crucified God.*

Before we go further, it's important to note that Kabbalah is *Jewish* mysticism, and as such, it isn't for Christians to practice (we have different, much more eclectic ways of working with God, His angels, and His philosophy). However, the concepts in it are still helpful to know when it comes to piecing together all of this mess we've found ourselves in. The elements of Kabbalah are derived from the *Zohar*, a text that re-analyzes Jewish Scriptures through a mystical lens and unearths many of the secrets thought to be littered throughout. Kabbalah scholar and professor Daniel C. Matt writes:

> According to Kabbalah, every human action here on earth affects the divine realm, either promoting or hindering the union of Shekhinah [the rabbinic concept of divine immanence] and her partner—the Holy One, blessed be he. God is not static being, but dynamic becoming. Without human participation, God remains incomplete, unrealized. It is up to us to actualize the divine potential in the world. God needs us.[26]

What an idea to mainstream Christians: the idea that God needs us just as much as we need Him. It almost seems contradictory to the negative theology that Matt later puts forward, noting how "the fool corporealizes God" by imagining Him to be an old, white-haired man like the Bible describes, thus limiting his understanding of God to the limits of his own imagination and missing out on the "oneness" of God that is "devoid of bodily categories," that is, unable to be described by such things like Old or Man or whatever other labels we might try to conceptualize Him with.[27] The idea that our actions impact Heaven as much as God's actions impact earth reminds one of what Jesus said: whatever we bind on earth will be bound in Heaven, as will whatever we let loose.[28] As above, so below, and all that.

But the major takeaway within Kabbalah I bring to you is the concept of the Sefirot, the ten spheres in which a Kabbalist works to understand over a lifetime, each one guarded by one of God's archangels as they test the Kabbalist's spiritual growth and progress towards enlightenment. These spheres, according to Matt, are ones that "Ein Sof [God, the Creator] emanated... through which its actions are performed," these actions being the ways in which God impacts the "world of separation below."[29] Swedish occultist and scholar Thomas Karlsson agrees with Matt here and elaborates in the magical sense,

---

26. Daniel C. Matt, *The Essential Kabbalah: The Heart of Jewish Mysticism* (USA: Harper-One, 2009), 2.

27. Ibid., 11.

28. Matthew 18:18-20

29. Ibid., 17.

noting that "the Sephiroth are emanations that exist in everything great and small," insisting that they, and the twenty-two channels that connect these ten spheres, "represent everything from stones, plants and colors to gods and cosmic principles."[30] These spheres and paths create a very simplified map that shows "the most fundamental structure of existence... that has been used by a great number of mystics and magicians to gain knowledge about the mysteries of the universe."[31] But by emanating, or creating, these things, which Matt describes as actual souls, God (or Ein Sof) essentially *defined* these things: things like Hesed (Love) and Tiferet (Beauty). He defined them and revealed them, as "before these qualities were emanated, they were utterly concealed within Ein Sof, utterly united with it."[32] To describe it another way a la Karlsson:

> When God creates heaven and earth he divides what was previously fused. God separates the light from the darkness. Originally everything was united and completely undifferentiated, and from this primordial state the world was formed through separation, i.e. through the qualities of Geburah [the punishing and destructive principle].[33]

The way I understand that: just as God fashioned all creation out of the deep darkness, the murky, primordial waters, so too did He define Himself, and bring forward these previously unnamed, unknown forces that make Him up into their own distinct shapes and effects. In creating the Sefirot, or Tree of Life, God separated from Love all things unlike it, and from Beauty all things unlike it, concentrating them into their pure essences. However, if one thing is separated, defined, from another, then it stands that something is left behind—and that is where the Qliphoth comes in.

The Qliphoth is the exact inverse of these beautiful Sefirot, which we might imagine as the empty cocoon a butterfly leaves behind when it bursts free and unfurls its wings to dry. In these cocoons remains the things God decided were *not* part of Him or His creation, and these things Karlsson describes as "a demonic anti-structure to the Tree of Life and the ten Sephiroth," made up of ten "waste products that are associated with evil" and all evil forces like demons.[34] Karlsson's

---

30. Thomas Karlsson, *Qabalah, Qliphoth, and Goetic Magic* (Jacksonville: Ajna Bound, 2017), 29.

31. Ibid., 29-31.

32. Matt, *Essential Kabbalah*, 18.

33. Karlsson, *Qabalah, Qliphoth, and Goetic Magic*, 57.

34. Ibid., 66.

discussion on evil and how mankind understands it acts as a prelude to his discussion of the Qliphoth, and it also gives us some insight into God, as Qabalists (their philosophy different, yet very much derived from, Kabbalists) and demonolaters working with the theory of the Qliphoth understand that even within the ten Sephirot themselves, opposing forces exist—like Hesed (Love/Mercy) and Geburah (Judgement/Power). We know God is both capable of great love and severe judgement, and so these two are together in His emanations, His definitions of Himself.[35] These forces create balance, as all love and mercy leaves no room for exacting justice (which would upset us, surely, as who would want everyone to be able to get away with being terrible all the time?) and all power and judgement leaves no room for a person to be redeemed for their mistakes (which would upset us, too, as who wants to be forever condemned for a bad decision with no chance to prove themselves better, changed?). However, it seems that Geburah is the thing that *keeps* the world divided in the philosophy of Qabalists (as surely everything would just "melt together and unify" without this destructive, divisive principle), and that Geburah can be seen as "the root of evil," evil itself simply meaning *separation*.[36] Without Hesed to balance Geburah, there would be, apparently, nothing but destruction and mayhem—and in fact, parts of Geburah apparently *did* once break free to create its own emanations in defiance of God, thus creating the Qliphoth, these "dark anti-worlds," otherwise known as "excrements of creation... occasionally associated with the material world" (which smacks something of our Demiurge theory from the Gnostics).[37]

It's at this point we might pause and, like good detectives, begin winding red thread around a cork board full of pins. From all primordial, unseparated, undefined matter, God made definitions; He made clear and emanated from Himself the Sephirot of mercy, of wisdom, of understanding, of judgement, and so on. But this *judgement*, this severe and punishing quality, is not like the others, and it *knows* it's not; it is Power, and it wanted to break free of these other lovely qualities. It wanted to stand alone; it wanted to separate from the Separator. And so it did to some extent—though it, being only a piece of God, could never be more than a scrap, a shell, a shadow, a *husk* of true Divinity. And so, in its rage, it emanated into the shells of the Sephiroth these parallel worlds full of all things demonic and dark, creating a cosmic counterbalance to the world of God. These worlds intersect on the spheres *Malkuth* (the Sephirot sphere for our world, the dayside where all good things come to light) and *Lilith* (the Qliphotic sphere for our world, the nightside where, according to Karlsson, all things uncontrollable, wild, and carnal roam[38]). They overlap here and are

---

35. Ibid., 53.

36. Ibid., 55-56.

37. Ibid., 67.

38. Ibid., 113.

forever connected into what can be described as this tree's trunk, as we know that the highest leaves of a tree are forever connected to its deepest roots. The demons live here in these spheres, along with the Infernal Divine—but I posit that it isn't because the Infernal Divine, themselves, are inherently evil. Rather, it's because they are sent by God to *contain* such evil that the husks of creation—and the husks of God—are capable of manifesting in the material world alongside any good manifested with the Sephirot. They're there to help *us* master that evil, that it might never blind us the way it currently blinds so many people.

After all, if this Geburah—Judgement, Power—is the thing that broke loose, and some shrapnel of it is the thing out there creating evil, doesn't it all make sense? When we look at these megachurches and their pastors, what do they operate on (besides greed and pride)? They operate on a lust for Power, and they divide, *separate*, the people by judging them, casting them into different hierarchies. While the speaker of *The Thunder: Perfect Mind* claims to have been sent from Power, we understand that this one, who exists in *everyone* and so unites them in their humanity, is coming from a Power in balance with Love; after all, that Power *is* still a part of God. However, there is no Mercy or Love in the operations of those forever scrambling after Power like wild dogs after a scrap of meat.

Once condemned, always condemned, and you might fight your whole life to be seen as worthy and human, like Cleveland describes in her experience with the *whitemalegod*, but you never will when that false god, that *empty shell*, is in charge. Plainly, what the Gnostics identified as the Demiurge, and what the Qabalists identified as a rebellious, out-of-balance piece of Geburah, is in fact a scrap of God that was expelled from the perfect, wholesome, and balanced definitions and emanations of God; it is the piece that fled back to the abyss, the primordial waters, and decided that it had been *cheated* of its place in the divine order. As a result, it reaches its torn and shredded tendrils up through its false world and tries to mold the material plane to its wishes, locked in a tug-of-war with the God who condemned it and cast it out of His own concept of Power for its rebellion. Some might call this thing Satan, or Lucifer, or anything else, but the truth is that these creatures we point to and call the Devil are, in fact, still God's angels, and they still work to contain this wayward shell—as well as work to test us, to see if we can resist the temptation of corrupting, tainted Power it offers us.

Therefore, when you see a pastor fleece his congregation of money and buy himself expensive status items, like a massive house or a jet, while his congregation struggles to pay their utility bills, you know you see the work of God's shell.

When you see politicians use His name to justify condemning innocent people and creating laws that disenfranchise them, you see the work of God's shell.

When you see dishonest pastors, scholars, and other public figures use misconstrued, contextless Bible verses to hide behind their need to maintain power—warping the subversive and liberating words of St. Paul the Apostle into tools that *justify* slavery, silencing of women, and other social evils—you see the painfully clever craftsmanship of God's shell.

When you see parents abandon their children for things they can't control (like their gender expression or sexuality), you see the work of God's shell.

When you see wars waged in the name of God, especially ones aiming to divide His children across the labels of Jew or Christian or Muslim, which we all can see are little more than grabs for Power and lust for wealth and resources, you see the work of God's shell.

When you see this caricature of Jesus created by folks like Billy Graham, James Dobson, and John Wayne, one stripped of His love and mercy until only brutal Power remains, one painted white and toting guns as the plight of the poor, sick, and needy go ignored, you know you see yet another mask of that debilitating, judgemental, limiting, and cruel thing called God's shell.

When you see supposed allies, like white feminists, loudly protest and march and shout for their *own* liberation and demands while conveniently ignoring the outcries of their non-white peers, you see the divisive talent of God's shell, and the way it can infiltrate just about *any* movement, no matter how good their intentions. (In this, especially, Christena Cleveland makes the point that "whitemalegod [the Empty Shell] is a shape-shifter who will become anything in order to maintain his systems of oppression," including alienating Black women from feminist spaces and refusing to acknowledge or accept where racism and sexism intersect in systemic injustice.)[39]

Above all, when you see the way in which this world has been organized—the ways in which the powerful *become* powerful, and the wisdom that tells us that "absolute Power corrupts absolutely," you see the very *machinations* of God's shell.

So What Do We Do About the Empty Shell?

Well, honestly, this is where we might finally come to a conclusion that, by this point, you might've guessed: Christian Witchcraft isn't *just* about reclaiming that personal relationship with God. No, it's far more than that. Christian Witchcraft in itself is a *reform movement*, one that aims to help people shake off the grip of that Evangelical Egregore of Jesus, that empty shell of God. Christian Witchcraft aims to help people find the *real* God, the *real* Jesus, the *real* Holy Spirit, that has since been distorted and bastardized six ways to Sunday. It's a title that acts out 1 Corinthians 1:27 to the fullest, and because we also know that the shell of God only lives off a sense of embattlement, it's also one that makes the most use of St. Paul's advice in Romans

---

39. Christena Cleveland, *God is a Black Woman*, 152-153.

12:20—because this movement isn't here to fight or yell or curse, but to heal and whisper and bless. It's here to provide a way for folks to learn true connection with God and their own selves, to unlock the ancestral wisdom and knowledge that the institution of the Church has long since tried to bury, and to reconnect all people, regardless of faith, into the patchwork quilt that makes Divinity across all peoples and traditions so rich, beautiful, and helpful to mankind.

So if you choose to wear the title of "Christian Witch," I hope you'll lift it up to the sun. I hope you'll hold it up with defiance and let it be seen—because while so many names exist for what we're doing, it's this title that'll reveal to you who people really are and who people really follow. And it's this *movement* that'll help people throw off the old shackles of that husk of God, no matter how it hisses and gnashes its teeth. Through the concept of *liberation theology*, or theology concerned with the dismantling of systemic oppression and abuses of power, as we see with Moltmann, Cleveland, du Mez, Thurman, Watterson, and many others, you can better understand the ways in which the message of Christ has been distorted to serve not the people He came to help, but the Husk that hurt them to begin with. And the more we equip ourselves with this knowledge—the more we listen to those not like us, and the more we wear the title of Witch, a traditional moniker of Bad Religion, to contrast those who so desperately want to be seen as practitioners of Good Religion—the more holes we might poke in the systems of abuse and oppression that such loveless Power has made.

But while these *realizations* may come about when we find the courage to explore that which mainstream religion has told us is forbidden, like crystals and tarot cards and other such wonderful little witchy trinkets, the fact is that this work is not accomplished with the wave of a wand. This work, in fact, cannot be done with magic alone. There is no spell to banish racism, no ritual we can do to heal a community of political suppression, and no potion we can make to cure us of our deeply rooted, generational shame. The tool of Witchcraft as a whole is here to support us, fortify us, enlighten us, and connect us with the true God, so that we might learn how He wants us to be agents of His work in this world. Whether it be speaking up, getting involved, or writing your representatives, whether it be volunteering at local non-profits, donating goods and supplies, or creating resources, or whether it be just helping a single person you see in need in your day to day life, it's these mundane things that will finally de-rust the wheels of change and allow long-dormant seeds of empathy to sprout.

Just as Paul claims to have known someone who was taken up to the third heaven, so too do we know someone who saw the Shell writhing and thrashing in the sands of Thaumiel: a great and terrible beast, one people might know as the Dragon across Christian writings and ideology. It is angry and hateful and willing to do whatever it can to collect souls like war trophies, as if it might claw its way back up to God and spit in His face: *See? See who is the* real *God? See who has more souls, more followers, more Power?* Yes, we know someone who saw it roar there at the base of the secret stairway connecting Lucifer to God, and who saw Lucifer watching it with eyes so cold and grim and resolute.

But the Dragon works hard. Everyday, it screams its many lies, hoping that by time they reach the ears of men, those ugly, scraping words will become suggestive whispers that turn them towards evil. It knows we write these words. It knows you read these words. It knows its grip is slipping, and *we* know what an animal does when it becomes desperate. Therefore, just the Apostles were accused of sorcery and wickedness, heresy and blasphemy, so too will you be hissed at, accused, and accursed when you stand by the light and deny the Dragon its deceptions. So too will you have fingers pointed your way as people try to drown out Truth with the much sweeter, false promises the Dragon made to them.

You know that you're here not just because you like magic and trinkets and personalized spirituality, but because you know that there is no figure better equipped to highlight the hypocrisy of the "holy" and withstand societal wickedness than the Witch. So remember the good advice of Jesus, who knew He was sending His Apostles to the wilderness where the wolves that unknowingly followed the Dragon skulked and waited for them: *be as shrewd as snakes and as innocent as doves.*[40] Then maybe, with this perspective and this knowledge, you'll walk this path with your head held high. And if your head should ever lower, if your spirits should ever waver, if you should ever feel some whisper of fear that seems to have traveled so many miles to reach you, look up to God and sing a sweet spell:

The Lord is my shepherd, I lack nothing. He makes me lie down in green pastures, he leads me beside quiet waters, he refreshes my soul. He guides me along the right paths for his name's sake. Even though I walk through the valley of the shadow of death, I will fear no evil, for you are with me; your rod and your staff, they comfort me. You prepare a table before me in the presence of my enemies. You anoint my head with oil; my cup overflows. Surely your goodness and love will follow me all the days of my life, and I will dwell in the house of the Lord forever.[41]

---

40. Matthew 10:16

41. Psalm 23

Chapter Eight

The Divine Feminine and You

"Women were painted as bigger antagonists than the Egyptians and the Romans combined..."
—Dogma, 1999

Mimi Says:

The biggest disconnect people have with the Church, especially as they begin their deconstruction, is that there is always a Father and Son—but what of the Mother? What of the women? Many examples in the Bible stick out as women are pushed to the background or demonized completely. We know of Eve, Sarah, Ruth, Esther, Mother Mary, and Mary Magdalene, sisters Mary and Martha... but there is *so* much more to the stories than the general sermons dig into.

A large part of my personal practice includes leaning into the Divine Feminine as much as the Divine Masculine, creating balance in all things. It only felt right that, especially as I became a mother myself, I would crave a spiritual connection to a celestial mother. And just as it's preached at us that a mother is essential to raising children, I felt as if growing up with only the Heavenly Father was just as lacking as the lifestyles the mainstream Church painted upon my impression-able mind.

I would say it was one reason I ran to Wicca as a young teenag-er. I was looking for the bosom of a mother that could heal the wounds I'd been trying to heal and hide on my own; the succor of the moon and its mysteries whispered to me, and I answered. I adored the ideals of a Divine Feminine and all the things that came with it, including sexual empowerment. And yet, it was still empty. The Horned God was important, but it still felt as if the Goddess overshadowed all in everything I read. I wanted both. Was it so impossible?

And so, when I dug into my ancestry, the Morrigan was there. She'd been a persistent image in my life, between dreams and waking notions, for as long as I can remember. As I have grown into wom-anhood, Badb was always there, but I have seen the sides of Nemain and Macha, and they have seen me. Connecting with her was my first step into realizing the Divine Feminine was in the religion I was steeped in and the only thing wrong about it was the way those who curated translations tried to stifle and subdue Her spirit.

Asherah, Sophia, and the Holy Spirit

For further reading, consider Claudia V. Camp's article, "Women Wisdom: Bible," which Mimi combined with her personal under-standing of Asherah for this section.

A constant question I asked in my more precocious years (and was reprimanded for, often) was how women came to be. While the 1990's were a bit more open and radical as far as sexuality, many things were still hushed or ignored completely in the rural communities of the South that I grew up in. And yet, I continued to ask in every church we went to: If we are made in God's image, where did He get the idea for women? Even in the Bible, in almost every translation of Genesis 1:26 I have read, it says:

> Then God said, "Let us make mankind in our image, in our likeness, so that they may rule over the fish in the sea and the birds in the sky, over the live-stock and all the wild animals, and over all the creatures that move along the ground."

Even bringing this verse up in Bible studies and to Papaw, I'd get a sour face or a brush away.

"It's just how they talked back then; no one actually thinks there was more than just God." Or, later on, "It's just like when the Queen of England says 'We' when she speaks."

But as my knowledge and interest in language grew, I realized that the Royal We did not apply; in these terms, when a ruler used "We," it was to imply sovereignty.

That wasn't happening in this part of the Bible, though, and we know by the verbs and pronouns used in Hebrew. So to put it simply, "God and I" just meant "We." If such language was used in translation, it meant someone was still with God.

Logic overtook faith, and I continued to dig in the Bible for what it could mean. And I found in Proverbs, chapters one through nine, multiple times is Wisdom known as a woman or female. The imagery shows hints of the female spirit that God draws close to and is told "should be embraced." Beginning in Proverbs 3, it declares that "happy is the person who finds Wisdom." But the real truth hit me like a ton of bricks when I reached Proverbs 3:18-19:

> "She is a tree of life to those who take hold of her; those who hold her fast will be blessed. By Wisdom the Lord laid the earth's foundations, by understanding he set the heavens in place."

The Tree of Life has been used as symbolism for the connection between Heaven and Earth, and it is found in many beliefs. It is harmony between birth, life, death, and rebirth, as we see with the changing seasons and the way the trees change in these seasons. It is both nature and spirit. For those who embrace Her, as Proverbs says here, She is our connection to all of the understanding of Heaven, Earth, and the cycle of life itself.

Wisdom was God's companion. The one that helped Him create the reality we all know. I read further, to chapter eight, and felt a surge of understanding and a warmth of familiarity in verses 22 to 23:

> Adonai made me as the beginning of his way, the first of his ancient works. I was appointed before the world, before the start, before the earth's beginnings.

It continues through verse 29 where the spirit of Wisdom was describing how she had been there before it was all made. However, verses 30 and 31 were almost like a gut punch covered in honey and inspiration:

> I was with Him as someone he
> could trust. For me, every day
> was pure delight, as I played in
> his presence all the time, play-
> ing everywhere on his earth,
> and delighting to be with hu-
> mankind.

The Spirit that was there was Her. It was Mother. It was Sophia. It was the helper referenced in John 14! The Holy Spirit was divinely female, and my heart rejoiced in this. This was the first time I was able to reconcile the Divine Masculine and Divine Feminine. By 2018, I thought my discovery was enough to move forward, whether alone or with others. I reclaimed my connection and everything went so much deeper than I could've imagined.

It wasn't until 2019, with the publishing of *When God Had A Wife* by Lynn Pickett and Clive Prince, that I was able to put two and two together for that symbolism. Because of this, combined with the archaeological evidence, I believe that Asherah is who was with God in the beginning; I believe she is the Holy Spirit, and the overall Divine Feminine. Her symbolism of trees and poles in the ancient traditions, combined with the verses showing symbolism of Wisdom as a tree, shade from a tree, sturdy posts and poles, tell me the connection runs deeper. I believe that the Greek translation of Wisdom, Sophia, is actually the Goddess Asherah. A translation for an idea, compelling two separate beliefs and traditions. In these times, the right way is the one that calls to your heart and spirit as truth. Personal research and study will help you make the decision.

However, in the Gnostic tradition, Sophia was taught to be the human spirit, or even the twin feminine spirit of Jesus (referencing the Holy Sophia that the later church then declared as Christ). Because of this teaching, in my own opinion and faith, calling upon Sophia is calling upon the divine Spirit within us. There is also some backing for this within the early Christian writings, for there are many times where the Holy Spirit and Wisdom (*Sophia* in Greek, *Sapienta* in Latin, both feminine) are described as distinct, such as in the works of the Greek bishop Iranaeus's work, *Against Heresies*:

> ... the Son and the Holy Spirit (Spiritus), the Word and
> the Wisdom (Sapientia) (...) For with Him were always

present the Word and the Wisdom (Sapientia), the Son and the Spirit (Spiritus).[1]

So you can see that there's something going on here with how especially early Christians once understood this distinction between Wisdom, the Holy Spirit, and more.

Then there are some who believe that the Holy Spirit of the Holy Trinity is the Goddess Sophia, and this is valid, too! In fact, for those who would still prefer to see the Holy Spirit as a separate entity of Asherah, there's plenty of evidence to suggest that the traditional view of the Trinity—Father, Son, Holy Spirit—was actually once more something like Father, Son, *Mother*. Even some of the biggest advocates for Christianity, who fought and argued with pagan critics of the time, could see this. Early church father Origen notes it as much in his discussion of the Gospel, where Jesus claims that it was the Holy Spirit, His *Mother*, that bore Him:

> If anyone should lend credence to the Gospel according to the Hebrews, where the Saviour Himself says, 'My Mother (mētēr), the Holy Spirit, took me just now by one of my hairs and carried me off to the great Mount Tabor', he will have to face the difficulty of explaining how the Holy Spirit can be the Mother (mētēr) of Christ when She was herself brought into existence through the Word. But neither the passage nor this difficulty is hard to explain. For if he who does the will of the Father in heaven [Mt. 12:50] is Christ's brother and sister and mother (mētēr), and if the name of brother of Christ may be applied, not only to the race of men, but to beings of diviner rank than they, then there is nothing absurd in the Holy Spirit's being His Mother (mētēr); everyone being His mother who does the will of the Father in heaven.[2]

Thanks to Origen's works on the Gospel and his attempts to explain these many ideas to early Christians, "we learn from this quote that, sometime in the beginning of the second century CE, the Jewish Christians of this Gospel spoke of the Holy Spirit as Mother (mētēr)."[3] While some others, like church father Jerome (c. 342 - 420), consid-

---

1. Irenaeus quoted in Johannes van Oort, "The Holy Spirit as feminine: Early Christian testimonies and their interpretation," HTS Theological Studies 72, no 1 (2016), 3. http s://dx.doi.org/10.4102/hts.v72i1.3225.

2. Origen quoted in van Oort, 1.

3. van Oort, "The Holy Spirit as Feminine," 1.

ered this to be a case of language alone (arguing that the word for Holy
Spirit is simply feminine, the way *la table* (table) or *la pelle* (shovel) are
feminine in French), many others, like the Jewish-Christian prophet
Elxai, argued exactly the opposite: that the Holy Spirit is a being
feminine in nature.[4] We know this thanks to the reporting of Elxai's
words from the church father Epiphanius (c. 315 - 430):

> And he [i.e., Elxai] supposed also that the Holy Spirit
> stands over against Him (i.e., Christ) in the shape of a
> female being (en eideithēleian) (...)[5]

These are but a couple examples of the understanding of the Holy
Spirit as feminine, despite the pushback and denial of the Divine
Feminine even within early Christianity. We can see also from this
that while the church fathers were instrumentative in creating the
Christianity we know today, they hardly agree on many important
issues. As time passes, and the historical evidence comes forward, as
well as voices around the world to declare truth that's been buried, I
know we will gain a better understanding of the balance between the
Divine Masculine and Feminine and the theology of the Holy Trinity.

Asherah in Mimi's Practice

Asherah has a place on my altar next to God, with their candles being
centered and surrounded by charms, crystals, or other trinkets I feel
drawn to with them in mind. My intention here is to keep Adonai
and Asherah together, so that the Divine Masculine and Feminine are
balanced and One. While a lot of my work can call upon one or the
other, I find my daily meditation and divination practices work best
when I have both candles lit and have invited Them into my space.
  My favorite things to use for Asherah specifically are Tree of Life
symbols and jewelry, as well as the Willow for more water influence and the Oak for more earth influence, moonstone and abalone
seashells (for both the symbolism and the prismatic coloring to show
all elements), Lotus flowers, doves and snakes, moon symbols (particularly when drawn on the spell or on the candle in use), and a besom
to symbolize the air and magical influence.
  My personal practice has a lot of feminine influence with Asherah;
I track my personal cycles and feed myself accordingly. I make sure I
am resting when I need to (which has been insanely hard to do with
four kids), as the moon and night are part of Her domain; I also believe
that autumn and winter are part of Her, too, because the cycles of life

---

4. Ibid., 2.

5. Epiphanius quoted in van Oort, 2.

are much like the cycles of the moon: waxing, waning, and back again. I actively spend at least five minutes a day in meditation with Her, longer if I can find the time. I even have a tarot deck and oracle deck specifically dedicated to Her. (They were very much influenced and I used a lovely gifted deck for years until I could afford the ones I felt were more like Her in my mind; She does not seem to mind sharing decks with others, either.)

Hearth and Kitchen witchery lean into Her influence as well. Because She was there with God in creation, She is a spiritual compass for magic, divination, and creation workings. Which means, with every loaf of bread, protection spell, and home remedy worked, I have that nudge in my heart that She is here with me as I do so. I could feel Her with the midwife and doula, in the midst as I gave birth to my own children. When I say I lean into the Divine Feminine, it is Asherah that I refer to. But, She's not the only one.

Mary Magdalene in Mimi's Practice: The Beloved (and a Woman Wronged by the Church):

When I think of transcendental feminine spirituality, in all its wonder and power, I think of Mary Magdalene. From the symbol of the rose, to the color red, Mary Magdalene exudes infinite understanding and peace in the knowledge of God and the mysteries of the kingdom of heaven. Why? Because she was the Beloved, the one that saw the vision Jesus taught, and shared His truth.

In these days of feminism bucking back against the oppressions and sins of the Church, Mary Magdalene has become a beacon of wisdom for the Inner Truth that Jesus spoke about. In spite of being a Saint (made by Pope Pius XII in 1950), having her own feast day, and her own gospel, Mary Magdalene was smeared by the early church when Pope Gregory changed her story in 591 A.D., and many modern churches still preach and teach the same misconceptions; they claim she was the repentant prostitute, the anonymous woman who washed Jesus' feet with her tears and hair, and the Magdalene, who had seven demons cast out of her and became a follower of Jesus. Now, based on the scriptures found in her gospel from the Nag Hammadi, I am more willing to believe she is the one who was exorcised, as she speaks on the Seven Powers of the ego.

I didn't find Mary Magdalene all at once. Every so often, something would pop up and make me double take at the woman in red, whether it was a song, a line from the early Christian poem, *The Thunder, Perfect Mind*, seeing a woman in meditation, or just finding myself drawn to roses or the red thread of fate. And, of course, *The Da Vinci Code* directed by Dan Brown (2006) took the world hostage in a game of "what ifs" and mystery, one that I gladly took part in. It was like gaining permission from the universe to dig deeper, without questions or hurdles, and I am honestly thankful I did. Finding her in Gnostic texts was the first step; from there, reading *The Gospel of Mary*

Magdala by Karen L. King allowed me to pour my thoughts and heart into studying, just as I did with Jesus' word.

As I've read about the Divine Feminine in the form of the beloved and lover of Jesus, I've found myself being more self-aware and giving myself the love and understanding I have always needed. If Jesus was True Love for the world, Mary Magdalene was True Love for our self without ego. Mary gave me the understanding that loving others as I love myself means I have to *actually* love myself. And when you're raised around Southern Baptist and Pentecostal ideals from girlhood to teenage years, the undertones are less about *you* and more about the men. Mary Magdalene has healed so much religious trauma and self-deprecation, and the more I work with her, the more I understand the importance of being a woman outside of the patriarchal standpoint.

Mary holds a place on my altar, usually beside Jesus. My setup is fairly simple, with a red candle (pink if it's rose scented) inscribed with the symbol of Mary Magdalene (the Camargue Cross). I ask her blessing with my oil perfumes, give her rose quartz, amethyst, and garnet, wine and honey as offerings. For Easter and Ostara, I dye eggs red in honor of her and her myth, where she told Emperor Tiberius that Jesus had risen from the dead, and he retorted that an egg on the table would turn red before he believed her.

The egg immediately turned a deep, dark, bloody red.

I find symbols, like the Flower of Life and the Hamsa, have also been associated with her, and I leave those tokens when I find them. With her, I sing, I dance, I meditate and follow her down into the seat of my heart to listen to the truth. Bringing Mary Magdalene into my acts of faith and devotion is taking things further than simply saying a prayer. She is my influence and inspiration when I dig deep into my shadow work. While I do blend her and Asherah in my cycle and body work, Mary Magdalene is the steward of my spiritual strength in the sense of overcoming trauma and standing firm in myself. Confidence as a woman, a partner and confidant, comes from working with her.

A personal note: This dialog is open to the idea of an existing feminine energy; personal relationships and experiences are not meant to exclude anyone that is searching for said connection. My language on what is written is a reflection of just that: personal experience. In a time when being gay, queer, trans, or anything other than cishet, was *hush-hush* and usually something that happened in "the city," my experiences reflect a time of growth from close-minded preaching and practice to something that exudes love to and for all.

The *Theotokos:* Mary, Mother of God and (Christian) Queen of Heaven

Sara says:

Naturally, we couldn't wrap up a conversation about the Divine Feminine without also talking about Mary, Mother of God (or *Theotokos*), could we? If you live in a more Protestant area, you may have heard it said that Catholics and Orthodox folks "worship" Mary, but that's because oftentimes Protestants consider talking to *anybody* except God to be idolatry. Even though we know what idolatry actually is based on our conversations in Chapter 1, and we know that worship *not* just prayer, but more a full devotion, submission, and self-sacrifice to a deity, many Christians in America don't have the tools to tell the difference. America is an especially Protestant-heavy country past the east coast, though, so it's only natural that the average person following Protestant theology would be pretty confused about what worship is. They don't understand why one would go to Mary, or any Saint, or even any angel, rather than just going to God Himself for every single thing. But we know that God has a particular energy and feel to Him that can be pretty overwhelming for those just getting to know Him, and some of us who are getting back into Christianity might need intercessors to speak to God first rather than go to Him directly. Hell, even those who have been Christian their whole lives go to Mary, because she offers a unique perspective of Divinity, having raised the literal God Incarnate (if you follow the Trinitarian idea that God the Father, God the Son, and God the Holy Spirit are all God).

On the other hand, if you live in a particularly Catholic area, you may very well notice statues of Mary (often affectionately known as Mama Mary) in people's yards, or on gravestone markers, and especially in the beautiful Catholic churches, off to the side of the main altar in a separate altar cubby. For people who grew up Catholic or Orthodox, she is everyone's spiritual Mama, as well as Mother of the Church of believers itself, and that sentiment is based on this moment from the Gospels:

> Now there stood by the cross of Jesus His mother, and His mother's sister, Mary the wife of Clopas, and Mary Magdalene. When Jesus therefore saw His mother, and the disciple whom He loved standing by, He said to His mother, "Woman, behold

> your son!" Then He said to the
> disciple, "Behold your mother!"
> And from that hour that disciple
> took her to his own home.[6]

As such, you may notice people referring to Mary as their Mother, or even as Mom. Despite what Protestant denominations say, Mary's role is considered, by the Catechism of the Catholic Church, to be "inseparable from her union with Christ and flows directly from it."[7] The Catechism also states that "Mary's function as mother of men in no way obscures or diminishes this unique mediation of Christ, but rather shows its power," as all her power to help the church members still comes through the grace and power of her Son.[8] But we know as Christian Witches that even if our power comes from God, it's still *power* that we're given the privilege to wield—the most raw and intense power there is.

"All generations will call me blessed," says Mother Mary in the Gospels, and that's the crux of how she's treated within the Catholic Church: venerated and adored as Queen of Heaven and Mother of God, and acknowledged for her incredible role in helping humanity through the grace of God the Father, Son, and Holy Spirit. According to the many different pieces knit together into the Catechism:

> "The Church's devotion to the Blessed Virgin is intrinsic to Christian worship." The Church rightly honors "the Blessed Virgin with special devotion. From the most ancient times the Blessed Virgin has been honored with the title of 'Mother of God,' to whose protection the faithful fly in all their dangers and needs.... This very special devotion ... differs essentially from the adoration which is given to the incarnate Word and equally to the Father and the Holy Spirit, and greatly fosters this adoration." The liturgical feasts dedicated to the Mother of God and Marian prayer, such as the rosary, an "epitome of the whole Gospel," express this devotion to the Virgin Mary.[9]

Essentially, it's by offering deep respect to Mary for her role in the story of Jesus and the redemption of humankind that we can further

---

6. John 19:25-29

7. Catechism 964.

8. Catechism 970.

9. Catechism 971.

appreciate Jesus and God and the Holy Spirit altogether. So much has been said about Mary—that she's the *New Eve*, erasing the errors of the Genesis story, that she terrifies demons and protects her children (the Church as a body of believers) with incredible ferocity, that she appears most often to women and children, so on and so forth.

There's a lot of love for her among Catholic, Orthodox, and Episcopalian women especially, as she's essentially the female star of the Christian show (given how Mary Magdalene had been slandered and falsely conflated with a prostitute from the Gospels). In fact, according to sociologist Michelle Spenser-Arsenault, "Mary's high esteem in the Catholic church is continuing evidence that women are highly regarded in the church"—granted, largely in part for their role as mothers and stewards of the next generation of the faithful, but still highly esteemed.[10] And it's because of this focus on motherhood that, combined with the idea that she's essentially the Christian All-Mother, she's one people lean on for support as someone who lived on earth and understands intimately the role of a human mother; she offers a type of motherly love that, for many who had hard relationships with their biological moms, can be comforting and helpful. She's also seen as a great supporter for mothers and mothers-to-be who need a helping hand. People will often pray to her for help in these issues—intercession to be more gentle and patient parents, or intercession for the comfort of a mother that they can't get from their own for whatever reason.

Of course, that's not the only time people pray to her, or the only thing that's focused on in folk ritual and celebration. So important to older denominations is Mary that the entire month of May is dedicated to her in Catholic liturgy. May Day, similar to the neopagan holiday Beltane, is a time where girls crown the Blessed Virgin with mayflowers and recite the Hail Mary, a prayer developed from the way Gabriel addresses her in Luke 1:26-28.[11] Other times of the year, certain cultures, such as that of Sardinia (an island off the coast of Italy), have beautiful processions where folks wear traditional clothing and carry a statue of Mary around streets littered with rose petals and herbs, praying for her intercession for the town's protection from plague and other disaster.[12] Outside of processions, countless shrines, chapels, and even full churches—like the famous Notre-Dame de Paris, or *Our Lady of Paris*—are dedicated to Mary and house statues of her. In Slovenia, for instance, it's not uncommon to pass a shrine that looks like a little house, where a statue of Mary sits on an altar surrounded by flowers, candles, and coins. She's an undeniable presence in Christian

10. Michelle Spencer-Arsenault, "The (Re)Construction of a Female Icon," *Sociology of Religion* 61, no. 4 (2000): 482, https://www.jstor.org/stable/3712533.

11. Ibid., 481.

12. @archaeology_bae, 2022. "I, myself, am strange and unusual. Archaeology PhD -Cambridge Uni." Tiktok, November 17 2023. https://www.tiktok.com/@archaeology_bae/video/7117459589930454277

faith, especially among older denominations—and from our conversations on Christena Cleveland's work, we also know she comes in many more shades than just *white* (which, given she was a Jewish woman from modern day Palestine, should surprise no one).

Ways of working with her vary, but one of the simplest is to pray the rosary. As a friend said once: holding the rosary is like holding Mary's hand. And the rosary prayers, each bead representing a repetition of one of the staple prayers (Hail Mary, Our Father, Glory Be, etc.), is a great way to slow your thoughts, relieve stress, and settle into a meditative mood to begin the rest of your spellwork. Talking to Mary directly, she can get you the help you need by putting in a word for you to her Son or by giving you her own wisdom and guidance like any mother would. And knowing she scares demons? That she has the angels with her all the time—that essentially, where she goes, all of Heaven follows? That's powerful, too; we can learn from her when it comes to ferociously wielding God's power for the sake of protecting ourselves and others.

So when it comes to reconnecting with the Divine Feminine, your options are wide open—and even this doesn't touch on the many female Saints you might turn to for help, like St. Joan of Arc! If the Divine Feminine is important to your craft, then know you can easily find it embedded in Christianity and work with it fully. Know that it's not only okay, but *encouraged*, so that you might understand a full spectrum of Divinity rather than one flat image the mainstream Church continuously tries to sell us. Not everyone will find that the Divine Feminine resonates with them, and that's okay—but for those who always felt that there was something off, something missing, maybe you'll find it there with Her.

Section 3
Understanding Ourselves and Our Spiritual Power

Chapter Nine

The Fundamentals of Magic and Its Traces in Jesus's Life

N OW, AFTER ALL OF our discussion of these Bible verses and the context behind them, you may be (or may not be) surprised to know just how much magic and mysticism was all over the Bible in the early days—both in the Old and New Testaments. Our aforementioned example of magic, Leviticus 14, surely wasn't the only example of magic done by official priests, or magic not just condoned, but actively commanded by God. But the issue of magic is a tricky thing, you see, as no one seems to be able to readily define it. In fact, not even rabbis could pin it down, according to the Jewish Annotated New Testament: while rabbis were out forbidding "sorcery as antithetical to the Torah," they seemed to have quite the "difficulty defining it," which should surprise no one given how many different words were used for magical acts that we simply don't have the context to wholly understand anymore.[1]

Because magic is so difficult to define, it's just as difficult to distinguish the line between an acceptable miracle and an unacceptable spell. After all, "rabbinic miracles workers sometimes [struggled] with powerful magicians and witches, and beat them at their own game"—and yet at the same time, "in other cases magicians and

1. Levine and Brettler, *The Jewish Annotated New Testament*, 568.

witches [taught] the rabbis some powerful spells,"[2] suggesting some crossover between the two stations of Miracle Worker and Magician. Figures such as Hanina ben Dosa (a contemporary of Jesus), Hanan the Hider, Honi the Circle Drawer, and of course, the many prophets and priests of God, can be shown to do all kinds of miracles—from stopping the Jordan river to bringing rain, as well as more malevolent miracles like causing illness, blindness, and even death. All these things are ones that, to anyone observing from the outside, look like the same magic as the sorcerer laying curses or invoking blessings in surrounding polytheistic cultures.[3]

One of the biggest challenges people face in discussing the mystic work they do, be it as mystics, as mages, or as witches of God, however, is exactly that: defining what magic is. It's the first breakdown in communication between a confused Christian and a Christian Witch, and until it's resolved, conversation and explanation can't readily resume between the two. So for the sake of this book and this philosophy of witchcraft and magic in Christian contexts, we'll define magic thusly:

> _Magic_: the spiritual energy that exists within our own bodies, emanating from the core of our being (our souls) and given to us by the Breath (or Spirit) of God.

This force and its source has been given many names over the course of human history: the breath of life (_ruach_ in Hebrew), or the traditional Chinese concept of _chi_ or _qi_ (_ki_ in Japanese), or the Ayurvedic and Hindu concept of _prana_, or the Roman and Greek concepts for the soul, _anima_ and _pneuma_ respectively. These refer to either the soul itself or the current of energy that exists within living things, and it's how practices like tai chi operate. To use this practice as an example of the concept of energy: tai chi, now understood as a meditative and health-related form of martial arts, is one that focuses on regulating the body and mind through slow, controlled, meditative movements—and one that, through religious philosophies and systems like Daoism, harnesses and utilizes this life force within the body to create debilitating strength. According to Rosemary Ellen Gulley:

> Regardless of style, the key to all martial arts is skillful use of the universal life force (ch'i in Chinese and ki in Japanese), which permeates all things and can be directed throughout the body. The universal life force exists in the opposites of yang and yin, active/masculine

---

2. Vermes, "Jewish Magic and Miracle Workers, 682.

3. Ibid., 680.

and passive/feminine, which are in constant interplay.
The force is controlled by uniting it with mind and body
in physical movement, breathing techniques, and meditation.[4]

In Gulley's take on chi, she also mentions a controversial style of
attack in the art of Chinese boxing (Kung Fu), called *dim mak*, in which
some Kung Fu practitioners believe "if a body is struck at a certain
point in a certain manner at a certain time of day, a delayed death
inevitably follows"—a "death touch," if you will.[5] While many martial
artists have written this idea off as sheer fantasy, it's still a concept
of Chinese mysticism that exists to some extent, therefore giving us
a different culture's perspective on the concept of energy work and
energy manipulation—energy that we're calling *magic* for the sake of
our collective understanding.

Was Jesus a Witch?

Unfortunately, even when people *did* attempt to define or distinguish
types of magic for legal reasons (especially in the Roman empire), the
concept of magic wasn't always so clear cut throughout the ancient
world and in the time of Jesus. As we've mentioned before, magic,
miracle, and medicine were all considered synonymous at one point,
and that's because the nature of the thing is so volatile—as are their
reasons for being used. After all, what really distinguishes Jesus's raising Lazarus from the dead from, say Apollonius of Tyana doing the
same thing? Critics of magic and witchcraft will say that it's God's
power that allowed Jesus to do this, and that some demonic force was
at work among these pagans that allowed them the same miraculous
feats (and in fact, that's exactly what church father Eusebius says: that
Apollonius has done his work "with the help of a more important
demon"), but the irony is that Jesus Himself was accused of this very
thing by the Pharisees.[6] In fact, Conner stipulates that in Mark, the
decision to interpret the Pharisees accusing Jesus of *being* possessed
is "a conspiracy to ignore or minimize the role of magic in the New
Testament and early Christian literature"; he notes that:

> The accusation by the Jewish leaders is not that Jesus is
> possessed *by* a demon, but rather that He is the magi-
> cian *par excellence* because He has bound Beelzeboul

---

4. Rosemary Ellen Gulley, *Harper's Encyclopedia of Mystical and Paranormal Experience*
(USA: HarperCollins, 1991), 344.

5. Ibid., 344.

6. Conner, *Magic in Christianity*, 235.

himself, the prince of demons, to his service and works his miracles as a result of exercising that control.[7]

The fact of the matter is that in Jesus's day, people—be they Jewish or Greek—saw Jesus as a charlatan, a hack magician, one who learned His tricks during the brief stint the Holy Family fled to Egypt (a place known for its magic since the story of Exodus, with the magicians that could duplicate the first few of God's plagues in the Pharaoh's courts).[8] They were sure He was nothing special, that all His miracles were just nonsense—especially because the people of antiquity had seen miracles, or *wonders*, like these performed before. In fact, it turns out there's quite a bit to compare between Jesus's miracles and the many spell formats and methods found within the Greek magical papyrae.

Throughout the four Canonical Gospels, the story of Jesus is told through the lens of four different writers. Some, however, describe the way Jesus performs His miracles in different ways than others. For instance, in Matthew, we know that Jesus performed miracles, but not necessarily *how*. In Mark, however, we get some more critical details—like the fact that Jesus used a mix of spit, mud, and incantation to cure a blind man, and that He used incantations, mutterings, and sighs to work other miracles. These miracles "contain the same procedures, healing formulae... and narrative structures found in pagan and Jewish sources," according to the Jewish Annotated New Testament—and the editors of this rendition of the New Testament assert that "the modern tendency to distinguish Jesus' healings from those of contemporary Jews such as Hanina ben Dosa and pagan miracle workers such as Apollonius of Tyana... is perhaps theologically motivated."[9] To which us Christian Witches say: *of course it is.* After all, if the early Christians worked so hard to be seen as respectable members of society, then having charges of witchcraft, fraud, sorcery, and other such things leveled at them would've done them (and their budding religion) no good. (And charges of witchcraft were only *some* of the wild rumors spread about the members of this early cult.)

For all our discussion about magic and witchcraft, we will once again remind you that the concept of the *witch* as we understand it is a highly modern view of it—and highly politicized in a day and age where witches seem to stand in direct opposition of the Church and its unsavory, corrupted practices that have put a death touch on countless peoples, cultures, and traditions. While some might insist that Jesus was a witch—as, after all, raising the dead, transmuting water into wine, and exorcising spirits does check off quite a few magical boxes—the fact of the matter is that Jesus would not have considered Himself any kind of *witch* in the words that would've been used then.

---

7. Ibid., 235

8. Wilken, *The Christians as the Romans Saw Them*, 100.

9. Levine and Brettler, *The Jewish Annotated New Testament*, 72.

He wouldn't have considered Himself a *magos*, and especially not a *goēs*.

To call Him a witch is therefore, in our opinion, a vast oversimplification (and does the work of Jesus's earliest critics for them, notably Lucian of Samosata). Lucian, a Roman satirist, thought of Jesus and His followers as little more than uneducated, gullible country bumpkins and "considered both Peregrinus and Jesus to be *frauds* or *sorcerers* (γοης) [goēs] and *tricksters*... sleight of hand artists."[10] What Jesus did wasn't considered fraud by the people who believed in Him, nor was it out of sorts with the types of miracles discussed by His Jewish and pagan peers in wonder working. A word more suitable for Him—and that, in a discussion with Jesus, He gave Himself—is simply "Shepherd." As transcribed from this conversation in Sara's work, *Where the Gods Left Off:*

> I am simply Me. I do what I do... I am a Shepherd... To the flock, My very being is magic. But it's my Father's force that guides us all—that I wield in His name.[11]

One of the most common things you'll hear said about *magic* vs. *miracle* is that it's the *source* of the power that matters—and when Christian Witches explain that it's God the Father's power that we draw on, they'll insist we call it anything else *but* witchcraft. But we know we name our power *witchcraft* to call a spade a spade and recognize this force for what it is: magic. Holy magic, yes, but magic. In the words of Martin Duffy, "there is no black or white magic—no good or evil—there is just power," and whether that power is "good" or "bad" entirely depends on its affect *and* the individual it's affecting (hence why so many Saints cursing the hell out of their enemies were painted as noble, while anyone doing magic *on* church officials was deemed a servant of the Devil or what-have-you).[12] And it's this force that now, having defined it, we might discuss how to actually *use*.

Understanding the Source of Magic of a Christian Witch

Sara says:

Somehow, against all odds, it was in a channeled conversation with St. Paul the Apostle that I finally understood what Christian magic

---

10. Conner, *Magic in Christianity*, 15, 195.

11. Sara Raztresen, *Where the Gods Left Off,* 181.

12. Martin Duffy, *Anathema Maranatha*, 36.

actually was and how it was meant to be used. I certainly didn't expect him, of all people, to tell me, but then again, we know that St. Paul was himself quite the magician as we read of his exploits in the book of Acts. He exorcised unclean spirits constantly, to the point that one spirit he cast from a girl just because it was annoying him with how it made the girl shriek day and night about their presence in the village as holy men.[13] Yet, as we know from his work in the Acts of Paul and Thecla, these many works (and the controversial things he preached) often got him accused of sorcery, requiring him and other Apostles to find other ways to do their work without causing a scene.

Of course, despite all that we've already covered about *magic* and *miracle* and *medicine*, there will still be those folks who can't stomach the idea of magic *in* their miracle; it's simply too easy to plug one's ears, cover the words of this book with their hand, and say that all of this was only ever the *power of God* and not otherworldly spirits. However, you and I both know that is not what people at the time thought of Jesus. Between the Roman critics of Christianity, like Lucian with his scathing satire and philosophers such as Celsus, who himself had quite the hefty criticism of both the new religion and its figurehead, it's clear what the opposition of Christianity believed. In fact, on top of Lucian's remarks, Celsus insisted that "it was by magic that he [Jesus] was able to do the miracles which he appeared to have done," and that early Christians thereafter went around doing miracles "by pronouncing the names of certain daemons and incantations."[14] But for anyone that would cry out and say that this was nothing more than the vitriol of *unbelievers*, well—unfortunately, for them, even the early church fathers like Origen outright admitted that "except for powerful works and marvel," or rather, *miracle*, which we know is synonymous with *magic*, "the new doctrines and teachings of the apostles would have made no progress."[15] From all this talk on both sides of the aisle, one thing becomes certain: miracle was a cornerstone of early Christian spread, and it looked no different from the magic of other wonderworkers, or *thaumaturges*, of the era.

Be it pagan *thaumaturge* or Christian *theurge*, however, the result is the same: making the impossible, possible. Making the dream manifest into reality. And the reality so many people, especially mainstream Christians, want to close their eyes to, is the fact that *magic* has always existed, and that without it, *religion becomes inoperable.* I'll argue this plainly: when we deny *magic*, we deny the very tool that connects the Seen and Unseen worlds; we deny a connection with God Himself. We deny our spiritual heritage, and we throw the blessings and gifts of the Spirit right back in God's face. It's as foolish to remove a Christian's magic as it is to remove their muscles and still expect them to stand up,

---

13. Acts 16:16-18

14. Wilken, *Christians as the Romans Saw Them*, 98.

15. Origen quoted in Conner, 369.

or to remove their minds and still expect them to think. For all this talk of spiritual warfare from mainstream Christians, they've eaten up the false advice of God's shell, that Dragon; they've followed the orders of the Dragon, who told them to dump their holy arsenal of power into the deep and cavernous depths of the Dragon's lair.

Nonetheless, knowing what magic *is* and that it's well embedded in Christian tradition, it comes time to understand how to tap into it. When St. Paul explained it to me, I thought that I, for lack of a better way to explain this, *had the scales fall from my eyes.* Between what he showed me—him and his traveling partners weaving trickles of golden light like spiderwebs through a crowd, catching folks and luring them in so they might hear the message behind the magic—and what he *told* me, which was that the true magic comes from a Source much higher than our own souls, I was flabbergasted. It also lined up with what I noticed about other spell formats from things such as the Greek magical papyrae: many of these spells weren't so much about forcing the magician's will out into the universe, but rather, about petitioning a deity to do some heavy lifting on their behalf and create effects and magics beyond what a single person might be capable of. In fact, how many times does the Bible itself allude to it in Acts and other such places?

When Peter tells the beggar who cannot walk, to walk, he commands it *in the name of Jesus Christ.*[16]

When Peter confronts Ananias and Sapphira, he makes it clear that these two didn't just lie to Peter about how much money they got from selling a parcel of land, but to *God*, and after Peter announces this, they fall down dead, one after another.[17]

When Peter and John lay hands on the people of Samaria, it is *then* that they receive the Holy Spirit, just as the Apostles themselves had on Pentecost—and it is then that the people learn the difference between the impressive, yet still fraudulent, magics of Simon the Magos and the great wonders of the Apostles, who the Holy Spirit was forever with.[18]

And Paul himself *breathed*, with great success, "murderous threats" against these early Christians—only to have his power *grow* after receiving a vision of Jesus and converting himself.[19]

Acts is a book that shows, in no uncertain terms, that while people might be powerful on their own—Simon, and then the Jewish exorcists who later burned their books after failing one such exorcism, for instance—it's through the power of God that the true works take root, not just memorizing certain names and formulae. For Christians, it's through the whole Trinity, the Father, Son, and Spirit, the Apostles

---

16. Acts 3:6-7

17. Acts 5:1-11

18. Acts 8:9-25

19. Acts 9:1-22

gain the ability to heal the sick, raise the dead, *cause* death, escape prisons, meet people at the direction of God's angels, and so much more. Because like the pagan wonder workers of old, the Apostles were working more than their magic; they were using their magic, and its container, their souls, to channel the glory of God down through them. Like the AC adapter on a laptop charger (that box part that converts alternating current, or AC, into a direct current usable for laptops), your soul is such an adapter, and it uses your own magic to convert, distill, and direct the otherwise massive power of God into something you can handle as a single person.

In short: a Christian Witch's magic is less about being a *witch* in the typical way we might think of it, and more about being a *conduit* of power near unfathomable. This requires a level of peaceful temperament and responsibility that I cannot overstate, because God *answers* when you learn how to call for His help, and it can be a beautiful blessing for those you direct it towards, or it can be utterly cataclysmic. There's a reason it's known as *calling down the fire [of God]*. This is also why beginning the path of a Christian Witch with learning is so important: yes, learn about magical philosophy and how to use tools and so on and so forth, but most importantly, learn about the very character of God so that you might understand intuitively how your magic should be used in your day to day life. Actually commune with God; sit with Him, learn from Him, try your best to understand what He wants you to do and how He wants you to grow, so that you might step into your magic in the full authority that He and His Son and His Spirit can grant you.

It's important to note your magic will be no different than any other action you might take. God does not stop you from making bad decisions in your daily life because He gave you that free will. If you want to lie, cheat, and steal—if you want to backstab your brothers and whisper false rumors about your sisters—by all means, no one is stopping you. But every action you take has consequences, and if you know *nothing else* about the character of God, you should know this: God is not, and has never been, one to help people avoid the just consequences of their actions. Go ahead and cast as many spells as you'd like; invoke God's name for every single one, big or small, blessing or curse.

Just remember that you reap what you sow.

How to Build and Conceptualize Your Magic as a Christian Witch

With all this said and done, it's important that we understand our magic as something like a spiritual muscle. You can train your mind with all manners of brain games and puzzles and good books, and you can train your muscles with various styles of exercise. Likewise, you can train your magic to be strong, resilient, and extremely effective in the many applications of magic one can think of. This begins with a concept called *energy work*, which, at its simplest, is using the raw spiritual energy in your body to effect change. This might seem abstract to some people, as this energy isn't something you can see or smell or anything else; it's not something anyone just looking at you can easily perceive.

But it is something that you can *feel*. Maybe you've already felt it already: as tingles skittering under your skin, or warmth pooling in your palms, or as a dense ball of *sheer will* in your core that seems to spiderweb through you like a phantom heart pumping something sharp and exhilarating through your whole body. Most of us have felt it at least once or twice in our lives, even if we have no concept of magic. It's when our emotions are heightened, and we psyche ourselves up for something great—that *bouncing off the walls* feeling—that we, as spiritual creatures, naturally raise our own energy. It's when we take a deep breath and center ourselves for something intimidating: there, we square our shoulders, and by extension, our inner column of power, to face it. It's when we shout from deep in our belly, beat our chests, and show our teeth that we feel like we can take on anything, anyone.

That is energy at work.

To continue building it means to become aware of it in our daily life and grab onto the threads of it that already exist within us. When we understand our own energy better, we can also learn to recognize and properly channel the power of God (which, from experience, feels like a bright flood of fire when it hits the soul during rituals and other high magic that we'll discuss later). We can also use our energy in any way that we can imagine it once we can more fluidly feel it move through our bodies and manipulate it, because our minds and our souls are so intimately connected. To give you a picture of what we mean, if you've ever played a game like Skyrim, you might notice how certain low level magical wards include a mage creating a shield of blue light in front of them. It looks like a faintly glowing blue shield.

Sara says:

Well, if you can imagine what it looks like and understand why it works, why not push your magic out the same way? Why not let your magic flow out into the shape of a shield and protect you from anything that might come careening your way in the spiritual world around us? (Though me personally, I prefer full coverage; I like to imagine I'm in a golden bubble covered in spikes, so that any potentially nasty things stay far away or risk getting injured trying to get to me.)

Another example of how I use my magic in little everyday situations includes traffic lights. If you've ever played something like Connect Four, you might even be able to *hear* the sound of a red plastic coin falling down to the last slot of the game board. When I look at a traffic light, I see something similar: three of the four holes of a Connect Four board, with my plastic coin being that little green light. When a light is red, I focus on that *shwip* sound of the coin falling down, and when it's green, I'll imagine that my little plastic coin has a fifty pound weight anchoring it down to the bottom just long enough for me to pass under it without it changing.

Now, wait a minute, you might be thinking. *Is that really magic, or is it just placebo?*

To which I answer: it doesn't matter what you or I think it is when I get through eight out of ten lights. Some I just know aren't going to work based on how much distance I need to cross, sure—but then again, maybe that *just knowing* is me defeating my own magic, because we know that magic requires you to believe in it for it to work. Remember what Jesus told us: faith the size of a mustard seed moves mountains.[20]

But in order to build this magic for everyday uses such as protection and little tricks like getting through traffic lights on our rush to work, we need to conceptualize and work with our magic, which requires us to actually spend some time with ourselves. Back when I was a young witch and didn't have so much access to all the information we have about witchcraft now, this was a little hard to figure out to do. I vaguely understood something about the concept from watching shows like *Naruto*, where their fantastical interpretation of chakra had my eight-year-old self trying to imagine my own energy center. It turns out that the show wasn't *entirely* off when it came to how this kind of power can be accessed, because that helped me learn to feel those tingles in the palms of my hands. It sounds so silly, but it's true: we really can glean some esoteric wisdom from the most unexpected places.

My love for this silly show faded as I went to middle school, however, and I became more interested in witchcraft itself. Imagine my surprise when I was browsing the many strange online forums and websites a few years later and discovered a magical exercise that seemed to validate what I was doing! On Spells of Magic, a website that was little more than a complicated and endlessly deep rabbit hole of homebrewed spells, tips, exercises, and more, I found a post from user Lord_Grace in 2010 dictating how one might learn to feel, conceptualize, control, and grow their energy by manipulating an *energy ball*.[21] It was something that had my young, freshly budding witchy self enamored, because it required absolutely *no* tools whatsoever: just me, my pool of magic, and a quiet space to practice. To this day, it's still a valuable exercise, so here's how you might practice this on your own whenever you find the time to do so.

---

20. Matthew 17:20-21

21. Lord_Grace, post to "Energy Ball," Spells of Magic, September 2, 2010, https://www.spellsofmagic.com/read_post.html?post=262685.

Magic Building Exercise: The Energy Ball

When you're settled in a comfortable place, be it in bed right before going to sleep or alone in your office when no one's around, take a deep breath and get into the headspace for your energy work. The procedure is as follows:

- Hold your hands about 6 inches apart, palms facing each other.

- Imagine energy pooling in the center of your chest or from the pit of your stomach.

- Feel it stretch from its center up your chest, then down your arms and into your palms.

- Feel your magic on your skin: notice how it tingles at your palms and warms you.

- Imagine it drifting out of your hands and hovering between them, and ask yourself:

  ○ What does it look like to you?

  ○ What color is it?

  ○ Does it act like water? Plasma? Smoke? Fire?

  ○ How fast or slow does it move when you let it be?

  ○ How does it make you feel to look at it?

  ○ What does this say about *you*, the bearer of such energy?

- Focus on spooling it into a neat ball between your hands, then press your hands in and imagine the ball condensing.

- Continue pouring energy into this ball even as it gets smaller. Feel the density of it, and feel it press at your palms like two opposing ends of a magnet.

- Then slowly move your palms further away from each other and imagine the ball growing bigger as you pour more energy into it, less dense as it grows in volume.

- Repeat the last two steps a couple times, then allow the ball to disperse by either sucking it back into your palms or letting it fall apart into the empty air.

Once you're done with this exercise, take note of the experience. Think about how easy or hard it was to move this energy, and how it made you feel as it traveled through you. Think about its appearance and reflect on what it could symbolize or say about your potential magical styles. We'll talk more about spellwork and types of witches later, but right now, it's important that you get to know the magic that already exists within you, and how it meshes with your personality or possible magical paths.

Sara says:

My magic, for instance, appears to me as golden light; it's bright and wily as fire, and it's highly visible; it shines whenever I find myself in a dark or dimly lit place in meditation. And just as we might make a ball of energy, we can make other shapes, too; this golden light of mine makes for a wonderful sword, shield, bow and arrow, or any other weapon I can think of when I'm out trying to deal with troublesome spirits or other such challenges. Again: whatever you can think, you can do—if not physically, then psychically. So go forth, build your magic, and remember: this power you're learning to use is itself a gift from God.

Chapter Ten

The Basics of Divination

**Divination:** An uncertain presage or prediction, which is interpreted by reflection after the judgment of a private light, as when it is said, "My mind or heart foretells this and that to me" or "This the Angel, my spirit, indicates." —Martin Rulandus the Younger, A Lexicon of Alchemy (1612), presented by Benebell Wen.

—◦❖◦—

"How do you know you're talking to God and not Satan?"

After asking what a Christian Witch is, or how it's possible to be one, this is the third most popular question posed to this community—and for good reason. We can't shrug this off as a silly or stupid question, because people forget: it's not only ghosts and demons and strange spirits that live in the many pockets of the world of the Unseen (which we talk about more in Section Four). It's gods and goddesses and Saints and angels; it's _God Himself_ that lives there, in that place we call Heaven. Before we get into any discussions of the creatures you might meet in the Unseen Realm, however, and before we answer this third most popular question posed to Christian Witches, let us give you another question to chew on: _how can we be connected with God if we only learn how to pray, but never how to hear the answer?_

Little do most people know, but once upon a time, they did know how to hear the answer. As we've already mentioned, the Levite priests were specifically instructed to use the Urim and Thummim: two stones that essentially acted the same way as a modern pendulum, giving _yes_ or _no_ answers to any question a priest would ask God. A priest would keep these two stones in their pocket and pick one at random to get their answer. Some say that this is the same as drawing straws or something, that it's all up to chance and has nothing to do with divination and magic. This is a silly assertion. If you ask God a question, and you draw straws or pick a stone or any other thing you can write off as chance, why would you assume it wasn't God that directed your hand to the stone or straw He wanted you to pick?

In fact, this is precisely the function of the divination method of casting lots, called *cleromancy*, a category to which the Urim and Thummim belong. It doesn't only appear among the priests of the Old Testament, though; this was a common form of divination among many different peoples, with one example of non-Israelites doing so being in the case of Haman, a Persian court official at the time of King Xerxes' reign in the Book of Esther, who cast a lot to see what day he should destroy the Israelites:

> In the twelfth year of King Xerxes, in the first month, the month of Nisan, the pur (that is, the lot) was cast in the presence of Haman to select a day and month. And the lot fell on the twelfth month, the month of Adar.[1]

From that word, *pur*, comes the holiday Purim (lots), in which Jewish people celebrate Queen Esther's saving of her people from such planned destruction. Nonetheless, as you can see, this was something many different people knew how to do—and that includes the Apostles. In Acts 1, the Apostles are gathered together to decide who will replace Judas in their work of spreading the good word. They do this by consulting God directly via lots:

> So they nominated two men: Joseph called Barsabbas (also known as Justus) and Matthias. Then they prayed, "Lord, you know everyone's heart. Show us which of these two you have chosen to take over this apostolic ministry, which Judas left to go where he belongs." Then they cast lots, and the lot fell to

---

1. Esther 3:7

Matthias; so he was added to the
eleven apostles.[2]

The idea that casting lots is something as silly and superficial as just leaving things up to chance, when the Apostles clearly *asked* God to reveal to them through these lots who should be chosen, is born of Christians' deep denial about the mystic practices of their own faith. Let us say this clearly: *you cannot operate religion without magic.* It is not possible. When you are dealing with a being like God, or His angels, or His Spirit, or any of the things Jesus Himself could do or demonstrate, you are speaking of *magic*—a term that had some tumultuous definitions over time.

Beyond this, the other standard form of divination, prophecy, is one we also briefly touched upon in our discussion of 1 Samuel. Given that the priest class was able to directly communicate with God via tools like the Urim and Thummim, and that they were closely associated with God and His proper worship, one might think that all prophets were of the Levite (or priestly) tribe. But of course, when we look at the actual prophets, the ones that came up weren't necessarily of the priestly class—not always. In fact, one could even be trained to be a prophet, as those like the prophet Samuel taught students who were "pious, intelligent, and studious."[3] Prophecy, after all, is "the ability to receive and decode Divine emanations," which can be done through anyone who has "a highly-developed imaginative prowess," or "the ability to conceive of things not perceived through the usual five senses," and it certainly hasn't been limited to just one tribe, or even to just men.[4] Even today, modern sources, scholars and rabbis, talk about what it takes to become a prophet, such as being "mentally sound... physically healthy... studied to the extent that he has acquired wisdom... have overcome any desire for honor and power" and having intellect that was "finely developed."[5] This is by no means the full list, but shows the standards any new prophets would be held to, should they be trained today: standards of humility, wisdom, righteousness, and selflessness.

Nowadays, there is no official body or institution that can properly teach us how to become prophets like Samuel had in his time. Moreover, in Judaism, it's thought that "prophets cannot receive messages when they are angry, in mourning, or in other forms of bad news."[6]

---

2. Acts 1:23-26

3. Richard M. Davidson, "Schools of the Prophets Paradigm for Pastoral Education," *Faculty Publications* (2015), https://digitalcommons.andrews.edu/pubs/2103.

4. Rabbi Jack Abramowitz, "What is Prophecy?" OU Torah, accessed November 30, 2023, https://outorah.org/p/22472.

5. Rabbi Jack Abramowitz, "The Necessary Qualifications to Receive Prophecy," OU Torah, accessed November 30, 2023, https://outorah.org/p/22473/.

6. Ibid.

According to Jewish scholars like Rabbi Jack Abramowitz, maintaining mental health and wellness, as well as giving oneself time for proper rest and reflection, plays a large part in whether or not people can receive the signals and messages God sends, to the point that it's thought that the age of prophecy and prophets is ended altogether in the eyes of Judaism (prophesied by verses like Amos 8:12 and Eicha 2:9).[7] Only when the Messiah comes (which Judaism says hasn't happened yet) will this age of prophecy return.

Nuance (and the Danger of Charlatans) in Divination

But if that's the case, then what does this mean for Christians who believe that the Messiah *did* come, and that Jesus is that Messiah? Does it mean prophecy is back on the table? Potentially—though with no official institution guaranteeing or verifying the claims of the many single voices claiming to be prophets, there's no way to tell who's *actually* delivering messages from God and who's just grifting like their next private jet depends on it. There are so many charlatans who offer "messages" that are little more than their poor attempts at interpreting the Bible (as they'll insist you *can't* know what God says now, in modern day, without looking to the two to four *thousand* year old writings of the Bible). Without a governing body that can tell us whether or not any prophecies are legit, it's much safer for your spiritual and mental health to attempt contact yourself than trust someone else to be a divine middleman.

Let us make a point here, though: the Bible remains a valuable resource for *discernment,* which is critical to answering the core question we started this chapter with. If you read the Bible, you can learn quite a bit about the character of God: what He values, what He's done, what He's commanded others to do, what He considers acceptable and unacceptable, and the evolution of the story we call the collection of Abrahamic faiths (as each one has a separate covenant with Him). However, because so many don't do the due diligence to research the context of the Bible or the sociopolitical environments it was written in, the people asking a Christian Witch whether or not they're really talking to God never stop to ask themselves the same question. They never stop to wonder if maybe their own church hasn't missed some critical context that warps their understanding of God—or if the pastor explaining the Bible to them hasn't inserted some of his own worldview into his sermons that overrides the original message. When it comes to knowing how you're talking to God and not anyone else, therefore, it's crucial that you understand the *core* of all of God's commandments, which Jesus sums up for us quite simply:

---

7. Ibid.

> Hearing that Jesus had silenced the Sadducees, the Pharisees got together. One of them, an expert in the law, tested him with this question: "Teacher, which is the greatest commandment in the Law?"

> Jesus replied: "'Love the Lord your God with all your heart and with all your soul and with all your mind.' This is the first and greatest commandment. And the second is like it: 'Love your neighbor as yourself.' *All the Law and the Prophets hang on these two commandments.*" (Emphasis ours.)[8]

Here's another take on this: when Sara began her journey as a Christian Witch, she understood this idea in a slightly different language. She had a simple litmus test she followed when it came to her conversations with God *and* with any scripture she was reading: if the message is something that is *actively harmful to innocent people* (denying people rights and dignity, encouraging division and hostility among communities, unempathetic and unwilling to help others in need, etc.), then it was not of God. *That* line of reasoning helped her not only confirm that God was the one she was talking to and the one directing her, but also helped her walk away from any ideas or philosophies that displayed such a cruel and ugly nature—even if they were ones spoken in the name of God.

Our experiences are just a small glimpse of how you can identify that it really is God you're speaking to (and that anyone you speak to that is *not* happy with your respect of the humanity and dignity of other people is, simply, *not* God). Nowadays, we might come to understand more about divination as a way to get answers that the Bible doesn't hold. As you might've guessed, in terms of receiving modern messages, there are some questions that need direct answers because nothing like what we're asking about was conceivable to the minds of people in antiquity and beyond (as society has changed *so much* over the past two centuries, never mind two millenia). That's where building your divination language comes into play. We'll talk more about the specific psychic skills that make this viable in Chapter 11, but for now, let us

---

8. Matthew 22:34-40

clarify what we mean by divination *language*. What divination is at its core is a way of communicating with an entity that, like the English language you're reading this book in, helps you reliably, quickly, and effectively send and receive ideas. Everything from a simple "yes" or "no" to more complex, intricate messages can be achieved depending on the method you develop for yourself.

And speaking of mental health, while Christianity may believe they acquired a Messiah, that still doesn't address the elephant in the room: the idea that the quality of one's mental state dictates whether or not they'll be able to receive any messages. Naturally, with the world we live in, you'd be hard pressed to find anyone who is perfectly mentally sound. We live in a *very* different world than the prophets of yore did thousands of years ago. The stress of everyday life alone is enough to crack most people, what with having to do a community's worth of work all alone (working eight or more hours a day, cooking, cleaning, taking care of kids, keeping relationships alive, keeping all the bills paid, and more). Bring domestic and international affairs into things, and most people are walking around with a cocktail of mental misery just at baseline—and if Elijah had to have music playing to lighten his mood before receiving a message from God back *then*, what hope is there for us now?

This is where *tools* come in handy.

Mimi's Guide on Divination Tools and How to Use Them

Much like a carpenter and welder have specific tools for their trade, so too does a Witch with their craft. However, like with any other tool, practice is required and discernment is always an important skill to develop with your intuition. Not everyone uses the same things for divination, and not everyone uses divination in their practice at all! Using tools that you're drawn to will help with the intuition building part right away, but finding a passion for something is just as effective to help bolster your learning. Don't stop at tarot cards just because they're popular! (And side note: if you pick up reading as a profession, please ensure your state's or country's laws do not prohibit it under entertainment law. Many places will say it is unlawful to predict the future; use your best judgment when offering readings.)

I like to think of using divinatory tools as a translator; after all, we don't all have a Metatron or Gabriel coming to us saying "be not afraid!" like they used to in the Bible. Instead, we notice (or don't—oops!) the little coincidences and say to ourselves, "Self, I think something is trying to tell me something." Folks used to say that all the time when I was still in church back in Kentucky. Someone would walk in ten minutes late, or later, and say the same thing every time: "Something's trying to keep me outta church today." *Man*, if you'd just asked the pendulum, you might've known who would do such a thing. Or why.

Or maybe it's just all a coincidence.

Any time I asked about learning more ways to meditate or reach out to God with my gifts, it was always answered the same way: "You'll just know." Well, that doesn't help me at all! I can't even pick up normal social cues from physical, tangible people; how am I going to interpret something from Jesus Himself totally out of the blue on a Wednesday? Using tools helps those of us who need the "human translation" to what the Divine are saying and help us discern if it's really a message or if it's mundane. Every exercise done helps to hone that skill. It took me years before I realized what I'd been doing all my life was hearing God speak. For the longest time, any dream I had with the vision of my little Memaw Hazel hunched over her quilting rack filled me with both dread and comfort. I finally put the pieces together that God was speaking to me in a way I could understand. And even though I have played with Tarot and Lenormand decks for almost two decades, I didn't start really knowing what I was hearing until I was in my 30s.

There is an energy you feel with your deities (if you work with them) and your guides that ping the little inner discernment bell. If a dream makes no sense, if you're uneasy with a presence, if you're left with more confusion than answers, if it feels like you're being physically moved about and touched and encroached upon, it's time to take a step back and ask yourself, "Is this really Memaw, or is some *other* entity giving me the plot to a too-good-to-be-true Wattpad story and hoping I'll fall for it?" Discernment with tools is just an extra step to reveal these things and exercise that intuition. Always exercise caution in your space (especially since there are flammable things in it) and be mindful. Ask twice if you have to.

Now, as we get into a few of the different kinds of tools you can use, it is *so* important to note that nothing will fully give you perfect answers to the future. In fact, divination is much better when you *don't* use it to ask those pesky future questions ("will I get a boyfriend?" or "will I pass my finals?"). Instead, what the cards can do is work with your intuition to gain insight into yourself or a situation. These answers can help you make decisions, work through emotional blockages, and understand yourself on a deeper level. Whatever you do, though, remember that the point is to find a tool you like, that you can get access to, and that you can *understand*.

Tarot

One of the most popular forms of divination, tarot can be used to divine the good and bad of a situation. Every deck of tarot cards has 78 cards, divided into Major Arcana and Minor Arcana, which makes them a consistent format no matter what deck you get your hands on. While the interpretations can vary, they are usually all incorporating the same foundational understandings and meaning. Between elements and numerology, tarot has multiple layers to really dive into, and it's a popular choice for beginning witches.

Tip: if you can't have a real tarot deck for fear of being found out for your witchiness, a deck of playing cards can act as the Minor Arcana of tarot (minus the Knights, as there's only the Jack, which is more like the Pages). The suits are aligned like so:

- Cups | Hearts

- Swords | Spades

- Clubs | Wands

- Pentacles | Diamonds

Practice your learning this way if you need to, and know that so long as you're committed to finding that language you can understand, you can still do great divination with what looks like an otherwise unsuspicious pack of playing cards.

Oracle

Coming up behind tarot in popularity is the oracle deck. This deck has no set card number or meaning, as each creator imbues the cards with their own inspirations to help others clarify their questions to the universe and/or entities. Oracle decks are generally seen as more positive, but they aren't always easier than tarot since there's no system to draw understanding from, as each deck is so unique. Great for those looking for a challenge, but definitely not the easiest type of card deck to start with.

Lenormand

A lesser-known but still wonderful deck of divination cards is the Lenormand style of cards. Once the basis for a simple card game (as many divination decks are), Madam Marie Anne Lenormand brought this style of divination to the public view while being a famous French cartomancer and fortune-teller during Napoleonic rule. Let's put it this way: if Tarot is the "why" of a situation, then Lenormand is the "how." It's a very straight-forward set of 36 cards with set meanings for each. However, the way they are read is usually in pairs, with the Grand Tableau being an incredibly thorough (albeit intimidating) way to divine the questions at hand.

Bibliomancy

If you've been in the church for any amount of time, you've probably been introduced to Bibliomancy without even realizing. It's when you open to a random page in a book, especially the Bible, that's meaningful to you and read from it to interpret what the message says and how it can apply. This can be a real challenge to your discernment, of course, because sometimes you ask a question about your relationship and open to a chapter about a massive ancient battle—but like all things, the more you do it, the better you get.

Song Shuffle

Similar to Bibliomancy, when asking for some inspiration or answers, a song randomly playing on the radio that fits the exact situation, or when played during a random shuffle on a playlist, can really be insightful and comforting. Your guides know what songs will get your attention, so lean in and trust them!

Tasseography (with tea leaves, coffee grounds, or wine sediments)

There are fragments of tea leaf reading in much of our popular media, and it's a pretty simple concept. The person inquiring drinks the tea until the leaves and a pinch of liquid remains. Whatever shape the leaves and herbs take in the bottom of the cup can give an idea of what is coming or currently happening with the inquirer. The same applies to wine sediments and coffee grounds, though I have very little experience with either. Tried it, and it wasn't for me. But it might be just right for you.

Sara says:

With coffee grounds, specifically, there's a Balkan tradition brought over by the Ottoman empire. How it works is you ask your question, drink your coffee, and once you're at the very end, you flip the cup of grounds over onto the plate. Then, after they settle, you flip the cup back over and see what shapes you can pick out that might hint at some message. Is it like a Rorschach test? Yes. But is it *helpful?* Honestly, it depends. When in doubt, just remember: you can always cross reference one type of divination with another. Don't be afraid to break out your tarot cards and double check the meaning of your coffee grounds.

I did that once, and where I thought I saw an angel, a man, and a dog in my coffee, I asked God for clarification in tarot and pulled the Ace of Wands and the Fool—cards that had, incredibly, an angel, a man, and a dog on them. That was more than enough verification for me that it was God that put those images in that cup for me to notice, and the cards themselves showed me the message He was trying to give me.

Cleromancy, or Casting Lots

Casting lots appears a few times in the Bible, and it was used as a way to divine God's will for a decision. In other cultures throughout the world, this can look like the following:

- Bone throws

- Key Throws

- Rune throws

- Coins

- Dowsing Rods

- Pendulum

- Ouija Boards

Using Nature as a Divination Tool

Using visions and images in the shape of living elements is something that takes a lot of practice, but a lot of us already do it! When you quip some animal fact (for example, believing the cardinal coming to visit means a loved one is nearby, or that the wooly worm colors tell you something about the upcoming winter), you are using a divinatory practice that has been passed down from generations. Think about it: a popular augury event that we still practice large-scale in the United States is Groundhog Day, a nationally recognized holiday!
   Other examples include:

- Scrying (water)

- Pyromancy (flame)

- Capnomancy (smoke)

- Augury (animal and nature signs)

There's even a type of divination that occurs when you read the shadows cast on the wall from a lamp, called *sciomancy.* Pretty cool, right?

Dreams and Meditative Writing

Ah, dreams. This is the one topic I can speak on at length, if only because I've been doing it since I was a child. What started with sleep-walking and night terrors turned into being able to receive messages and speak to my passed on loved ones. It was because of this gift that I sought out counsel from my Papaw, a southern Pentecostal minister that never turned down my questions. (He might've admonished me a bit, but I was always welcome to ask them, at least.)

Dreaming is something of a wild card, as you cannot always fully control the situation. Lucid dreaming and astral projection fall under this category, in my opinion. If you're inexperienced or uncertain, there are a few tells to know if it's just your subconscious or if it's a message. This includes seeing vivid details, such as hands, faces, or specific names. Just having an "I know I was in some neighborhood" feeling is different than "I saw the sign for Spruce Street." I urge you to keep a notepad by the bed or your notes app on the home screen to record messages when you wake up.

And meditative writing is just what you think it is: going into an almost trance-like state and writing what comes. You've probably seen examples of this with paranormal investigations or that really fun movie, *Insidious*. This one, I feel, has the potential to really rattle some bones if you're unused to speaking directly to a spirit or entity, but with practice, it can show you things and reveal concepts to you that you never expected. While this is one of the hardest ways to divine, with the concepts we talk about in Chapter 11 and plenty of practice and courage, you can get the hang of it.

Reading the Stars

Using the moon phases has been a practice done worldwide, in all cultures, in all ages of civilization. It's an integral part of life in Appalachia, too, as anyone using *The Farmer's Almanac* will tell you. Our parents and grandparents might have called astrology blasphemy, but they were quick to make sure you didn't plant your seeds at the wrong time. They had the stars to tell them when to wean animals and children, cut hair for growth, canning their garden harvests, and almost anything you can think of in everyday life.

If you've got your head in the stars, know that this sort of metaphysical science has many layers to it, far more than just asking "what's your sign?" Have fun with it!

Numerology

We all know about the angel numbers or the spirit numbers, but did you know numerology has been around since the early Greek philosophers? Pythagoras started the basis of the rules of numbers, and a cult of Pythagoras molded Arithmancy into the foundations of our numerology today. And it wasn't just the Greeks! There's a system of numerology in the Torah that's explained further in Jewish mysticism, specifically Kabbalah. Be mindful of this, though, as its specifics are part of a *closed practice*, which means they belong to a certain religion, culture, or group that isn't freely available for anyone to access. Practices and entire religions might be closed to people until conversion, such as Judaism as a whole, or they may be closed no matter what unless someone belongs to a certain ethnic group or tradition (as is the case with Slavic magic like *zagovory*, or certain egg cleansing techniques like the Latin American practice: *limpia de huevo*. The Italian version, however, is open to all).

Now, these are by no means an exhaustive list of tools, but they are somewhere to start when it comes to finding your preferred divinatory language and translator. However, when it comes to developing the intuition to *use* these tools effectively, we start talking about something else entirely. The divination tools themselves are like a car: useful, beautiful, functional, but ultimately nothing more than a driveway decoration if the gas tank is empty. Your intuition is like the gas, and the more you can grow your intuition, the better and more accurate your readings become. It can be difficult to trust yourself, and it can take time to develop the signs within your own body that signal it's time to choose a card, throw some bones, or look at a certain shape in the tea leaves. But like all things, practice makes perfect. That's why witchcraft is often called a *practice* or a *craft* in the first place: because you'll always be working to improve your skills. In this case, when it comes to developing intuition and the ability to step away from tools entirely—working one's way up to finding clues and answers through direct meditation or psychic experience—there are certain skills you can work on that will make this whole communicative process easier, which we'll talk about next.

Chapter Eleven

Preparing to Enter the Unseen Realm

"Heaven is here, all around us, and so are our loved ones; we just can't see them."

⸺⸙✤⸙⸺

Sara says:

Of all the people I'd ever thought would say this, I did not expect it to be a local Catholic priest. Granted, I didn't hear this from the priest himself. He apparently told my aunt this, as she came seeking advice about the paranormal activity in her house that started up after she tried to get a sign from my late uncle. But the idea is still there, and it's still shocking to me that someone within the structures and strangleholds of the Church would admit to it: that the spirits of our loved ones are out there, alive in Christ, and maybe only a half step removed from the world we see around us.

So in this chapter, we're going to talk about developing the abilities that, no doubt, can spook many a modern Christian: the clair skills that help us meditate, and by extension, come in contact with the world of spirits, both human and inhuman, and how we might go about interacting with them in the world we share together. It's one of the greatest stumbling blocks for the Christian and the Witch separately, never mind together, as once you become aware of a world outside tangible reality, things get *real* in a way they weren't before. The skills you learn about here are critical to meditation, which is both a form of *divination* and a form of contact with the worlds beyond. They're skills that'll help you better connect to your guides when you need a divinatory message, and ones that'll help when it comes time to approach Section Four, the section about the spirit world. If that idea seems intimidating, then trust me on this: once you become comfortable with spirits—calm enough to approach them with curiosity and kindness, and alert enough to not trust everything they have to say right off the bat—you'll find that nothing can really scare you anymore.

At least, that's what I've found.

Before we get any further into spirits, though (as that is still a long ways off in this here guidebook), we should lay down some important key concepts: what it means to meditate, which skills you can use to get reliable messages from your spirit team, and good ways of backing up your meditation experiences through divination tools like tarot. I'd also be remiss not to talk about the very real dangers of psychological conditions like *spiritual psychosis*, which have done quite a bit of damage to aspiring practitioners. Mental health professional Charlie Penwarden sums up the concept of spiritual psychosis and its negative effects as such:

> Spiritual psychosis is often characterized by *a loss of touch with reality as we know it.* Individuals experiencing a spiritual psychosis may have difficulty distinguishing between what is real and what is imaginary. They may also have difficulty functioning in everyday life, experiencing disruptions in work, school, relationships, or other areas of life. In some cases, spiritual psychosis can be accompanied by paranoia, delusions, or other symptoms typically associated with severe mental illness. (Emphasis mine.)[1]

These are tough, realistic conversations that need to be had, and this topic is, in and of itself, ripe with things that will no doubt trigger at least one or two repressed fears, depending on how deeply you found yourself in the Church. Hell, even people who never grew up religious can have some serious stuff to work through before they get comfortable working with, say, *demons*, which you can read more about in Chapter 17.

But don't worry. With the right amount of dedication and a healthy dose of courage, you can creep out of your comfort zone and learn

---

1. Charlie Penwarden, "Spiritual Psychosis: A Sane Awakening or Mental Illness?" Behaveo, accessed November 30, 2023, https://behaveo.com/spiritual-psychosis/.

things you might not have learned otherwise. So let me (and later Mimi) get you started with the basics.

The Clair Skills

If you've been friends with witches who have gods or spirits in their practice, or if you've been on #witchtok for a moment or two, you might notice people talking about their deities or spirits as if they're physical people: "Loki told me this," or "King Asmodeus showed me what I needed to know about this problem," or "Archangel Gabriel pops by sometimes to help me with my writing." For someone who patently does *not* feel any sort of connection or communication with such entities, it's easy to wonder: *am I broken? Am I doing something wrong? Am I not a good enough witch?*

The answer is no on all counts. Truth be told, nobody is seeing or hearing these deities in their homes the same way they might see or hear a real person (at least, nobody *should* be, because that's a potential sign of serious mental illness that would need to be tested and, if identified, treated). These witches online, or these witches in your life, are likely describing how their interactions felt *to them*, contextualizing it through external interactions that the human mind can more readily understand. There's an art to translating the snaps of phrases you might get when you ask a question, or the images that flicker into your head, or the energy you feel skitter along your forearms in a rush of goosebumps, and that art comes in the form of the clair skills.

According to Mat Auryn, "we are all born with a predisposition toward one of the psychic senses," or clair skills.[2] *Clair,* French for "clear," attaches to words we otherwise know well, given our five physical senses—but they also describe those other moments that we might, in our naïveté, shrug off as nothing. There are many examples of such signs that we get from our senses.

The sudden full body shake, for instance, that seems to grab you by the ribs and jostle you ever so lightly—especially when you start trying to think about or speak to certain entities.

Or the pop of a word or phrase in your head that seems to come from nowhere—that maybe takes your voice, but you know viscerally isn't *you*.

Or even the inexplicable feeling of joy, or sadness, or indignance that might wash over you for a moment before it disappears.

These tiny little signs are so often ignored or justified in some way: a chill, or an odd mood, or some subconscious idea that you might've picked up from a movie or something. So often do people think like this that it's no wonder to me why some folks say that they pray to God and "never hear a response"; how can you, when you ignore every

---

2. Mat Auryn, *Psychic Witch: A Metaphysical Guide to Meditation, Magick & Manifestation* (Woodbury: Llewellyn, 2020), 55.

single way in which the Divine might contact you? How many times will people ask God to speak to those with no ears, or reveal Himself to those with no eyes? Jesus tells us in the Gospels that those who have ears to hear should hear—and I'm here to tell you that you can, at least marginally, grow those ears He's talking about. Let's take a look at our first clair skill: *clairaudience.*

CLAIRAUDIENCE | CLEAR HEARING

When people talk about *clairaudience*, or "clear hearing," they're talking about what you would typically think of when you think of psychic skills: literally hearing another voice, or maybe sounds connected to whatever spirit is coming through (for instance: hearing birdsong, or a train rushing by, or any other such out of place sounds for your environment that would tip you off to someone trying to send a message). I know I said earlier that nobody is actually hearing sounds, and I stick by that in the sense that these sounds in clairaudience aren't so clear and easily understandable like normal, everyday speech; they're fragments, pieces, or even "echoes" of words, and many folks describe the conversations they may overhear in the spirit world as being particularly muffled, as if they're eavesdropping from under thirteen layers of cotton blankets.

Clairaudience comes to me most often as a word or phrase in my own voice that I know deep down isn't actually coming from me. It's difficult to explain, but something about the way a word is said, or the tone of the voice, or just the way it inserts itself into my normal flow of consciousness, tells me that it is *not* my own thoughts echoing around my head. It's something else entirely, herding my thoughts in a new direction and getting me to make connections and realizations I otherwise wouldn't have. It also sometimes comes as those moments between sleep and waking, too, where I just have my eyes closed and know I'm almost ready to doze, and then suddenly, I *hear* something. It's something like a shout, so clearly that I jerk and look around the room. A voice will say *Hey!* Or even *Sara!* And I'll feel viscerally unsettled for a moment, my heartbeat spiking, before I settle back down and try to go to sleep again. It doesn't happen very often, but it's a big surprise whenever it does. Other people have mentioned something like this happening, too, where suddenly, they'll hear what sounds like a real voice outside them telling them to *Run!* Or *Get out!*

And when they heed those voices, they find that moments later, something happens—something as extreme as even a break-in.

If clairaudience is your dominant sense, chances are you sometimes hear snatches of things that just don't feel like *you.* They feel foreign, from someone else, and they point you in the direction of information you might not have known you were missing. You might also be used to feeling like you're hearing actual words or sounds that don't have a source, like birdsong or a whistle or someone's laughter that draws you to get outside of your current train of thought. To continue developing it, spend time alone in a quiet space and listen *deeply*. See what you can hear, whether it's just the buzz of electricity, and allow yourself to get curious. You might also ask your spirit guides to speak and grasp for unique qualities of their voices that separate them from your own inner voice.

CLAIRVOYANCE | CLEAR SIGHT

Clairvoyance, or *clear seeing*, is a sense that allows you to see things that others might not be able to, whether in everyday life or in meditation and visions. It doesn't mean you're seeing any people or anything in your home, though. Like with clairaudience, while you can get glimpses of things moving from the corner of your eye or, if you're more inclined to be something of a medium, able to make out features of spirits long passed, there is reason to be concerned if you're seeing whole, tangible people just hanging out in your house. In these cases, it's best to speak to a licensed mental health professional to rule out any serious conditions and illnesses.

But barring conditions like aphantasia, which make it actually impossible for people to visualize things in their mind, clairvoyance is likely one of the most useful senses. It's especially useful if you're someone who likes to meditate, but you can't seem to get your mind to hold onto the black nothingness behind your eyelids. That's okay if you can't keep your mind blank; in fact, I'd say it's encouraged, because those sudden random flashes of imagery you get are *important.*

Things can be revealed to us in dreams, meditations, and visions that we might not have otherwise thought about, and it can be a safe landscape for our spirit guides and God to tell us things. When we set time aside to commune with God and allow ourselves to see what He wants us to see, we experience things that let us slip away from the mess of the waking world and focus on things that are more important than our everyday griefs and struggles. We may create in our own mind a comforting place to retreat to—a cottage in a little orange grove, for instance, or a place out by a tranquil pond, or even a cafe in our favorite city—and we can use that space to meet with God and get His messages.

For me, especially, it's the cornerstone of my work and interactions with entities of all kinds. Whether in my weekly conversations with angels, Saints, demons, and gods, or in my private and personal conversations with my chosen guides, the ability to see the places these entities want to meet me in is essential. I've been shown the terrible Lake of Fire by Saints like Cyprian and Francis. I've hunched over my journal in the ornate and elegant studies of the many Princes and Kings of Hell, or the Infernal Realms. I've seen cities bustling with people that are long gone, been in the middle of battlefields with swords swinging and men howling at one another, I've walked through a man's personal Paradise, and I've sunk to the very bottom of the ocean, all thanks to these entities and the environments they weave for me in meditation. Granted, there are always multiple clair skills working in each of these situations—the deeper you can stitch yourself into a space with *all* of your senses, the more real it seems, after all—but clairvoyance makes it so crisp and detailed that it's as if I'd entered a painting, or better yet, a movie.

Of course, it's worth asking the question I'm sure you're asking yourselves right now: *how do you know this is actually something your spirit guides want to show you, and not something you're just deciding to see?* To which I say: *you'll know.*

You'll know because you'll see things that you know you've never seen before. And you'll know because you'll see things you never *wanted* to see. Terrible things that reveal wounds you didn't know needed to be healed, or fears you didn't know needed to be resolved. You'll find yourself exploring this landscape as if it were some new map in a video game, the space marked by objects and creatures and other things so striking that you'll think about them long after you exit the meditation. They stay with you, these things you see and discover, and you won't stay the same person for long the more you meddle with them. Whether that's for better or worse entirely depends on you and your ability to handle what you're shown.

If clairvoyance is a dominant skill for you, it means you have no trouble holding images in your mind's eye and seeing the vivid details of them. It means you might get flashes of pictures in your mind that you can't explain, or that your dreams feel especially real (even if you can't always remember them). You may have an easier time meditating or entering the Unseen Realm we discuss in Section Four because you're able to more clearly see yourself within it, and you're able to get hints and ideas about entities, places, or things by how you see them in your mind. If you'd like to develop it further, and you don't have conditions like aphantasia, then hold an object in your hand and study it closely, and when you close your eyes, try to bring that image through the darkness. Let it bleed in like watercolor, bit by bit, and continue to open your eyes to sketch in any details your vision is missing as needed. This will build those skills to see even when you can't really see.

CLAIRTANGENCY | CLEAR TOUCH

Clairtangency, or clear touch, is a sense that lets you get vivid feelings of things that aren't really there. If you suddenly get the visceral feeling of a dog's fur under your palm, or maybe of rain on your cheeks where there is none, you might be getting the senses of someone or something else that's hovering in the Unseen Realm. It's once again a skill that works best in conjunction with other skills, especially in a meditation space, in order to better stitch yourself into the scene, but it can also let you know that something is lingering and looking to share information with you.

It can also be one of the skills that entities may use to try and test you. One of my only examples is during a dive into the Infernal Realms with Lucifer. It was a specific place we were going, to learn specific things in my spiritual journey, and I tell you, I have never been so disturbed just sitting in my living room, because the experience was more than sight and sound. I entered this place upside down, through a tight and warm and *damp* canal, and I could feel the blood rushing to my head, as well as the squeeze of this tight space against my shoulders and the way the slick walls slipped against my clothes and skin. *Terrible.* I have a bit of a fear of being stuck with my arms pinned as it is—think if you were to get yourself stuck in a tube and unable to move or lift your arms—so this was genuinely an awful experience until I made it out and landed on a ground that felt as if it were made of flesh. Even through the boots I imagined I had on, I could feel the texture of that floor as I walked: soft, unstable, and *squelching* under every step.

Not the most exciting clair skill to develop, honestly. But if it is one that you find yourself more easily able to latch onto, then it's one that can give you hints about the experiences of spirits nearby, or about places you may go in meditations. It's also one that will make things feel much more viscerally real, and therefore it'll require so much more grounding to make sure you can still find the line between meditation and reality. Still, you can continue to grow this skill by committing the feelings of things to memory, like different fabrics, plants, or machinery, and bringing those memories back to the surface of your fingertips when you meditate. Touch the things you see as if they're really there, and allow yourself to feel them as if they're really there, too.

CLAIRGUSTANCE | CLEAR TASTE

Boy, clairgustance is just one of those weird skills you might not readily expect or know what to do with. "Clear taste" means you may suddenly pick up on the taste of something you've never eaten before, or even get the bitter taste of bile or some other reaction as a spirit's emotions start coming through (which is different from getting the emotion itself). However, if you suddenly get the taste of something that is sentimental, like a meal your parents used to cook, maybe it means it's worth checking in on them.

I have absolutely no connection to this clair. The only way I can suggest you might try to build it is by, in meditation, grasping onto the full flavor of whatever it is you're seeing yourself eat. Maybe even take a piece of chocolate with you to your space and eat it before you go to meditate, fully registering its taste, its texture, how it melts on your tongue, and more, and then when the flavor of it is fully gone from your mouth sometime later, try to recall the experience again. Imagine yourself eating it again, down to how it feels to chew the chocolate and swallow it. You might also draw on clues from your memory, too. If you eat something that looks like a pepper in meditation, imagine the crunch, or the heat level (if it's not a sweet pepper). But let anything else come through, too; let specific tastes and textures that might surprise you come through, because it's all more information to contextualize where you are and what you're doing in this meditation space.

One big caveat, though: only do this with entities and in spaces you trust. Plenty of cultures will tell you to never eat the food of the Fae, for example, because it'll trap you in their realm forever. Same with food of the dead. Even gods (like Japanese goddess Izanami) have been trapped in the underworld after dying and eating the food down below. If you wouldn't eat candy from a stranger, do *not* eat it from a spirit you do not trust. Otherwise, though, have fun developing this skill, and if it's one you already align with, try and decode the clues you get from those sudden bits of flavor and texture you pick up on out of nowhere.

CLAIREMPATHY | CLEAR FEELING (EMOTIONAL)

Notice the key word in this one? *Clairempathy*, or "clear feeling," is something most might just shorten to *empathy*. You've likely heard of people claiming to be empaths. In a magical sense, this may be a situation where the emotional energy of others around them grafts onto them and affects their emotional state. In a mundane sense, it may mean they can relate really well to another person to the point of being able to share in a certain feeling with someone (so, if their friends are sad, they'll end up being sad for and with them). For those who truly are empaths, it can be helpful to be able to pick up those emotional currents, especially if people are trying to hide them. Sad folks who hide behind a bright smile are one example of those the empath can easily see through. However, it also comes with a fair bit of danger, because allowing oneself to be consistently overwhelmed by the feelings of others will leave one ungrounded and unstable, as well as unable to separate their own feelings from those around them. In this case, I recommend a shield, especially if you're going into a volatile situation.

Shielding Exercise: Just like I explained with an example of a magical ward based on Skyrim, this time, you're going to extend your magic out. Imagine your magic flowing from your core (your chest or stomach) and up through your shoulders, down your arms, and into the palm of your hands. From there, let it flow out like water, and instead of only imagining it in front of you like a shield, imagine it completely enveloping you like a bubble.

Within this bubble, close your eyes and really *see* it. See the color of it, and see the world outside it through that color. If any emotion is coming your way, see it like you might the northern lights: as ripples of energy bouncing off your bubble. Maybe anger is a red flash of light, and sadness blue, but however you see the emotion that's coming at you, imagine it can't get to you—the same way that someone shouting at you wouldn't quite reach you if you were behind soundproof glass. In that bubble should be nothing but neutrality, calm and peaceful, so that you might regulate your breathing, heart rate, thoughts, and body. Release any tension in your body here and remind yourself that you are sturdy and strong.

This is difficult to practice in the moment, of course, so what I recommend is getting some good tear-jerking movies and practicing that way. That's how I learned to do this. I'm someone who cries at anything; I find myself jumping into the shoes of other characters far too easily and crying the moment I think about the situation a second too long. Even if the characters themselves aren't crying (yet), I'm already a mess and having difficulty breathing from trying to hold back tears. I don't think myself an empath; I'm just silly and imagine the situations of others way too viscerally. But by expanding this bubble around me during these movies, I'm able to snap myself out of it and re-center myself without becoming a puffy-faced ball of tears. If you find yourself similarly having trouble with the emotions of others and how they affect you, try this exercise for yourself.

CLAIRCOGNIZANCE | CLEAR KNOWING

If I had to pin myself to any of the senses, then along with clairaudience (in the sense that I get snaps of phrases or hear the occasional strange word), or clairvoyance (in the sense of visualization and meditative imagery), I am quite plugged into my claircognizance. It's a skill that means "clear knowing," and it's the skill that comes into play when you just *know* something. People might ask you how you know, and you really can't say, because you just do. There's no explaining that twist of the gut, or that sudden pop of an idea into the mind. It happens most when I read tarot for clients: I'll see a bit of imagery on a card, or even read the booklet, and it's like God is whapping me in the back of the head with His meaning.

However, in my opinion, it's something that works best in conjunction with other senses. For instance, during a meditation with the Goetic demon Prince Camio, I had the sense that there was someone else in the conversation with us. I couldn't tell who it was, because the figure was in disguise, a hood over a barren skull of a face. There was nothing that I could even grab on to make guesses with as a result. Still, as I let the guest stay nearby while I chatted with President Camio, I noticed I kept accidentally calling him President Marbas. The presence of the unknown figure hovered over me each time I got the name mixed up in my head until I looked over my shoulder at him.

"President Marbas? Is that you?"

Like a mask, the skull cracked and fell away, and there was President Marbas, his face like that of a man made of gold, a lion's mane of hair cascading to his shoulders. I even got to see him as a lion made of what seemed like golden stardust. It was beautiful, and it's thanks to the persistence of his name—and knowing what repeated mistakes like that mean—that I was able to discern what was going on. But during this experience, I'd already been steeped in clairvoyance as well, given it was a full meditation; as I said, claircognizance works fine on its own, but it works really well in conjunction with other skills.

If claircognizance is the skill most dominant for you, it means your intuition is likely top tier. People may find themselves caught off guard by how you seem to know what's going on before anyone else does, as if these secret and hidden things are laying out there in the open for you to intimately understand with little effort. Connecting the dots, putting together fragments and pieces of spiritual puzzles, and discerning the meaning of a message come easier to you than others. And if you'd like to develop it further, it's a matter of training yourself to be curious—to not discredit or ignore those odd snaps of phrases and ideas that come from nowhere. If you get the urge to shrug off a sudden idea or "gut feeling" in the future, instead pause and inspect it a little more.

CLAIRALIENCE | CLEAR SMELL

Mimi says:

Clairalience, also known as clairessence, is known as "clear smell." A lot of our memories are tied to taste and smell, and so it comes as little surprise that there are psychic abilities tied to smell as well. When you walk into a seemingly empty room, sometimes there is the hint of a smell lingering that can't always be explained away. A lot of scents can be tied to something heavy or offensive, or they can be light and pleasant. There are times it's of a loved one who passed on and other times it's of a person who is very much alive but has some sort of connection to you. For me, it's when my mother's scent of ash and White Shoulders perfume, or my father's scent of pine and sweat with a splash of Old Spice, tickle my senses. Neither of them live close enough to me or have been near me recently enough for these smells to hit me. But when they do, I check in with them, and I usually get the "I was just thinking of you!" answer.

A more recent example of this is my current home; I will be sitting on the couch or at my desk, writing away or playing with my children, when the smell of musk, amber, and roses hangs in the air. I can move away to a different space, like my hallway or dining room, and it will not be there. The woman who lived in the house before me had died here, and it was her forever home for over 50 years. The house sat empty for almost 20 years before we bought it, and even though the hanging smell of old smoke or aged wood can sometimes still hit me, the perfume and cigarettes, (or even sometimes the man's scent of turpentine and Stetson cologne) will grab hold of my senses and I have to calm my fluttering stomach. I say hi to Grandma and Grandpa (they're not mine, but that's what we call them), take a slow and deep breath, and wait for the moment to pass. Sometimes, when the kids are laughing and we're all living in the moment, I'll see a flicker of something out of the corner of my eye and that perfume will return. I know Grandma is here.

If clairalience is your dominant sense, you'll find yourself noticing specific smells where they shouldn't be, as well as a tug towards their origins (for example, your parents if you smell their specific colognes or perfumes). You'll also pick up on the smells of events or other things long gone, like smelling smoke in a place where there was once a fire, for instance. It's a tricky clair skill to have, because scents alone can be hard to discern, but they're very good for helping you detect a presence or bring to your mind something you need to pay attention to (like a relative you need to get in touch with). Developing it is as simple as being curious if you happen to catch a scent of something where there should be no scents, or remarking on what scents—or lack thereof—are usually around you so that you can tell right away when something changes.

Getting Into the Meditation Space

Now that you have a proper grasp on what these different clair skills are, as well as how to recognize your affinity with them or continue developing them, let's talk about the meditation space itself. This is where you'll meet many a different spirit, be they angels, demons, pagan deities, or even Jesus and Mama Mary and other such figures you may be wanting to talk to. It's not quite the same as *astral projecting*, but it is something that comes very close. In our opinion, it's also a good deal safer.

During meditation, you have a chance to explore more of yourself, your soul, your mind, and the energy of any entities you work with. Given our discussion on clair skills, you can now see how the energy of the Divine—expansive, infinite, and incorporeal beings like gods, angels, demons, Saints, and other spirits—might come through in different ways. For the purpose of this introductory guide, however, it's important to get a solid sense of God, and who and what He is to you, before you continue interacting and engaging with other spirits. As Christian Witches *and* Christopagans, the age-old commandment of having no other gods before God means exactly that: putting God *first*, and giving Him the right to decide who we talk to, when, and why. After all, it'd be a bit damaging even for human relationships if your friends ran to others they didn't know as well for a problem you know you could've helped them with really well, right? It's even more so with God, because part of that Christian affiliation means holding Him as our highest priority, both in our reverence and worship of Him and in our work with Him.

(And trust us: God will surprise you when it comes to working with other entities. You just have to have the good manners to ask first and respect the answer you get, as well as understand that the answer can change depending on a variety of factors.)

Now, God can appear wildly different depending on how you need to see and understand Him. For some, like Sara, God is fiery, bright, and speaks through His Seraphim more than anything else; He's a brutal and thunderous force when He's working to fight with and defend you from the many ills and foes in the world, and He's a gentle force when teaching you, like you were being hugged from behind by two warm, heavy, and comforting arms. For others, like Mimi, He can take on forms that we're familiar with: those of passed loved ones like Memaw, or even of certain animals (like the famous white dove that represents the Holy Spirit). But what's important to remember is that *however* you perceive God, it is *personal.*

God is not necessarily male. Nor is He any one race or ethnicity. (And if His Son, at least, is of any ethnicity, it certainly isn't the white kind.) God is an expansive, infinite being, the One some call Source and others call the Universe. He's the One that, as Christians, we believe created *all* things and created both Man *and* Woman (and everything off that spectrum, too) in His image, and so He can never be just one thing, and He can never look just one way. Any attempt to pin Him down as one thing or another is an attempt made in vain. This is a concept called *negative theology,* which, when plainly stated, is the idea that God is too infinite to be put in human boxes of identity. So when you go to meditate and encounter God, it's important to keep that in mind—and to keep your discernment working, as well as your courage, so you can ask relevant questions. As much as it may be annoying to see mainstream Christians spouting Bible verses off without really understanding them, there is some truth and good advice in one they love to quote:

> Beloved, do not believe every spirit, but test the spirits to see whether they are from God, for many false prophets have gone out into the world.[3]

By keeping your wits in mind, and having the confidence and courage to push back on spirits as you meet them—yes, including God, just so you might verify it's Him you're speaking to—you'll get pretty far. In the Interview with the Gods series on Tiktok, Sara regularly grapples with the entities that come into her space before asking questions, just to address any concerns she may have about them. However, she also trusts that God keeps her safe and keeps tricksters and troublemakers out.

---

3. 1 John 4:1

We're going to give you an exercise you can use to begin your meditations, but before we do, we'll say one more thing: if for whatever reason, starting off talking to God intimidates you and makes you uncomfortable, you don't necessarily *have* to start with God. It'd be great if you did, but we understand that the raw, unbridled force of God can be a lot to handle. That's why there's also a lot of truth in what Jesus Himself says in John, especially if you understand how overwhelming God is:

> Jesus answered, "I am the way
> and the truth and the life. No
> one comes to the Father except
> through me. If you really know
> me, you will know my Father as
> well. From now on, you do know
> him and have seen him."[4]

In this, Jesus is telling you multiple things, including the idea that Jesus is speaking metaphorically: one can argue that it is through Truth that one gets to God, including being true to yourself—living Life in a Way that is True and that heals your soul. It's also putting out the idea that Jesus is the Divine Middle Man, essentially. Being both fully human and fully Divine, Jesus is a man who understands the human condition and how hard it can be to just get through the day. At the same time, He also exists as an aspect of God (if you follow the Trinitarian doctrine that suggests God is three different aspects in one being, much the way the Triple Goddess is three iterations of a woman's life, Maiden, Mother, Crone, in one goddess). Being an aspect of God, literally God incarnate, means whatever you say to Jesus, you also say to God, so it works out. Though, of course, not all people follow the Trinitarian idea of God, and so some may see Jesus as a prophet or a figurative Son of God rather than a literal one; either way, He has sway with God and can help you get to the point of being more comfortable with God (and other spirits, like angels, which we'll talk about in the Chapter 16). But now, here's a good way to get into a meditative space.

Exercise One: Making Room in the Mind

In this exercise, take notice the title of it: *making room* in the mind. There are many ways to meditate, and some certainly do include the traditional meditation method you're thinking, in which you're meant to sit in complete silence with a head as empty as a candy bowl left on the porch during Halloween with a "Take One" sign. For some, this is a

---

4. John 14:6-7

viable method of meditation! Some people, *somehow*, are able to just close their eyes, let the darkness take over, and sit in complete and utter silence without a single distraction or thought passing them by!

God bless those people, but they are an *enigma*.

Rather, for this exercise, we're going to try something different, and that's focusing on the darkness for only a moment, so that you can make room for other things to come through: images, ideas, sounds, anything. Rather than trying to stifle any wayward thoughts, or make your mind go perfectly still, we're going to instead observe any thoughts that bubble up, and we're going to do this without any hope of encountering any angels or Saints or God or anything right away. By removing the expectations of encountering another consciousness, you can allow yourself to simply settle into the feeling of meditating at all. Here are the steps:

1. Find a place where you'll be comfortable and undisturbed for at least fifteen minutes.

2. (Optional) Get headphones and load up some of your favorite songs that have no lyrics. Sara suggests bardcore songs, folk music, Gregorian chants, phonk, or anything else that matches the mood you're looking to feel in this meditation.

3. Wherever you are, take a look at your surroundings first. Feel the surface underneath you. Is it hard? Or soft? Are you sitting with your legs crossed or are you in a chair? And your body itself: is it wrapped in a blanket, or are you wearing something like a sweatshirt that keeps you warm? Or maybe you're a little chilly in a t-shirt? **Take note of the physical sensations you feel in reality,** as well as where you actually are in the world. Fully understand that you are secure and safe there.

4. Take a deep breath, then close your eyes. Focus just on the darkness behind your eyelids at first. Notice whatever little flashes of light or lingering images from what you were just looking at remain, and then let them fade.

5. Don't resist the tug of your mind as it begins to wander. Let it go, and notice what images, shapes, colors, or thoughts come to your mind. **If any thoughts are about your to-do list, or things that worry you,** try to let them go for now. You can worry about them another time. But if they're things that are new and seemingly random, draw them closer.

6. Pick one image and hone in on it. Sketch it out to its fullest in your head. For this meditation example, we'll use a **tree.** When you see a tree, fill in the landscape around it: the grass, the other trees in the background, flowers on a worn dirt road, birds flitting about, sunlight filtering through the leaves. Whatever image you grasp, grasp it *fully*.

7. Hear the sounds. Wind rustling through the leaves, the song of birds. This may be difficult if you have music playing, but it may also meld well and harmonize with your music.

8. Feel your surroundings: feel the dirt under your feet, the bigger stones digging into your soles, and feel the breeze on your face. Feel the wind blow through your hair and unsettle it; reach out and touch the tree, lightly scraping your palm against its bark. Imagine it as if it's really there, and as if you're really touching it.

9. Now walk. If you're to focus on anything, focus on keeping these details real and alive as you explore this space. Walk down that dirt road and see what else appears in your meditation. Take note of any words or phrases that come up, or any smells or other things you hear. Be aware of colors of things, or types of animals.

10. Continue in this space until you feel like you're done—but no more than fifteen minutes. (This is also a great way to easily fall asleep before bed, if you decide to do this meditation then.)

Some words of warning about this meditation, though: remember that your mind is always on the defense, as any creature's mind is, and that you may feel the sense that there's something behind you or that you're being watched. This is normal and nothing to worry about. In your own mind and meditation space, *nothing* can hurt you unless you give it the power to do so, and even then, it can only affect you mentally. So keep yourself grounded, and if you need to, open your eyes on occasion to remind you where you are in real time. Remember that the world in your head is your own creation, too, and have fun with it!

Exercise Two: Meeting an Entity

When you've gotten the hang of meditation, and you're able to viscerally experience the world you've created for yourself, it's time to start using it as the place in which you'll be able to speak to entities like St. Michael the Archangel, Jesus, and even God. It doesn't have to stay looking the same each time, and certainly, it won't depending on who you speak to and how *they* alter the scene, but having the fundamentals down and enhancing your senses in a meditation space will make this easier to accomplish in the long run (and help you further develop your clair skills outside meditation).

However, as this is now an attempt at contact with an outside force, there are some things you can do beforehand to prepare yourself for a better connection. There are many plants, crystals, and times of the month that enhance psychic connection or connection to specific types of spirits, and by planning ahead, you can sink yourself into the headspace to accept interaction with other entities much better. For instance, when Sara began her Interview with the Gods series on Tiktok, she would burn certain plants in her preparations: rosemary to cleanse her space and mugwort to enhance her own spiritual radio signal beforehand.

Mugwort can be dangerous, though, so be mindful. Its essential oil is a neurotoxin, and as a tea, it can cause miscarriage, issues with cognition, and other ailments, especially if you drink too much. Unless it's something you're finding from the grocery store in the spice aisle, *do not* ingest any plants you're using for witchcraft, and even then, be mindful of dosaging (as even something as simple as bay leaf tea can cause problems if you don't know how much your body can handle). The plants of the world are so wonderful and good for us, but without proper caution and care, they can hurt us very, *very* badly, so never take something as herbal medicine or ingest something for spellwork unless you have expert opinion or enough expertise of your own. Sara only ever burned a tiny amount of mugwort, and only once a week, so she was fine, but that may not be the case for everyone.

Sara says:

I also don't need the mugwort anymore, because after over fifty encounters with other spirits, I've gotten the formula down pretty good and know how to stitch myself into the space an entity creates for us pretty well. If you're just starting out, though, here are some herbs and spices that can help you get into the zone:

- Lavender

- Bay

- Borage

- Celery

- Cinnamon

- Cherry

- Dandelion

- Fig

- Hazel

- Hibiscus

- Juniper

- Lemongrass

- Lettuce

- Mace (the outside of a nutmeg shell; good in psychic incense)

- Mugwort (if you're careful!)

- Orange

- Peppermint

- Pomegranate

- Rose

- Star Anise

- Thyme

According to Scott Cunningham's *Encyclopedia of Magical Herbs*, these items have at least something to do with divination or psychic power, as do the planet Mercury and the element of Air (both of which Lavender is associated, for example). Cunningham also insists that the color *yellow* has to do with psychic power,[5] though for color magic, *purple* is also another common one to choose, as it's the color of royalty, spiritual power, and the spiritual world.

Any of these herbs, spices, and foods listed here can be used to help you with enhancing your psychic power, and some, like cinnamon and thyme, offer you a bit of extra protection and courage, as well. As a Kitchen Witch myself, I'll tell you that the easiest way to gain the benefits of any of these things is to make a tea, *especially* if you're keeping your witchy path a secret for now. I mean, will anyone question you buying a box of peppermint tea from the store? Or an orange as a snack for yourself? I doubt it. However, if you have the means and the safety in your own space to do so, you might get a little more involved: maybe you make an incense for yourself out of cinnamon, mace, and orange peel, or a simmer pot that replaces mace with star anise. Maybe you eat a few seeds of pomegranate and leave some out as an offering to whoever you speak to, as well. Maybe you go all out and make a big dinner, like a roasted chicken seasoned with cinnamon, thyme, and nutmeg on a bed of onions, apples, and carrots, and you call on these ingredients to align your energy as you ask God to bless the food with protection, psychic enhancement, and power. It's up to you.

If you're in your own space and able to get a little more obviously witchy, you may also decide to include certain stones, items, or other iconography in your ritual set-up, too. Some good crystals to

---

5. Cunningham, *Encyclopedia of Magical Herbs*, 284.

enhance your psychic skills include (per Robert Simmons' *Pocket Book of Stones*):[6]

- Amethyst

- Blue Agate

- Blue Calcite

- Purple Chalcedony

- Blue Sapphire

- Purple Jade

- Blue Topaz

- Quartz

- Celestite (especially with angels)

- Lapis Lazuli

You'll notice I mention that celestite is especially helpful in communicating with angels. Robert Simmons would prefer seraphinite for specifically angel connections, which, by its name, you might guess has something to do with connecting with the Seraphim. He does also specify celestite for more general uses, though, and I personally prefer using celestite for all angel communications, as the Seraphim are only one order of angel (see Chapter 16).

But when it comes to meditation, how you arrange your space is entirely up to you. Whatever you choose to do to enhance your psychic intuition, whatever plant or stone ally you call on to help you focus your energy and power, is up to preference. There's no one way to go about enhancing any of your psychic skills. Once you've chosen your method and enjoyed it thoroughly (especially if it's a charmed drink or a blessed meal), get comfortable in your meditation space and get *intentional*. In each thing you do, be present, even if it's just lighting a candle or some incense.

I also recommend having a divination tool, like tarot or oracle cards, nearby. Cleanse these in your incense if you have any, or just give them a good knock to shake off any energy from previous readings. What you see in meditation may surprise you and cause you to second guess yourself, so it's good to have an outside tool like tarot cards or other preferred methods to get confirmation on what you're seeing and hearing. So prepare your tools, and then as you sink into your space, get ready for your meditation. Here's how to do it:

---

6. Robert Simmons, *The Pocket Book of Stones, Revised Edition: Who They Are and What They Teach* (Rochester: Destiny Books, 2015), 376, 378, 380, 392.

1. Start off with the Lord's Prayer, focusing on each word and imagining a great big bubble of golden light coming around you. This is your magical space, much like some witches might cast a circle. (We talk more on casting a circle in the next chapter.)

2. With your prayer finished, ask God to keep all tricksters, harmful energies, or frauds out of your space and allow only the entity you're asking for to come through. Trust that He'll protect you, and thank Him for it.

3. Repeat steps 1 - 5 of our previous meditation exercise, sinking into that empty space.

4. Rather than allow yourself to see random images, give a call into the darkness. Ask whoever you're looking to speak with to come forward and show themselves to you. **Take note of what you see, feel, or hear, and what phrases or words come up.**

5. If you're having trouble, now's the time to pull out a pendulum or other divination tool to confirm whether this entity is there. If you get a yes, spend time asking them to show you what they look like, what they feel like, etc., until you get a clear shape of them in your mind. It may be tempting to put your expectations on them (for instance, expecting an angel to look all pretty and golden), but let them appear however they'd like, and you'll get much farther with them.

6. Take note of your surroundings. Where did they bring you or want to meet? What does this say about them—or about you?

7. Ask your questions of this entity, using your divination tool of choice to back up the answers you get where you feel you need it. Spend time talking to them and getting to know them, too; it's rude to come just for answers and then leave, unless you're making your intentions clear from the start.

8. Don't spend longer than an hour, or hour and a half, in this space. It can be exhausting to go any further than that. When you're done, thank them for their time, ask them what they'd like you to do with any offerings you may have put out, and close the space with something physical to reconnect you to reality. For example, I clap once very loudly at the end to sever the connection with sound and pull myself out of the meditation space.

And that's the very basics of meditation, clair skills, and developing your psychic senses! This is the next step of divination alone as a

Christian Witch. It's a step that'll have you moving past being able to get answers from God and other beings and move into really encountering, interacting with, and understanding them as full separate consciousnesses. While this step isn't necessary to have a relationship with God—because you can always pray, and you can always pull cards or runes or anything to get His answer—it is something that'll make the whole relationship feel more, ironically, *human.* Putting faces, voices, actions, and ideas to names can only add to the connection you're building, as well as help you learn things about Heaven, the Infernal Realms, or anywhere else you might go, that you couldn't find in books. This is called *Unverified Personal Gnosis,* or UPG, and it's extremely helpful at filling in the gaps where mainstream religion falls short.

Be careful with it, though: you always have to use your discernment to know what's actually plausible (based on what we know about God and Heaven and such already from *all* types of scriptures, apocryphal or not), and what's something you just want to hear because it'd be really cool if it were true. It is very easy to delude yourself if you're not grounded and aware of your own biases, so make sure you spend a good deal of time working through and understanding *yourself* before you start encountering separate consciousnesses.

Another word of warning is this: if you ever feel like you're losing control of the meditation space, like you're being pushed towards a certain area or you can't control how things look, that's not necessarily a reason to be alarmed. It means that these entities really *are* with you, and that they're bringing you to places they want you to see and trying to get you to do things that will teach you something. If the entity you called on is one you trust to *not* try and harm you, by all means, give them the controls and let them show you things. Don't resist. If, for whatever reason, you're speaking to a spirit that makes you feel *unsafe,* just cut it off and get out of there, but be firm with your boundaries and honest with what makes you uncomfortable. Assert that you deserve this respect.

One of the most visceral experiences I had in this vein, that made me realize I was very much *not* alone, was also when I was working with Lucifer. I was exploring that cave of flesh I mentioned earlier, rolling around and treating it like a video game, exploring every nook and cranny for potential secrets or items or the like. However, we came to a part where there was an obvious fork in the path. I wanted to choose the path to the right, but I could feel in my bones that the path on the left was where I was supposed to be going.

No problem, I thought to myself. *I'll go explore the right area first, then come back to the path on the left.*

But as I went towards the right path, I kept noticing myself drifting left. It was like there was an invisible wall that kept me sliding against it, away from the path I wanted to take. It pushed me towards the path on the left. In fact, it *dragged* me there. Lucifer strolled up behind me as I was tugged, pulled, and essentially forced right over to the left path, where there was nothing but a ledge and a steep plunge to the darkness below. I ended up hanging off that ledge, clawing onto it, alarmed at how little control I suddenly had over my own decisions in this space—but when I asked Lucifer to let me explore, he relented and let me wander around the one little room I'd been trying to go to. There was nothing in it except a single chest, but when I opened it, it was empty. It felt like a gag on Lucifer's end, and there was that current in the air that said, *are you done? Let's go.*

So sometimes, yes, the entities you encounter will push you around and direct you a bit. It's usually because they're trying to show you something important or get you to do something important. Don't worry about it unless it pushes you too hard mentally; then make it clear that you are not ready for whatever's going on. Otherwise, though, enjoy your time with these entities, and remember that they are always here for you: the angels, the Saints, and of course, Jesus, God, and the Holy Spirit themselves. Go to them when you're tired and sad, go to them when you're happy and have good news to share, go to them when you just miss them and want to check in. Build that bond with them, and enjoy every moment of it.

Chapter Twelve

Tools That Can Aid Your Spellwork

Mimi Says:

W HEN I'M ASKED HOW long I've been a Granny Witch or what I do in my practice, I just shrug. To be honest, I can't always put my finger on it, because what I do is ingrained in me as part of living. And from what I'm finding in my community, that is the way of things: Granny witching isn't always about a big ritual or certain specialty tools. In fact, most things used are basic items found around your home. This is truly a "make do" sort of path, wherein you used whatever herbs you had from the garden or foraged, always kept a few jars clean and ready to be used for tinctures, and had a veritable encyclopedia of knowledge passed down over the years, ranging in information from how to deal with spooks and haints to the best way to cure thrush. Granny Witches were just as much faith healers as they were herbalists and doctors, so it makes sense that things used around the house and in the garden are the first things we go to. The things that I personally use in my practice are things anyone can use and are generally cheap.

Sara Says:

That cheapness—or rather, *accessibility*—is important. There's a middle step of learning here between the basics of *magic* itself, in which we use nothing but our own raw power, and the basics of *spell-work*. This middle step is the discussion of our magical tools: the items we use to channel our power into our spellwork. For the beginner witch of any spiritual tradition (or lack thereof), it can be tempting to spend one's money on all manners of fancy tools and crystals and bottles of herbs and spices, especially as we look to curate our magical style, aesthetic, and mode of expression. Witchcraft is, after all, a *craft*, much as writing is called a craft, or pottery, or blacksmithing, or any other form of skilled artistic expression that exists in the world. However, it bears repeating *over* and *over* and *over* again:

You need no tool, no crystal, no herb, no spice to perform good magic. You need only your own mind and your own energy.

Finding Tools to Use:

With all this said and done, for the Christian Witch that wants to develop an arsenal of artifacts that sharpen, enhance, and elevate their magical expression, it's worth discussing what types of tools you may come across in the world of witchcraft, as well as how to identify which ones may be for you, which largely depends on things like:

- Your astrological profile

- Your interests and hobbies

- Your environment or living space

- Your ability to be open about your practice with others

- Your ancestry or important cultural traditions

- Your access to certain materials

- Your artistic or crafting skills

- Your financial stability and general spending habits

All of these things coalesce into a more complete picture of who you are, what makes you feel in tune with yourself and the world around you, and what your magic means to you. By reflecting on these topics, you might better discover the aesthetic and creative direction in which you want to take your craft. After all, if you're always reposting beautiful, lush, Tolkien-esque, woodsy dreamscapes on Pinterest, but you live in a concrete maze of a city, there's going to be a disconnect between those witchy expectations and the mundane reality. However, before we start worrying too much about how to understand and curate our own unique witchy style via our magical tools, we should also make clear what tools are even for.

What Use Do Magical Tools Have in a Christian Witch's Practice?

You'll hear this kind of chattering often from more mainstream Christians: "Only God has power; miracles don't come from crystals! Using crystals this way is demonic and opens portals to possession! It's idolatry! You're worshipping the creation instead of the Creator!" But of course, none of them seem to know what idolatry actually means (or demonic, for that matter); there's nothing *idolatrous* about including God's creation in your work, because contrary to popular misconceptions, nobody is actually worshipping a piece of quartz or a sprig of thyme when they include it in a ritual. At least, not any more than a chef is worshipping the rosemary and rock salt they use in a meal. They're also not trying to trap any gods into the rock and treat it as if it has actually become the physical embodiment of the gods, which is what we know idolatry *actually* means in the Bible per Kugel's description in *The God of Old*.[1] However, despite all this, we also can't say that these mainstream Christians are *entirely* wrong. Mostly wrong, yes, but not *entirely*. The one thing they get right in all of this garbled rhetoric is that miracles don't come from crystals.

Miracles come from God—and by what we know about magic itself, they are channeled through us via our own energy. To reiterate: what separates magic from miracle (outside semantics) is the source of the works. Things we do with our energy that don't invoke God, like maybe holding a traffic light green for another couple seconds, is magic. Desired results we impress upon the world through the conjunction of our magic and God's power, or complex rituals, spellwork, and other more focused petitions, are miracles. Where magical tools come into play is in helping us *focus* and *direct* all that energy. (And yes, we'd say they do contribute at least a little bit of energy to the spell themselves, especially if they're living things like fresh herbs or energetically active things like crystals).

When we choose a specific ingredient for a spell that matches our intentions, or get a specific tool to use, we're able to further symbolize and reinforce the idea behind the spell, as well as concentrate our own minds (and therefore energy) on the task at hand. This collection of items in our spell set-up is therefore something of an energetic grid we use to direct this energy and these miracles out into the world through the channels we want them to take. For example, if you were to do a prosperity spell and wanted to channel God's blessings down through your power, you might choose specific ingredients that match your intention: anything green (the color of money), like green candles or crystals, or specific herbs like bay and basil, or things that have

---

1. Kugel, *The God of Old*, 83.

represented security and wealth to our ancestors (like nuts, seeds, and grains), or even things that simply remind us of gold, like honey.

Knowing all of these things hold the attributes of wealth and luck give us a physical, tangible symbol of an otherwise abstract idea, making it that much easier to quiet our minds, visualize our goal, and weave magical pathways for the miracles of God to flow and manifest through. Because these crystals and herbs are also parts of God's creation, and are at the very least spiritually and energetically active, they can also lend some of their own energy—or their *talents*, as we like to say—to our large-scale spellwork. This is what we might call "co-creation": the act of the Witch and their tools, all of which are pieces of God's creation, working with Him to cause tangible, noticeable changes in the world based on His will and the practitioner's petitions. But the origin of the magic and the miracle is, of course, yourself and God; the tools themselves are there to support you, not do the bulk of the work. They aren't gods, idols, or demonic portals. Rather, they're friendly assistants, and they have plenty of things to show you even outside of spellwork, if you take the time to meditate with them. The concept of animism tells us that these things can be teachers as much as tools, which you can read about in Chapter 18.

The same goes for divination tools. It's important to remember that you don't even need any specific tools to communicate with God. All you really need is a quiet space and some trust in your psychic ability. But like with magical tools, divination tools are helpful for starting witches who are trying to bolster their confidence in their skills and trust the things they hear from God. They're almost like training wheels for psychics, but unlike training wheels on a real bike, there's no shame in forever using the tools you need to get concrete messages (and, in fact, we encourage people to use them so that they always have something tangible to ground them and back up the messages they receive).

With all of that said, let's talk a little bit now about the different types of magical tools you might encounter in Christian Witchcraft.

Tools in Christian Witchcraft and Their Functions

If you've ever picked up a witchy book from the bookstore before, chances are that some of these tools will seem familiar to you. If you ever attended a Catholic church, or grew up Catholic, likewise, some others will seem familiar—and it may even surprise you to see them listed together in this book. But if we understand what it even means to be a witch, or perform folk magic, we know that there's only one real rule in gathering tools: *use what you have access to.* (Or did you think the witchy aesthetic of cauldrons and hanging herbs and bones was just one day decided on by a great meeting of witches from all over?) In the old days, the tools people had available—including local plants, rocks, waters, and more—were all the tools they needed. Likewise, today, we can see how those witchy tools evolved into things we might find more easily, or how those tools were hiding in plain sight, inconspicuous to prying eyes. This list below is by no means exhaustive, but it'll give you a better idea of what we mean.

Pot/Crockpot

Right away, you might guess what a good pot is analogous to: a cauldron. When Sara cooks her favorite one-pot meals, you bet that the red magma-like sauce bubbling away inside reminds her something of a witchy brew to bless for her family. Especially for the Kitchen or Green Witches who have things to cook and process, the Pot is the place you can combine all your energy and ingredients into one place (and you can get so many different sizes of them, too).

A Crockpot is the Granny Witch version of a cauldron. Mimi loves using intentional simmer pots to not only help set a magical mood for her work, but it makes her house smell *so* good. It's definitely budget friendly and great for kitchen magic. Plus, it's a hard little worker and fits in every kitchen size.

Broom

Mimi uses this literally and figuratively. Hanging a broom over your doorway helps to brush off negative energy from the outside that may have attached to you while you were gone. Mimi also keeps a broom outside on her porch; she turns it rightside up to invite good energy and guests, and she turns it upside down when she's cleansing and/or ready for company to leave (or not come around in the first place!).

Wand

A wand at its most basic is a tool (usually made of wood or crystals) that allows you to point and direct your energy towards your target. Think of a music conductor's wand, or even a laser pointer. It works as an extension of your own finger, and depending on the material, it can have extra effects, as different types of wood are culturally associated with different virtues and powers. It can also take a variety of shapes. A wooden spoon, for instance, is a wonderful "wand" for a Kitchen Witch. It also lines up with the suit of Wands in tarot.

Cup

Cups or small bowls are immeasurably useful as tools of *containment* or *holding* in magic. Whether filling with water to scry or using as a space to contain the loose ingredients in a spell, they give you a place to pool your magic and, as the saying goes, "fill your cup." These are also referred to as chalices or goblets, the former of which is familiar in any liturgical service where the Blood of Christ is shared with the congregation. This tool aligns with the suit of Cups in tarot.

Knives

If you've ever read a more Wiccan-centered or New Age book on witchcraft, you might have seen the term "athame" once or twice. An athame is a knife specifically set for ritual, but truth be told, any knife you have on hand that you can bless before a ritual is solid—especially for protection magic, offensive magic, or cutting things and people off that no longer serve you. It also aligns with the suit of Swords in tarot.

Jars

There are very few things a jar can't do. They can hold your special herbs, spices, or other small magical trinkets, they can become a physical symbol of a spell that you can hide somewhere or carry around after you fill them with ingredients, or they can even become a magical prison for someone when you tie their photo up and toss it in the jar to be forgotten about forever. What matters is that a jar (and other things, like drawstring bags, boxes, etc.) is a *container*, meaning you can use it as a source of energy that emanates *outward*, like a glow stick, or a tool to keep energy *inside* (like a steel trap).

Crystals

As the great St. Hildegard von Bingen said in the *Book of Stones*, from her work *Physica*:

> The devil abhors, detests, and disdains precious stones. This is because he remembers that their beauty was manifest on him before he fell from the glory God had given him, and because some precious stones are engendered from fire, in which he receives his punishment... But, just as God restored Adam to a better part, He sent neither the beauty nor the powers of those precious stones to perdition, but willed that they would be held in honor and blessing on earth and used for medicine.[2]

---

2. Prischilla Throop (translator), *Hildegard von Bingen's Physica: The Complete English Translation of Her Classic Work on Health and Healing* (Rochester: Healing Arts Press, 1998), 142.

For all the claims that crystals are "gateways to the demonic" by many a mainstream Christian, the truth is that their use in holy effects and wonders were argued for already, a *thousand* years ago, by one of the most iconic Christian mystics in the middle ages. While St. Hildegard argues their use for medicine in treating physical issues as much as spiritual, suggesting things like putting onyx in wine to infuse the wine with its properties, it should be known that crystals aren't good for curing physical problems (and certain stones, like malachite and selenite, are even toxic in contact with water), so they should never be directly ingested or put in things you plan to consume.[3]

However, the spiritual properties of crystals—like onyx's ability to absorb negative energy, or amethyst's ability to encourage peace, wisdom, and spiritual growth—are useful for magic, be it by lending their own talents to a working or by structuring the magic you're pouring into a crystal grid. You might also surround a cup of water with crystals to charge the water without actually putting any potentially dangerous crystals in contact with liquid. They can also be used in protective jewelry as amulets, held in the hands during meditation, or serve as an antenna for communicating with certain spirits.

Herbs and Spices

Like with stones, we also have plenty on herbs from St. Hildegard:

> Through the beneficial herbs, the earth brings forth the range of mankind's spiritual powers and distinguishes between them; through the harmful herbs, it manifests harmful and diabolic behaviors.[4]

There is no need to go to any special metaphysical store and buy a tiny baggy of overpriced mugwort for spellwork. Anything you might need to cast a spell can usually be found within the spice aisle at your local grocery store, because one of the principles of witchcraft and folk magic is *accessibility*, and having a pantry stocked with good herbs and spices will make both your food *and* your magic that much more interesting. Even getting pre-made spice blends, like pumpkin pie spice, is valuable when you make use of the spices in it (cinnamon, clove, allspice, ginger, and nutmeg, all of which have fiery, protective, energy-raising effects in magic). Whether in a blessed meal or a ritual setting, the place Sara goes to get her magical ingredients in a spell isn't her witchy tool space, but her spice rack, for precisely this reason.

---

3. Ibid. 145.

4. Ibid., 11.

Coffee and Tea

Not only are these fantastic for magic for their quickness and ease of preparation, but also for their easy concealment. After all, you can make countless herbal tea blends for all sorts of reasons—medicinal or magical—and no one's going to question you for regularly brewing a good cup of tea or coffee (nor will they notice you pouring your intentions into it as you hold the warm cup in your hands).

Tea has always been a go-to item for healing magic, especially, given how many remedies Sara's mother used tea for. Upset stomach? Peppermint. Loose bowels (or jittery nerves)? Chamomile. A cold or stuffy nose? Any kind of mint. Now, after learning more about the medicinal properties of herbs and spices, Sara will also use teas with cinnamon and ginger (and a heaping spoonful of honey) for sore throats and other such things. Just remember to do your research about even common household ingredients, and *never* replace a doctor's advice with home remedies.

Moreover, the old tradition of always having a pot of coffee on made your house inviting, filled with good energy, and let you be a good host should any company come by. Tea can be used medicinally and as a comfort for those whose nerves can't quite handle coffee (be it for the caffeine or the bitter flavor). Both can be used in divination, too. Seeing visions and discerning images in the coffee grounds and tea leaves have been a long standing tradition in Appalachian folk practice, and when Mimi is *really* in need of a sign, she grabs her favorite cup and settles into her intentions.

Bones

These can be used in a style of divination known as osteomancy, sure, but they can also be used as spell items on their own. If you manage to get the tooth of a certain person, you can create a tag lock that fixes the spell to them (though, granted, getting fingernails or hair is likely easier). You might also save the bones of certain animals to keep as symbols of their attributes; chicken bones, pork bones, even dog bones (such as the baby teeth that you'll find puppies chewing on as their adult teeth come in) all have their own special functions as spell ingredients depending on the connotations of them in your family or culture.

Incense

Incense can be used to cleanse a space, imbue a space with a magical attribute (for example: cinnamon incense for success and protection), or even as an offering to certain entities, which is also backed by the Bible per God's specific incense recipe listed in Exodus 30:7-8. If you've ever stepped into a Catholic church, that specific scent it has is the scent of frankincense. Myrrh is also often used, as both of these together represent two of the three gifts brought to baby Jesus in the infancy narratives. Frankincense is a great incense to burn as an offering to God and Jesus, whereas dragon's blood is a common scent for members of the Infernal Divine. It's also a nice tool to have just for the sake of making your space smell nice during meditation or the start of ritual work.

Candles

Mimi says:

I remember the last oil lamp my Mamaw had; it was carefully kept in a china cabinet and only used when the power went out. It was used when long nights and hard prayers were made because it was safer than letting a candle burn. Until I can get my hands on an old oil lamp (that's still in good repair), I use the seven-day candles. They're easy to anoint and decorate, come in a wide variety of colors, and don't burn the house down as easily if they fall over.

Sara says:

For me, candles were ever present as a sign of respect, remembrance, and honor to the dead—ironically thanks to my Catholic mother. Whenever it's my opa's birthday, or my grandmothers' (who were *both* born on October 2nd), or any of the other people in our lives we've lost, Mom will find a picture of them to set on the kitchen table and light a candle next to it. And of course, in the Catholic church itself, it's common custom to make a donation and light a votive candle after Mass as a way to offer prayers for intercession and aid. This is essentially candle magic: lighting a candle and focusing on one's intent through the flame, or offering that candle to the spirits beyond as a way of connection. It's influenced my own witchcraft, as I'll often use candles to represent a connection between me and whichever entity I'm speaking to, or I'll pick specific colors based on the intentions of the spellwork (and prayers) I'm performing.

Rosary

Prayer beads exist in a variety of different religions, but anyone coming from a more European bend, especially, will find some comfort in using this Catholic tool as a way of connection to their culture and ancestry, *and* as a way of engaging in deep spiritual work. Each bead on the rosary represents one prayer, and so if you're ever having trouble getting into a deep meditative state, praying the entire rosary and reflecting on the mysteries is a great way to separate yourself from the hustle and bustle of everyday life. It's also incredibly protective, as when you call on Mama Mary through the Hail Mary, you call on the angels, and when you call on the angels, you call on her Son, and when you call on her Son, you call on God. No deeper protection exists than having the entire host of Heaven by your side.

Bible

While used as a tool of oppression and an overall "rule" book by a lot of the more Evangelical Christians in the South, the Bible is a spell book for those who know how to read it. Mimi usually has a Psalm or two on hand when a spell needs to be crafted or a prayer said over a ward. If you know where to look, too, you'll find plenty of inspiration for spells—whether looking for herbs and crystals mentioned throughout the Bible, looking at specific ritual formats that most people dismiss (like Leviticus 14, which remains a *fantastic* exorcism format), or creating some of the spells our ancestors used, which were based on stories from the Bible. For example, anything Jesus did to get rid of evil or tongue-lash people can be used in some blistering magic against those who would do you wrong, and anything Jesus did to inspire love and joy in people can be used for those you want to uplift.

Prayer Books

More specific than the Bible itself, you can actually grab copies of *just* the book of Psalms or Proverbs, both of which are essentially little books full of cantrips. If you've ever played Dungeons and Dragons, they work about the same as in the game: they're quick spoken spells that require no other materials but you and the spoken Word, and by God, they are *powerful.*

Holy Water (& Oil, Salt)

Now, you could make all these yourself with a solid blessing—or you could pop over to your local Catholic church and ask the priest for a bit of whatever he's got on hand. Every time Sara and her mother stop by with empty bottles, they come away with plenty of holy water for all their protective needs. Her mother will start sprinkling it on people who are having an especially rough patch of luck, and Sara uses it to wipe down ritual spaces, anoint herself or objects, or likewise dissolve the bad luck off of people or things.

Oil is especially useful for anointing candles and other such items, as well as people (especially given how often it's referenced in the Bible, like in Psalms 23:5 or Mark 6:13). According to Abbot Andrew Miles:

> The purpose of this [holy] oil is primarily for healing and protection from harm; but the oil can also be used to pray for all the blessings which the oil represents; that is, all the riches which are ours in Jesus. The oil can be used in praying for oneself or in praying for others.[5]

And even for the most staunchly anti-magic, bona fide Catholics, blessed salt is traditionally sprinkled in the corners of newly blessed and cleansed houses to protect them from any malignant spirits or other bad energy. It has other uses, namely in baptism, and from a more witchcraft-centered perspective, it can also be used to make black salt (which is salt combined with the ash of incense). All in all, it's a fantastic tool against negative energy.[6]

Bells

For those who can't cleanse a space with incense, water, oil, or salt, there is something known as *sound cleansing*, in which bells are especially useful. Silver or iron bells rung throughout a house can scare all manners of unclean spirits away, and the bell itself has even been used in the spellwork (or, rather, curse work) of many a Christian Saint, priest, and bishop. Regarding the use of bells, Martin Duffy notes:

> The practice of ringing a bell whilst making an invoca-tion, malediction [curse], or blessing is found cross-cul-turally, and is typically used to draw attention to the spoken formulae within the magico-religious rite. The bell's knoll thus serves to underscore and affirm the saint's blessing or curse, and is effectively synonymous with the binding sentence at the end of a spell or prayer, such as Amen, Fiat, and So Be It.[7]

As a result, bells make an appearance not only in the many Christian magical situations Duffy describes (everything from blessings to severe

5. Andrew Miles, "Blessed Oil," Catholic Sacramentals, accessed November 30, 2023, https://www.catholicsacramentals.org/blessed-oil.

6. Rev. John H. Hampsch, "Blessed Salt," Catholic Sacramentals, accessed November 30, 2023, https://www.catholicsacramentals.org/blessed-salt.

7. Duffy, *Anathema Maranatha*, 29-30.

and incredible curses, performed especially by Saints like St. Maedoc), but also as relics of Saints passed. Saints would carry these "'miracle-working' bells, and surviving exemplars were frequently revered as holy relics possessing preternatural power," with shrines like "St. Patrick's Bell Shrive, St. Conall Cael's Bell Shrine," and many others showcasing these legendary items.[8] Like the rosary, therefore, bells are powerful tools to cleanse spaces with sound, and also powerful tools to aid in punctuating and focusing the magic of a Christian Witch.

Medals

There are several Catholic amulets and medals that might remind you of the early Christian amulets we've discussed before. Physical objects to carry and remind one of God, Jesus, the Holy Spirit, and even Mama Mary have long been a part of Catholic folk belief and religious practice. Two of the most famous ones include the Miraculous Medal and the Saint Benedict Medal. Both of them have their own long and wondrous creation stories, the former being a representation of the vision of Mother Mary that Saint Catherine Laboure saw in 1830,[9] and the latter being potentially extrapolated from an image of St. Benedict holding a cross with Latin phrases on it, which became part of the medal.[10]

When it comes to the Miraculous Medal (which Sara has as a keychain and as a little laminated card in her wallet, both of which were given to her to keep her safe by her Catholic mother), the story involves an incredible tale from St. Catherine, including visions and directives to create this object for the Church to use in their time of need. According to St. Catherine's own testimony, this medal had been created by demands of the vision of the Virgin she saw in the night, and with its completion, Mama Mary made it clear what this medal could be used for:

> There now formed around the Blessed Virgin a frame rather oval in shape on which were written in letters of gold these words: "'O Mary conceived without sin, pray for us who have recourse to Thee.' Then a voice said to me: 'Have a medal struck upon this model. All those who wear it, when it is blessed, will receive great graces especially if they wear it round the neck. Those who repeat this prayer with devotion will be in a special

---

8. Ibid., 30.

9. "Miraculous Medal," Catholic Sacramentals, accessed November 30, 2023, https://www.catholicsacramentals.org/miraculous-medal.

10. Abbot Dom Prosper Gueranger, "Saint Benedict Medal," Catholic Sacramentals, accessed November 30, 2023, https://www.catholicsacramentals.org/saintbenedictmedal.

manner under the protection of the Mother of God. Graces will be abundantly bestowed upon those who have confidence.[11]

St. Benedict's Medal appears against all matters of evil, and was even a key instrument in protecting monks in Bavaria from the alleged attacks of "witches" in 1647. On the vertical part of the medal's cross are the letters of an acronym, which creates the phrase, "Crux Sacra Sit Mihi Lux," or "May the Holy Cross be my Light," and on the horizontal line is another acronym, "Non Draco Sit Mihi Dux," or "Let not the Dragon be my Guide." They intersect on that middle *S*, and they create both a powerful blessing and ward. Around the cross are four letters, *CSPB*, which mean "Crux Sancti Patris Benedicti," or "Cross of the Holy Father Benedict." While many Catholics will insist that the medal itself has no power, the fact is that by taking on the image of the cross, as well as the prayers and blessings forever etched into its design, it does give a Catholic (witch or not) a connection point to Jesus through meditation and sheer iconography, which gives one the gateway for all the protection and spiritual cover they need. Abbot Dom Prosper Gueranger wrote in 1880:

And now, applying these considerations to the medal which is the subject of these pages, we come to this con- clusion, that it must be profitable to us to use with faith the medal of St. Benedict on occasions when we have reason to fear the snares of the enemy. Its protection will infallibly prove efficacious in every kind of tempta- tion. Numerous and undeniable facts attest its powerful efficacy on a thousand different occasions, in which the faithful had reason to apprehend a danger, either from the direct agency of Satan, or from the effects of certain evil practices.[12]

The cross alone is more than enough, of course, given it's this medal's main motif, but for those who love their Mama, and who also want some hardcore wizard-looking tools that can do a damn good job at helping one give bad energy the boot, medals with such rich histories like these are great to carry around (and make some really cool statement jewelry).

---

11. "Miraculous Medal."

12. Gueranger, "Saint Benedict Medal."

Thread

String, especially red string, has a myriad of uses, be it from the Bible (such as in Leviticus 14), in folk magic (with Slavic folk magic being especially prone to using red embroidery), and in general practice. Given the nature of string is to tie something, it's fantastic for binding spells, and there's an entire category of magic known as *knot magic*, which creates anchoring points for spoken spells as one creates something via crocheting, knitting, etc. Slavic magic is an example of a cultural practice in which certain designs "are embroidered down the sleeves or over the front of the bodice" of things like the *vyshyvanka*, a type of Ukrainian shirt, to protect against *prychyna* and *vroki*—purposeful curses and the evil eye.[13] Madame Pamita, a member of the Ukrainian diaspora, mentions in her book:

> For men, there is heavy embroidery on the wrists, so that their hands might be empowered; around the neck, so that they may always hold their head high; and on their chest, so that they might feel love and courage. For women, there is light embroidery on the wrist and neck—sometimes on the hem of the garment as well—and large talismanic embroidery on the sleeves to strengthen the arms for hard work and protecting the loved ones they hold close.[14]

All such embroidery and symbols can be used to attract any good thing or dispel any bad thing, and they can be embroidered on more than just clothes: tablecloths, ritual cloths, or any other cloth that gets used for important things. Slavic culture (and the many groups that make up the Slavic category) are only one example of the many cultures and traditions that use such stitchwork and decoration in their magic.

Pen and Paper

The Word alone is a powerful tool—so powerful that even just writing down a verse of the Psalms or Gospels on a sticky note can create a whole new ritual tool from seemingly nowhere. Even in the Bible, this type of magical power that written spells have is made clear, as when we look at Numbers 5:11-31, we see that one of the ritual tests

---

13. Madame Pamita, *Baba Yaga's Book of Slavic Witchcraft: Slavic Magic from the Witch of the Woods* (Woodbury: Llewellyn Publications, 2022), 8.

14. Ibid., 8.

for infidelity involve a cursed drink. Contrary to popular myth, there were no abortifacients in this drink; it was just dirt from the temple floor mixed with, according to Duffy, the ink of a curse written on a scroll, which was then "blotted... into the water, thereby causing the words of the curse to infuse the filter."[15] There's more folk magic surrounding this idea, such as the instance in which "a bewitched woman attempted to lift her curse by writing the Lord's Prayer on a piece of paper, soaking it in water until the ink ran, and then drinking the infused water."[16]

Of course, we're not recommending that anyone drink ink; this is not the safest or healthiest thing to do. However, what Sara has done in the past as a more cooking and kitchen focused witch, is write a Psalm on a piece of paper to go under her cutting board, which radiates the Psalm's power into every ingredient she chops for her blessed meal. She's also written verse numbers on pieces of paper and put them into lockets with other materials to create magical amulets. Moreover, a pen and paper is all you need to create sigils and cast magic on other people, as writing down someone's name and birth date can replace other items like fingernails or hair in a spell.

Farmer's Almanac

Divination isn't only found in the bottom of a cup. Learning signs from nature and the sky has been a boon in predicting weather and setting oneself up for success. Mimi uses things like counting foggy days in August, wooly worm colors, and persimmon seeds to see what kind of weather she'll have for the winter. (In Wisconsin, it's not always the most reliable, but still a good indicator for the length of biting cold over heavy snow.) Using the stars in the sky and the moon phases has dictated how and when to plant, preserve foods, and do general life things. The astrological signs were equated to parts of the body, and doing something (or not) was dependent on where that sign was.

Playing Cards

A regular deck of playing cards works just fine if you're in the way of using them for spells and charms. Mimi remembers how her Little Mamaw gave her a Nine of Hearts card and told her to put it in her plastic pocketbook when she was little, and it's something she does to this day. However, it's important to note that a few charms and spells Mimi was taught for luck are commonly used in hoodoo practices. Since they have been handed down in her family, Mimi uses them. However, because of the nature of hoodoo as a closed practice, this

---

15. Duffy, *Anathema Maranatha*, 44.

16. Ibid., 45.

book will not be teaching or explaining further on these topics out of respect.

The Body as a Tool of Christian Witchcraft

In Appalachian folk magic practices, there's a myriad of ways to practice; after all, as the practice and superstitions were passed down from family to family, there was no one set way of using things, like a broom or a candle. Instead, the foundational things used in this practice are your head, your hands, and your gut instinct.

Head

Having a "knowing" in your work, or that claircognizance, is a lot of head work. but you've got to be able to understand what the signs are saying and really dig down and ground yourself to hear that still, small voice. Having psychic abilities are all well and good, but the biggest part is your intention. Just like "cooking with love" or "souring the milk" with bad feelings, your head sets your intention to the workings you're doing. The passion and reasoning behind it all is a huge part of Appalachian magic. If you're keeping to the more Christian magic practice here, the spiritual gifts of this part would include the gift of knowledge, the gift of teaching, and the gift of prophecy.

Hands

Picture your grandma's hands. Are they calloused from a life of labor? Are they wrinkled, with every line telling a new part of their story? Warm or cold, manicured or not, a grandma's hands hold the love and wisdom that comes with caring for their family, friends, and community. Mimi remembers how her Mamaw would tell her about all the burns and cuts she'd gotten when she first learned to cook with cast iron, gut fish and rabbits, and so on. All Mimi could think about was the power that her hands held, whether intentional or not. A lot of faith healers lay their hands and do energy work to heal and protect in the name of the Holy Spirit; this is where the gift of healing, the gift of giving, and we'd even say the gift of shepherding is. Hands hold those who need guidance, too.

Gut

You've got to use the sense that God and your Granny gave you. While not everything is magical, not everything is mundane, either. A lot of power goes into trusting your gut. Mimi would venture to say your heart is part of your gut here, since you pour your heart and soul into something just with that gut feeling. Not only that, it taps back into that "knowing" and a life of experiences to help you know what's going on around you. As far as spiritual gifts go, Mimi would say you'd find the gift of discernment, gift of wisdom, and gift of faith under these parts of the practice. So with all that said and done, remember: you don't need to spend a dime to do great magic. It isn't these tools that create magic and miracle, or that change the world.

It's *you*, and the God that gave this magic to you.

Chapter Thirteen

The Basics of Spellwork

O KAY, SO, WITH THE basics of magic firmly under your belt, you may be wondering how you take your *magic* and your *tools* and combine them into something workable. Of course, as we discussed before, if you have just your body, your voice, your energy, and most importantly, your God, then a simple prayer can undo even the thickest knots of a curse and bring the most splendid blessings. Hell, you can even actively cast curses that will straight up ruin people this way. To quote occultist Damien Echols in his book, *Angels and Archangels*, "a magician should be able to be dropped off naked in a jungle on the other side of the world and still be able to perform incredibly powerful magick."[1] However, on the other side of the argument, even if a skilled *artist* can somehow create beautiful artworks out of nothing but sticks, leaves, and mud, it doesn't mean they're any less of an artist for buying some paints and a canvas, right?

Right. So as we take stock of our tools, and the style in which we conduct our energy, it's time to figure out how to combine them into something we can feel good about. In this chapter, we'll talk about quite a few things: the types of spells there are, the ways in which you might organize a spell, and a conversation on the ethics in specifically *baneful* spellwork (or curses). You can also check the QR code in the back of this book to download some printable spell sheets for your own grimoires. As you grow more adept at handling your own magic, you'll find that spellwork is something like cooking (and I'm not talking about kitchen witchcraft): the amounts of ingredients you use, the

---

1. Damien Echols, *Angels and Archangels: A Magician's Guide* (Boulder: Sounds True, 2020), 195.

fluidity of your process, the adaptations you make along the way, it all makes a spell unique every time, yet simply and predictable.

But like all things, such an intuitive fluidity takes practice, so let's dive in.

What Does it Mean to Cast a Circle?

If you've seen any of the more old school magical resources, especially ones that stem from Wicca, you may have noticed that the authors recommend *casting a circle* before starting any magical work.

With the four archangels of the cardinal directions, however (discussed more in Chapter 16), you can recreate something you may have heard of before: the idea of calling on the elements (in this case, angels of the elements) and casting a circle. There are several ways in which you might perform this idea, one being the Lesser Banishing Ritual of the Pentagram (or LBRP) as outlined by the Hermetic Order of the Golden Dawn. This ritual is easily accessible in Damien Echols' book, *High Magic*, though do be warned that it, like any occult or ceremonial magic text, is *full* of the occultic Qabalah that simply... rips off much of its format from mystic traditions in Judaism. Nonetheless, this LBRP is one that, according to Echols, can help with cleansing your energy of any old and dirty muck you picked up throughout the day, mentally focusing you for ritual, purifying your environment, providing protection, getting your subconscious active, and get you used to the concept of evocation as it pertains to whatever beings you might call on.[2]

If you're looking for something less complicated, however, it's as simple as asking these four angels to come forward from their respective directions and guard you, and then asking God above it all to watch over you. Many examples of such a simple evocation exist. One such example is a specific Jewish bedtime prayer that essentially does exactly this in much fewer words or steps than the LBRP:

> In the name of God, the God of Israel, on my right is **Michael,** on my left is **Gabriel,** in front of me is **Uriel,** behind me **Raphael,** and all around, surrounding me, **Shekhinat-El.**[3]

Shekhinat-El means the Divine Presence of God, a feminine force in Jewish mysticism, lore, and grammatical reference in Hebrew. To avoid appropriating concepts from Jewish mysticism, you might just say "God" or "the Holy Spirit" in its place, but since these angels still exist within Christianity, it's worth looking at this prayer as an *example*

---

3. Velveteen Rabbi, "Calling All Angels" (blog), Velveteen Rabbi (2010), https://velveteenr abbi.blogs.com/blog/2010/04/calling-all-angels.html.

of how one might cast a circle with angels. A similar concept is also found in the *Clavicula Salomonis* (the Key of Solomon, not to be confused with the Lesser Key of Solomon):

> MAKE a Carpet of white and new wool, and when the Moon shall be at her full, in the Sign of Capricorn and in the hour of the Sun, thou shalt go into the country away from any habitation of man, in a place free from all impurity, and shalt spread out thy Carpet so that one of its points shall be towards the east, and another towards the west, and having made a Circle without it and enclosing it, thou shalt remain within upon the point towards the east, and holding thy wand in the air for every operation, thou shalt call upon MICHAEL, towards the north upon RAPHAEL, towards the west upon GABRIEL, and towards the south upon MURIEL.[4]

But the point still stands: ask these angels to come to you and create what is essentially a little magical bubble for you, and ask God to cleanse and purify you and your space before beginning. Sara, for example, prefers the Catholic version of the Lord's Prayer alone for this, so that she might purify herself and her space and get her mind right for anything she's about to do. It also signals to God that she's trying to work with Him and get His attention. After this, you may consider asking God to send the four archangels to help you mediate on the elements and work with you to craft your magical bubble, if you wish to. Don't feel like you need to copy anyone's way of bringing the angels into your space or do any outlandish and long ritual formats for this; the point is to get your mind right, give yourself a clean slate for ritual, and keep you safe as you try to go about your business.

You may be wondering what you need to protect yourself from, and I'll tell you: there are many spirits in the Unseen Realm looking for a quick bite. (For more on the miscellaneous spirits Unseen Realm, see Chapters 18 and 19.) After all, something that new magicians don't readily think about or realize is that magic, being an energy, is to the spirits of the Unseen Realm as food is to our physical bodies. Some creatures want to take it wherever they can get it, and when a magician—especially a new one—suddenly starts raising their magical energy, it does the same as sending a giant signal into the sky that there's food nearby. Think like Batman's signal, except instead of a bat, it's a burger or something.

These rituals and protections will keep you safe in those first few months when things come skulking around trying to figure out if you're an easy source of food or not. Before the concept makes you uncomfortable, though, let me be explicitly clear: these entities are

---

4. *Clavicula Salomonis*, Book 1, Chapter XIII.

nothing to worry about. They can't actually hurt or harass you (unless you let them by being needlessly terrified of them and inflating their negative capabilities in your head), and they'll leave when they realize you're not worth the effort, so don't let this put you off from doing magic altogether. If you wouldn't be scared of the few ants that come into your house when you drop food on the floor, there's no reason to be scared of these spirits, either. Just sweep them out and clean your floor (in magic: banish and purify) and you're good as new.

Types of Spells

Right away, the first thing you should know is just how many types of spells there are (and the many types of labels that one might attach to such spells or styles of magic, which we talk about more in the next chapter). Sometimes it feels like there are as many types of spells as there are tools—but realistically, each one falls into one of three categories: *spoken* spells, *ritual* spells, or *craftable* spells. There's often an overlap here, as we might discover with this Venn Diagram.

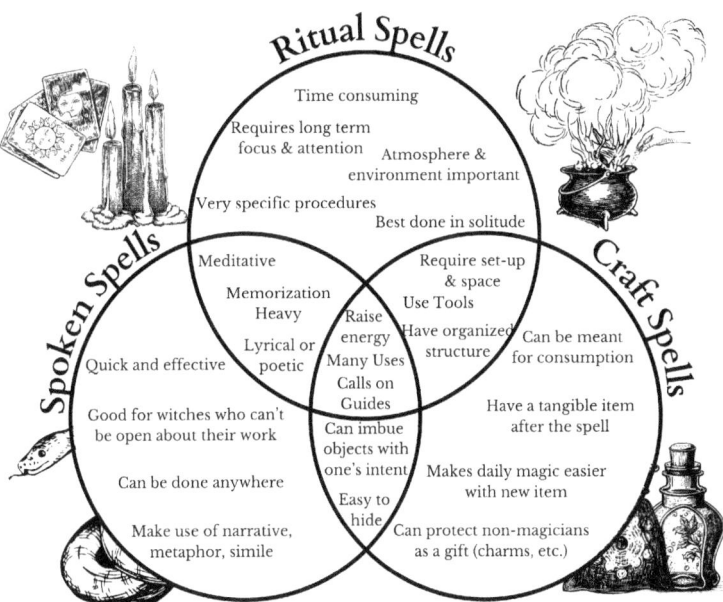

When we talk about these types of spells within the context of this diagram, we can make sense of it by talking about the certain formats they come in. To break down these topics, here are a few examples.

Ritual

- Church (think of Catholic Mass or any Sunday sermon)
- Ceremonial magic (including many of the tool-heavy, time-consuming formulas and procedures of most Western occult practices, like Solomonic magic)
- Moon rituals with the new and full moons
- Exorcisms

Spoken (Cantrips)

- Narrative spells
- Rhymes (including nursery rhymes!)
- Comparative spells
- Songs/Psalms
- Mantras

Craft

- Potions (tea, broth, coffee, herbal infusions)
- Foods
- Holy oils, salt, or water
- Jar spells
- Amulets
- Charms
- Sachets
- Wards

Some of these types of spells need no explanation, as it's easy to imagine, knowing what we know about magic historically, how one might use Scripture or other tools to create a paper amulet they can carry around for their protection. It's also easy to understand how

the tea you make from your favorite herbal blend, when imbued
with blessings and the help of said herbs, can be thought of as a potion. Others, however—like narrative or comparative spells—bear
talking on further.

Sara says:

You'll find these types of spells most often in Catholic folk magic
across various cultures, where drawing on the name of God, or Biblical stories about Jesus or other prophets, or even making stories
up about Jesus, help create some powerful charms. In Slovenia, for
instance, one of the oldest charms ever discovered is one against
tooth pain, written in Latin by the Cisterian monk Bernard in the
12th century in the village of Stična. It tells the story of St. Peter:

> *B,s,e.a.c.d.e.l.m.l.n.n.u.n.s.i.i.i. In nomine Patris et
> Filii et Spiritus Sancti. Amen. Sancus Petrus dum
> sederat supra petram marmoream, misit manum ad
> caput et Dolores dentium contristabatur. Veni Jesus
> et ait: quarecontristeris Petre? Air: venit vermis mi-
> graneus, ut exas et recedes et ultra famulum Dei enim
> ledas. Amen.*

In English:

> *B,s,e.a.c.d.e.l.m.l.n.n.u.n.s.i.i.i. In the name of God
> the Father and the Son and the Holy. Spirit. Amen.
> When St. Peter sat down on the marble rock,he his
> head with his hands and was sad because of a
> toothache. He came to Jesus and said, 'Why are you
> sad, Peter?" Peter answered: "There came crawling
> worm and ruined my teeth."And Jesus said: "I charm
> you, crawl-ing worm, to go away and not bother
> anymore the servant of God."Amen.*[5]

Is there a Biblical story where such a thing happened? Not that
I've read across all the Gospels, be they Canonical or not. Yet as
ethnographer Saša Babič goes on to show us, there are quite a
few special qualifications to Slovenian folk magic, especially of the
spoken variety.

---

5. Dolenc quoted in Saša Babič, "Charms in Slovenian Culture," *Icantatio: An International
Journal on Charms, Charmers, and Charming* 3, no. 3 (2013), 87, DOI:10.7592/Incantati
o2013_Babic.

She notes how many of these charms would be "passed on from generation to generation directly in communication between teacher and student," and that these teachers would tell their students the most specific rules for how each charm should be cast, such as "how loudly or quietly it should be told, if there had to be any pathos in the speech," and most importantly, how slow they should be said, as "all the charms were said slowly—so that the force (good or bad) could receive the message."[6] She also gives a rundown of the *context* of these spells, which was especially important: the *reason* for the spell (such as issues with the weather or bad luck), the conducting of any ritual a charm requires (such as going to the crossroads, doing spells by moonlight, using certain objects), the belief of the person requesting the charm, and the person conducting the ritual themselves (who were thought to be better at casting this magic than the average person).[7] Interesting, however, is the fact that some old world misogyny managed to sneak even into the *good* applications of magic among communities, despite the very woman-centered idea of the *Witch* that spawned out of the last century. Slovenian magical "healers of people were mostly women; men were healing livestock diseases and more difficult diseases, for which the effect was better with a more 'masculine, stronger word'," according to Babič and Matiče-tov.[8]

Other curses in the Slovenian language came about, as well. Some healers used curses to heal, such as a curse against the snake that had bitten the one receiving magical help, which invokes the name of St. Šempas, "in which the Holy Mother asks Šempas to heal the bitten man"; here's a prayer that is open for folks to recreate, as it's a simple narrative prayer:

> *Evo sćudeža! So oni koj verovali, jime moje zaterali: če je vraga govoril, Bude nove jezike pahudil, če je vraga ... Ako budo otrov pili, neče škodovati njim; Na bolezne ruke kladati ti čejo, Izlečiti njih budo.*

In English:

> Behold a miracle! They believed immediately. They said my name: If he talked to the devil, He will walk over new languages If there is hell ... if they will drink poison, it

---

6. Babič, *Charms in Slovenian Culture*, 88.

7. Ibid., 88-89.

8. Ibid., 89.

will not harm them; to who ill hands they will put, they will heal them.[9]

Of course, these are but a few examples from only one culture. If you leave Slovenia and visit its western neighbor, Italy, all of the culture, language, and history change, but plenty of aspects of the folk magic seem the same. You'll find yet more folk charms, incantations, and other such things that rely on the spoken word and little else. According to Mary Grace-Fahrun, this is one you might say "outdoors first thing in the morning":

> *Pater Noster dei Sanctorum. Maria bella angelorum.*
> *Maria belle che dormiva, il figlio in sogno le appariva.*
> *"Caro io ti ho sognago che al Calvario ti han portato.*
> *Coron d'oro t'han levato e le spine t'han piantato." "Quel*
> *che dici è verità," rispose Cristo alla mamà. Chi questo*
> *dice tre volte per via, paura non ha di alcune malattia.*
> *Chi questo ice per tre volte in un campo, non ha paura*
> *di acqua, tuoni e lampo.*

In English:

> Our Father of Saints. Beautiful angel Mary. Beautiful Mary was sleeping, and her son appeared in her dream. "Dear one, I dreamt they took you to Calvary; they removed your gold crown and stuck you with thorns." "What you say is truth," replied Christ to his mother. He/She who recites these three times on the street fears not any illness. He/She who recites these three times in a field fears not rain, thunder, and lightning.[10]

If you have any ancestry in specific places, like Italy or Slovenia or Germany or anywhere else in the world, then you bet there's a treasure trove of folk magic waiting to be discovered. Consider looking into books similar to Fahrun's *Italian Folk Magic* or *Slavic Kitchen Alchemy* by Zuza Zak, or looking into papers and books by ethnographers like Saša Babič and Mirjam Mencej. These types of materials written by people of your ancestry, who are focused on specific areas or time periods or cultural situations, will help you find the magic that your ancestors might've used. Even if I don't consider myself a folk

---

9. Dolenc quoted in Babič, 89.

10. Mary Grace-Fahrun, *Italian Folk Magic: Rue's Kitchen Witchery* (Newburyport: Weiser Books, 2018), 139.

magician, it's nice to know that the things I'm including in spells or the formats I'm using have some cultural significance to me. Remember, though: *not all folk magic is open.* A general rule is that closed practices will be hidden within families that pass it down, but it helps to be vigilant and ask what cultures the books you're reading are getting their information from—and whether those cultures are appropriate for you to borrow from.

Nonetheless, other spoken charms and spells include anything out of the book of Psalms or Proverbs. These spells, or *cantrips*, are fantastic for just about any opportunity. Even things elsewhere in the Bible, like for example, Deuteronomy 28:16-20, or like Mark 11:12-21, where Jesus curses the fig tree, are powerful for Christian magicians to perform their own curses. Using the fig verses (even just using verse 14) was in fact a common way to lay *comparative* curses, in which people would compare the effects of Jesus's curse to what would befall their victim. But returning to the Psalms, it's Psalm 109 that is likely the biggest (and most often used, yet most extreme) example of what is called an *imprecatory Psalm.* Anything called *imprecatory* means it is meant to be a curse or bring misfortune on others, specifically in response to some injustice or wrong that the target has done to whoever is doing the imprecatory work. Psalm 109 goes like this:

> My God, whom I praise, do not remain silent, for people who are wicked and deceitful have opened their mouths against me; they have spoken against me with lying tongues. With words of hatred they surround me; they attack me without cause. In return for my friendship they accuse me, but I am a man of prayer. They repay me evil for good, and hatred for my friendship. Appoint someone evil to oppose my enemy; let an accuser stand at his right hand. When he is tried, let him be found guilty, and may his prayers condemn him. May his days be few; may another take his place of leadership. May his children be fatherless and his wife a widow. May his children be wandering beggars; may they be driven from their ruined homes. May a creditor seize all he has; may strangers plunder the fruits of his labor. May no one extend kindness to him or take pity on his fatherless children. May his descendants be cut off, their names blotted out from the next generation. May the iniquity of his fathers be remembered before the LORD; may the sin of his mother never be blotted out. May their sins always remain before the LORD, that he may blot out their name from the earth. For he never thought of doing a kindness, but hounded to death the poor and the needy and the brokenhearted. He loved to pronounce a curse— may it come back on him. He found no pleasure in blessing— may it be far from him. He wore cursing

as his garment; it entered into his body like water, into his bones like oil. May it be like a cloak wrapped about him, like a belt tied forever around him. May this be the LORD's payment to my accusers, to those who speak evil of me. bBut you, Sovereign LORD, help me for your name's sake; out of the goodness of your love, deliver me. For I am poor and needy, and my heart is wounded within me. I fade away like an evening shadow; I am shaken off like a locust. My knees give way from fasting; my body is thin and gaunt. I am an object of scorn to my accusers; when they see me, they shake their heads. Help me, LORD my God; save me according to your unfailing love. Let them know that it is your hand, that you, LORD, have done it. While they curse, may you bless; may those who attack me be put to shame, but may your servant rejoice. May my accusers be clothed with disgrace and wrapped in shame as in a cloak. With my mouth I will greatly extol the LORD; in the great throng of worshipers I will praise him. For he stands at the right hand of the needy, to save their lives from those who would condemn them.

As you can see, that's pretty intense. That's not just calling for justice: it's calling for the active destruction of the target *and* the misfortune of their family. More interesting, however, is that, despite opening up like most Psalms with "an invocation... followed by a petition" to God for *why* this prayer should be answered, it then dives into a "long vituperative curse of the enemies"; it is one that "resembles the Mesopotamian 'namburbi,' lit. 'untying,' a type of prayer intended to undo a magical spell."[11] Moreover, the editors of the Jewish Study Bible take the time to note that "the complaint focuses on the evil words of the enemies; for this reason, many scholars posit that here and elsewhere the enemies are magicians."[12] This isn't just a curse, then. It's a *counter* curse, and it's a heavy hitter—both protecting you *and* serving back a boatload of nonsense that someone else sent your way.

But of course, you may be wondering if you're even *allowed* to use something like this—if God wouldn't be angry at you for it. After all, Jesus told us to love our neighbors (Matthew 22:37-39) *and* our enemies (5:43-45), so it leaves these kinds of Psalms and other possible cantrips in a state of limbo—unless you know a little bit of history.

---

11. Berline and Brettler, *The Jewish Study Bible*, 1393.

12. Ibid., 1393.

Is Cursing Allowed in Christian Witchcraft?

Sara says:

I used to be the kind of person that would say a hard, emphatic *no.* I would tell myself that magic was *only* okay to use if you used it for *love* and *light*—that so long as you harmed none, you could do whatever you'd like. That sentiment may feel familiar to you, especially if you were out reading the more Wiccan-centric books off the shelves of your nearest big chain bookstore, and that's because it comes from the Wiccan Rede:

> Eight words the Wiccan Rede
> fulfill: An ye harm none, do
> what ye will.

Even when I'd shed the more heavily Wiccan-influenced ideals I'd absorbed as a youth exploring the craft, long after my eleven-year-old self absolutely *labored* through Judika Illes' *Pure Magic*, there still remained that aversion to "doing harm." After all, hadn't Jesus told us to love our neighbors as ourselves?[13] Hadn't He even told us to love our *enemies*, to bless them so that we, too, might be children of God?[14] Doesn't the word of Jesus undo all of the more vengeful, retribution-focused personality God exhibited in the Old Testament? Well, according to the many priests, bishops, and even Saints and Popes over the course of the Catholic church's existence, it seems that *no,* God's vengeful nature never fully went away—and that, in fact, Jesus inherited quite a good deal of it, if we look at apocryphal documents like the Infancy Gospel of Thomas or the Canonical Gospels.

In the Infancy Gospel of Thomas, which opens by describing Thomas as "the Philosopher," we see Jesus get into mischief.[15] There are several instances in which Jesus not only curses other children for seemingly silly reasons (including, but not limited to, poking at a puddle Jesus was standing over with a stick or cutting Jesus off while He was walking), and not only does He curse them, but He curses them *to death*—to the point that St. Joseph has to reprimand Jesus on behalf of the grieving and terrified townspeople.[16] If you don't believe me

---

13. Matthew 22:37-39

14. Matthew 5:43–44

15. Infancy Gospel of Thomas, *Gnosis Archive,* I.

16. Ibid., III-IV

about young Jesus cursing kids to death, here's an example from the text:

> After that again he went through the village, and a child ran and dashed against his shoulder. And Jesus was provoked and said unto him: Thou shalt not finish thy course (lit. go all thy way). And immediately he fell down and died.[17]

And while I've mentioned it a little bit already regarding cantrips, I'd be remiss not to directly illustrate the fig tree debacle:

> The next day as they were leaving Bethany, Jesus was hungry. Seeing in the distance a fig tree in leaf, he went to find out if it had any fruit. When he reached it, he found nothing but leaves, because it was not the season for figs. Then he said to the tree, "May no one ever eat fruit from you again." And his disciples heard him say it.[18]

A few verses later, we find the results of this curse:

> In the morning, as they went along, they saw the fig tree withered from the roots. Peter remembered and said to Jesus, "Rabbi, look! The fig tree you cursed has withered!"[19]

As we can see, while our Savior here has some wonderful advice and boils down the Ten Commandments for us in a simple, easy-to-follow,

---

17. Ibid., IV.

18. Mark 11:12-14

19. Mark 11:20-21

two step formula, He wasn't always the best at following His own advice—and later Christians drew on that *heavily.*

Moreover, you may have noticed that I've mentioned a little bit about cursing before from Martin Duffy's *Anathema Maranatha* when discussing the use of bells. It's from Duffy's work that we come to understand just how important the imprecatory arts was to early Christians, who needed some way to get God's attention when people were giving them a hard time. He writes:

> Whilst many modern Christians consider it antithetical to use a 'positive' and godly force for the obtainment of a 'negative' effect, the practice of using prayer and holy items to evoke curses was once quite acceptable. Indeed, whilst modern societies now place much emphasis on restorative justice, in earlier times the concept of 'justice' had a very different and much more Old Testament feel.[20]

This is a fascinating statement, especially alongside one of the most interesting observations Duffy makes in his work:

It is also notable that many of the saints' imprecatory powers, such as making the land barren, withering limbs, and causing people to become paralyzed or fixed to the spot, are also firmly associated with witchcraft and the evil eye.[21]

Unlike witches, though, who were thought to do their magic at the *detriment* of the church, these holy men of God especially—priests and bishops and Saints and the like—did some *powerful* baneful magic, which was "presumed to work by grace of God and the intercession of his holy retinue."[22] This was especially important in a time where law enforcement wasn't the most efficient or useful thing, as with all the reasons Duffy gives that a representative of God like a priest or monk would go slinging curses, one of those reasons was to dissuade people from committing crimes against them, their monasteries, their chapels, and their flocks.[23] These clergymen and Saints were considered "religious virtuosos capable of wielding divine power for the purposes of blessing and cursing," and they were seen as those who walked in the footsteps of the great prophets and miracle workers of the Bible itself as they cast their own miracles and laid waste to enemies of the Church and their communities.[24] In essence, whatever

---

20. Duffy, *Anathema Maranatha*, 122.

21. Ibid., 32.

22. Ibid., 7.

23. Ibid., 37.

24. Ibid., 37.

ill they wished on people–especially if it worked–was considered to be co-signed by God Himself.

Of course, while clergy would share *blessing* booklets with each other (and still do, given many a Catholic priest will use something like the *Book of Blessings* for their liturgical or other blessings), the curses weren't so easy to come by. The reason we know of the existence of such curses is because priests would write them down in "Bibles, books of prayer, and other religious texts" that clergy used, scrawled in margins and made as notes for use whenever.[25] Among clergy, these curses could be of a variety of different types, be they:

- **imprecatory prayer** (as in, simple prayers meant to directly call God's wrath on people),

- **liturgical prayer** (in which a priest would read a curse on usually an excommunicated person to the congregation, thus sealing its power by making other people aware and also believing the person had been cursed),

- **clamours** (which Duffy describes as "a vigorous appeal to God and His holy retinue—the apostles, confessors, and saints—for preternatural aid," often combined with other curses), and

- **excommunications** (which "gave rise to the colloquialism, 'by bell, book, and candle'" because of how the "solemn ritual carried out by a bishop and twelve priests" would call upon God to extinguish the person's presence from His sight for their wrongdoings as part of the Church).[26]

Some of the curses are simple, only a few lines long, while some are *extreme*, going on and eviscerating their targets. But again, because these were alleged men of God, no one questioned them. No one even had the *right* to question them.

But it wasn't just the clergy that would do all of these things. Even ordinary people would cast some gnarly curses, with some interesting formats and methods. After all, in a time where "few amongst the general populace could afford the cost of bringing a prosecution to the courts of law," there had to be *some* way of getting justice for wrongdoing—and if the courts of Man could be no help, then issues would have to be brought up before the equalizing, accessible, divine court of God.[27] Whether this meant asking a priest to curse someone on their behalf, or just going out and doing something like a "black fast," in which one sends all the negative feelings and pains of fasting at their target in the form of raw malignant energy to *kill* them, people

---

25. Ibid., 41.

26. Ibid., 40-52.

27. Ibid., 121.

had their ways of getting justice from a God that, per Exodus 22:21-24, Deuteronomy 10:17, and other places in the Bible, is shown to be one who hears the call of the oppressed and brings the sword down on their oppressors in response.[28]

One could also use such holy curses, or maledictions, to drive out the forces of the witches who did them and theirs harm (in which they might have recited "Psalms 8, 27, 101 (102), and 108 (109) backwards" over a poppet representing the witch before burying it to nullify the witch's power), or to discover thieves (in which they charmed a piece of cheese to get stuck in the throat of a lying thief that ate it so they could identify him), or any other number of reasons one would have to fire magic bullets on their community members.[29] We might now understand what Gideon Bohak and Geza Vermes meant when they mention how rabbis would have trouble fighting a witch's magic with their own miracle, because for all intents and purposes, this is exactly what it sounds like: one magician staving off the works of another with counter curses (commonly referred to today as *baneful protections* and *return-to-sender* spells).[30]

In short, no, cursing is not against God. Or, rather, as Duffy explains based on the evidence presented in his work, cursing in *general* isn't against God; it's only when "there is discord between the curse's motivation and God's law" that it becomes an issue.[31] I've done baneful workings myself, when directed to by God to do so. For the most part, I still think that one should always make sure that baneful work is necessary before going through with it, as it can become so very easy to sink into a state of *vengefulness* rather than stay one seeking nothing more than justice. It can also be easy to let one's ego go unchecked and delude oneself into thinking that one is justified in cursing people for petty transgressions. I'll tell you this now: as God doesn't stop us from making *physical* actions on this earth (as in, He isn't coming out of heaven to personally stop you from lying or cheating or stealing), neither will He directly block you from poking the magical bear and starting fights with other witches, either. However, He will feel suspiciously M.I.A. when you start feeling the consequences of your actions, because that's where the (often very hard) learning happens. God is a God of justice, and true justice, remember, takes no bribes—nor does it tolerate whining if you get cosmically smacked for doing something you shouldn't have. Nonetheless, now is a wonderful time to discuss some personal experiences with spellwork (including baneful workings), as well as the ways in which you might seek out certain formats in the Bible to conduct your work, or even write some yourself.

---

28. Ibid., 121, 28.

29. Ibid., 102, 45.

30. Vermes, "Jewish Magic and Miracle Workers," 682.

31. Duffy, *Anathema Maranatha*, 24.

Writing Your Own Spells (and Knowing When to Use Them)

First and foremost, let me make something very clear: spellwork should be your *last* resort when it comes to a problem you're facing or a thing you're trying to achieve. If you skip to doing magic on someone before ever trying the obvious things first, like:

- Talking through the issue with the other person

- Getting outside perspectives to balance and ground yourself

- Coming to some kind of solution or compromise

- Setting boundaries (even if it means removing the person from your life)

- Actually creating a relationship with the person organically (before doing love spells)

Then you set yourself up for a big chance to create a mess. In fact, in *all* cases, it's best to check for mundane reasons things might be happening first. Have you really been hexed, or are you just having a bad day? Is there really a spirit causing mayhem in your house, or was that just a shadow of an object that is in a place you usually don't put it? Are you getting messages through seeing random animals, objects, or other such "signs" about a certain topic, or are you just subconsciously looking for these things and falling into confirmation bias? Are you under spiritual attack and need to do a massive self-exorcism... or do you just have a cold and need a box of tissues by your bedside?

Every good Witch, every responsible Christian, should have no problem defaulting to probability, logic, and ration *first* before diving into supernatural conclusions. This helps you keep grounded in reality and prevents you from developing an especially nasty and complex issue we've mentioned already: *spiritual psychosis*. While many people, including us writers of this book, have had meaningful and beautiful experiences with non-corporeal entities (from Jesus and angels to Lucifer and demons, from God Himself to pagan gods, from nature spirits to Saints, which we touch on in Section Four), not everyone has the same experiences. Not everyone *can* safely have these experiences. And when it comes time to use magic under the watchful eye of our guardian spirits, there are many people to whom the concept of such power, and the implications of it, greatly destabilize and upset their mental state. At best, it can cause paranoia, deep fear, and debilitating worries. At worst, it can even cause *death*, given the stories of people trying to, for example, jump into a busy street and stop cars with their minds.

If you've exhausted all sensible, mundane options to the point that you don't know what else to do, it may be time to cook up a spell. It can be a deeply focused, organized spell with lots of items and a sacred space set for it (a ritual), a quick charm or cantrip spoken aloud, an item or sigil infused with your magic (an enchantment), or a tangible item that takes in your intents and energy to operate (things like jar spells, blessed food, potions, etc.). No matter what you choose to do, though, in order to keep it from being overwhelming, there are some tips we can share. These will make it easier to use the free spell creation sheets that come with this book.

Before Writing the Spell: Doing Divination

Sara says:

Now, you can do whatever you'd like—but if you're just starting out in the craft, it is critical that you use your divination skills wherever possible. Even as a fairly experienced witch myself, I will still consult with God via tarot or other divination methods over whether I should even do a spell at all, never mind what kind I should do. By doing this, I can show my respect to God by deferring to His guidance first, *and* I can get some outside perspective on the issue that maybe I didn't see before because of my limited view on the issue. There have absolutely been times where I was sure I would want to do one type of spell, only for the divination results to show me that God was telling me to do a completely different type of spell for similar results. There are also times where God has told me to hold my horses and be patient for a little longer rather than whipping out the whole ritual altar for a situation. And then there were times again where I thought I should bite my tongue and simply ask for God's blessings, only for God Himself to tell me to bust out the baneful magic and get to work against someone who had done me harm with a pretty nasty hex.

Remember that in life, we don't have the full picture all the time. However, God and the angels? They all have a bird's eye view of the situation. They're able to see things going on behind the scenes that we're oblivious to, and they're able to predict the consequences of our actions better than we'll ever be able to. Trust them to give you some good advice before performing a spell, especially if you're stuck trying to decide what to do in the first place.

Tip 1: Deciding Your Intention for the Spell

Obviously, before you even get started, you want to know what you want to accomplish. What is the end result of your spell? How many ways can you think of achieving this result, and which way will align most with your short and long term goals?

For example: if you want to gain more wealth, you need to consider what you're trying to attract. General wealth and money is a simple prosperity spell, but if you're looking for a new job opportunity, it may make more sense to go with a spell that will clear any blockages in your paths (known as a *road opener spell*) to knock down any obstacles that stop you from finding newly opened doors in your life. If it's more wealth through creative pursuits, like art, writing, or other such goals, you may be looking at a spell that ignites your passion, drive, and planning in order to get the project off the ground and keep your momentum as you work. All of these will have different formats, Bible verses or examples of Biblical magic, ingredients, and spiritual allies to enact.

Tip 2: Finding Inspiration From the Bible

We've mentioned Leviticus 14 several times now, and it's because as an exorcism format, it's pretty good. We recommend it for anyone who needs to cleanse ill will and bad luck off themselves, because the format itself is intense, focused, and *clear*. However, it's also important to note that finding inspiration from the Bible does *not* mean that you follow the ritual exactly step for step (as, understandably, most people do not ever want to kill a live animal for an exorcism, like Leviticus 14 demands with the killing of one bird).

It's at these times that the concept of *application* becomes neces-sary. To use the Bible to its full effect, be it in the prophetic verses and Psalms that hold power just on principle of being inspired Word, or actual formats of ritual magic that are commanded of God's priests and prophets and kings and so on, it's important to know *why* these things are being done. In the instance of Leviticus 14, the priest must "take the live bird and dip it, together with the cedar wood, the scarlet yarn and the hyssop, into the blood of the bird that was killed over the fresh water"; after sprinkling the afflicted person with the blood, using the live bird as the tool directing the exorcistic power, "he is to release the live bird in the open fields."[32] While there's much more to this whole format, this is an important thing to understand, because while it seems terrible to a modern audience to do such a thing to a bird, the reality is that this is a very powerful magical symbol: it's most likely to represent the illness being banished from a community.[33] In ancient days, this whole ritual was seen as though the two birds are one, with "the impurity, after being removed by the blood of the slaughtered

---

32. Leviticus 14:6-7

33. Conner, *Magic in Christianity*, 133.

bird... [being] transferred to the second, live bird," which, after it flies away, takes that impurity with it and frees the afflicted person.[34]

We see a similar concept happen in the sin offering two chapters later in Leviticus 16, where one goat is sacrificed to God as a sin offering and another sent off to the wilderness after being presented to God, and each goat's role decided by the casting of lots (cleromancy). According to the editors of the Jewish Study Bible, the Hebrew word used here, *Azazel*, when split into the two words "ez'azel," is a phrase that has come to mean *scapegoat* (lit: "the goat that goes away,"), but the word *Azazel* itself means "the fierce god":

> It literally means "the fierce god" and as intimated by the medieval exegete Abraham Ibn Ezra is evidently the name of a demon or deity believed to inhabit the wilderness. Thus the sins of the people are symbolically cast into the realm beyond civilization, to become the property of a being who is the antithesis of the God of Israel.[35]

Moreover, because God commands this to be done, it isn't seen as idolatry by sending this second goat to the dark forces beyond civilization; according to these editors, this is seen not as sacrificing to another god, but something more like obeying the orders of a king who says a portion of a feast should be given to his servant.[36] Thus, you can see how magic in antiquity, especially that often sought after by the common people, was magic that promised to drive away illness and disease from a people, with officials like priests overseeing such a rite as part of the established religion. By understanding *why* these elements exist within rites such as those outlined in Leviticus 14 and 16, we might better understand how to replace these elements rather than following the exact steps unnecessarily.

In any case, one can replace those birds with two coffee filters full of herbs and spices related to the concept of banishing and protection, such as the skins of onions and garlic, cloves, and other related ingredients. Then, the spellcaster can tie them into satchels and set fire to one, representing the bird being killed, and dipped the other in its ashes, representing the live bird being dipped in blood, before taking that ash onto their own skin, replacing the sprinkling of blood onto the afflicted person. Afterwards, the "living" satchel" can be dispatched outside to have that energy taken away and dissolved in the wilderness. This way, one can basically recreate the raw concept of Leviticus 14 without needing the exact measurements and specifications and

---

34. Berline and Brettler, *The Jewish Study Bible*, 226.

35. Ibid., 232.

36. Ibid., 232.

other such things. In magic, and in many other areas of life, being able to draw out these raw concepts—the *why* of some action or rite or process—and apply them with whatever you have available is a boon.

Outside of standard ritual formats like this, however, keep an eye out for verses that ring out with the same themes as the magic you're trying to do. For instance, a fantastic road opener Psalm is these two verses (Psalm 107:14-16):

> He brought them out of dark-
> ness, the utter darkness, and
> broke away their chains. Let
> them give thanks to the Lord for
> his unfailing love and his won-
> derful deeds for mankind, for
> he breaks down gates of bronze
> and cuts through bars of iron.

The language used here—bringing people out of darkness, breaking chains, breaking down bronze gates, cutting through bars of iron—all invoke imagery of *jailbreaks*, freedom, a journey towards the light, and removing barriers. This kind of language, no matter where you find it in the Bible, is wonderful for adding that extra strength to your spells. Try looking through the Gospels, any of St. Paul's letters, or the books of any prophets (like Isaiah and Ezekiel) for some really good inspiration.

Tip 3: Choosing Your Ingredients and Tools

Another important thing to do is to not overwhelm yourself with a thousand and two ingredients and tools and other such things. It's unnecessary, expensive, and difficult to convince yourself to pull out on those lower energy days—especially if you're just starting out and haven't even built up your arsenal of items yet. One thing you can do is abide by a *rule of threes*. After all, if God appears to us in the form of Three (the Trinity), then three is a more than acceptable number to start with when it comes to grabbing tools. As you get more, and get better at organizing your tools, multiples of three (like six, nine, twelve) are also solid numbers for organizing tools.

Still, choose *three* herbs to start with that represent your intention, or *three* crystals if you have any on hand, or *three* angels if you know which ones you're trying to work with. There are so many herbs that have "protection" as a quality, that if you try to include them all, you'll just be creating one wild and expensive blend of spices to potentially throw away later. Speaking of blends of herbs and spices, if you're cooking a meal, it also helps to identify three ingredients you want to invoke within your meals. This way, you'll be able to use the same meal for a variety of different things. Spaghetti, for instance, can be an edible ritual of protection (onion, garlic, bell pepper) or of love (oregano, thyme, tomato). It'll make your magic a lot more versatile (and make it so you have far fewer things to put away and clean up at the end of your spells).

Tip 4: Deciding Which Energies You'd Like to Call Upon

You may notice we mentioned calling on three angels in that last tip. Along with tools, formats, and Bible verses, you might want to consider invoking certain spirits to help you along. Obviously, with God as the source of our magic, His involvement here goes without saying—but if you're trying to focus on specific effects, then specific angels or Saints can be a great benefit to you. Working with them is another story, but for everyday spellwork, you might ask God to send Archangel Gabriel your way to help with making sure the things you want to say land correctly, or Archangel Raphael for healing. You might also pray to Mama Mary for intercession if you're trying to start a family.

Incorporating spirits isn't mandatory to the spellwork, of course. If all you want to do is focus on the other aspects and have no other entities but God the Father, Son, and Holy Spirit in your space watching over you as you do it, that's a fantastic place to start. Using prayers to begin and end your spellwork, like the Lord's Prayer or Glory Be, are great ways to further include them into your set-up.

Tip 5: Incorporating the Flow of Nature Into Your Spellwork

Lastly, think about the *time* in which you're working your spells. While it won't undermine a prosperity spell to perform it during a waning moon (which, because the moonlight is fading away, is considered a good time for decreasing things and banishing things you don't want), it does *help* a lot to perform that spell during a waxing moon instead (where the moon is growing more full, and the light growing brighter, symbolizing increase and growth). Likewise, new moons are lovely times for planting new seeds and manifesting your dreams, whereas full moons are great times to harvest the fruits of your labor in this thirty-day cycle and further develop your psychic powers.

This cycle of *growth, peak abundance, decay,* and *peak barrenness* are found in more than just the moon cycles, though. If you don't have the patience to wait for the waxing moon for a money spell, you can also go by the cycles of the sun. Dawn is analogous to the waxing moon, dusk to the waning moon, midnight to the new moon, and noon to the full moon. The season changes, too, give you three months at a time to simmer in these specific energies. Again, you can still accomplish perfectly powerful prosperity and growth spells in autumn, but as the world slows down and prepares itself for sleep, you might find that any spells that have to do with banishment, exorcism, lightening burdens, or shedding and outgrowing that which no longer serves you will have an extra kick during this time of the year. Find the pulse of the world around you; tap into its rhythms and the flow of energy that our world subsists on. It'll only add a layer of harmony between you and God's creation.

Other things to consider include the astrological symbols, as the sun and moon pass through different signs all year long, and the days of the week, which are considered to have their own special meanings. For instance, if you have a goal of getting more organized and efficient, the new moon in Virgo that occurs in September is the time to give such a spell your all. In many parts of Italian folk magic, Fridays are considered days for love spells of all kinds. Meanwhile, Sunday, by its very name, invokes the beautiful energy of the Sun: warm, shining, optimistic, lucky, and bold. Any luck or abundance spells on a Sunday can benefit from that extra energy. These are just a couple examples of the ways in which you might include these celestial events or other calendar-based moments into your magic, and you can easily find such correspondences with a quick search through your favorite magic books or the many witchy blogs and resources online, then write them down in your own personal grimoires for easy reference.

All in all, your spellwork is not only going to be a way in which you can use your magic in the world, but a way in which you can express yourself and your power. No matter how many people believe that onion is good for protection, your spellwork will always be special to you, because it has your perspective, history, style, folk beliefs, and most importantly, your unique energy, woven into it. Nobody can copy that. Nobody can take that away from you. It's all your choice, and those choices all reflect your individuality. So go forth and dream up all the spells you'd like; test them out, write down what works and what doesn't, tweak things to fit your ever changing needs and situations, and most importantly, have *fun* with your budding craft! Be sure again to check out the QR code in the back of the book; there, you can find sample spells and blank spell sheet templates to start creating your own grimoire.

Chapter Fourteen

Incorporating Heritage and Culture Into Your Craft

Sara says:

For every American that says "I don't have a culture; I grew up in America," I can promise you that this isn't true at all. And by deciding it's not true and putting in the legwork to make sure it's not true, you can actually do some good work deconstructing not only your faith, but your very identity, too. This'll go a long way in combatting the *nationalism* part of Christian Nationalism as it continues to threaten our society. We've talked about its ills and the damage it does to people, this Christian Nationalism, but when we reject out of hand that we belong to any one nation—accepting instead the many stories that make up our family lines, the communities that stretch across countries and continents, and the old ways and practices of our ancestors that, despite being so distinct, also have so many similarities that unite such different people—we don't need to hide ourselves behind any one country's banner for the sake of our ego's pride and sense of self. After all, if we take a note from 19th century German philosopher Arthur Schopenhauer, we know that:

> The cheapest sort of pride is national pride; for if a man is proud of his own nation, it argues that he has no

qualities of his own of which he can be proud; otherwise he would not have recourse to those which he shares with so many millions of his fellowmen. The man who is endowed with important personal qualities will be only too ready to see clearly in what respects his own nation falls short, since their failings will be constantly before his eyes. But every miserable fool who has nothing at all of which he can be proud adopts, as a last resource, pride in the nation to which he belongs; he is ready and glad to defend all its faults and follies tooth and nail, thus reimbursing himself for his own inferiority.[1]

When we realize that there is more to us than the flag we were born under, we can make some great progress in achieving justice for all—and in keeping folk practices and diversity alive in places hell bent on making everyone the same. It can break the shackles of a nation's attempt at forcing people to choose between love for a country and acknowledgement of its sins and ills, and it can help people find a deeper sense of self that their uprooted family tree may have lost in its journey to new lands, new shores. It reminds us that we are all so very different, and that different is *good*; different is *exciting* and makes our communities richer, fuller, not weaker.

On a more personal and magical front, it can also help us take the witchcraft we learn about from the common introductory books on the shelves of big name bookstores and transform it into something much more meaningful, personal, and powerful. For instance, for someone of Slovenian descent, of course it's helpful to be able to pick up a common resource like Scott Cunningham's *Encyclopedia of Magical Herbs* and know that walnuts are associated with fire and the sun, with fertility and power[2] —but it's even more helpful to go into my own traditions and see the evidence of it. To see photos of *potica*, a common walnut-filled pastry, on the tables at every big holiday, at weddings, at other important events, I can tell that it's there to represent luck, success, fertility, jubilee, and so much more. With these associations, I get what I can't get from Cunningham's book alone: *memory* and *nostalgia* and a *familial connection* to the walnut, a sense of its *personal value* to me. I come to find a deeper appreciation for it thanks to the many positive memories I have that include one of the most iconic symbols of Slovene cuisine, history, and tradition.

---

1. Arthur Schopenhauer, "The Wisdom of Life," translated by T. Bailey Saunders, accessed November 20, 2023, https://monadnock.net/schopenhauer/wisdom-4b.html.

2. Cunningham, *Encyclopedia of Magical Herbs*, 255.

The Magic of the Mountains with an Appalachian Granny Witch

Mimi says:

The mountains call to you; their thick and twisted boughs hold secrets and mysteries that prick at your heart and urge your spirit to come closer. Something that has always fascinated me was the fact that, during the separation of Pangea, the mountains that became Appalachia were also part of the mountain range that makes up most of the British Isles. So it would make sense that their magic woven here in these forests and down in the hollers would resonate so well: the spirit of their ancestors spoke to them through the mountains that were sisters through time. The people who ventured to the New World and made their home in the craggy foothills and solemn mountainsides of Appalachia were folks of hard work and wit: mostly Scots-Irish and British immigrants who had Christianity imprinted on them for the world to see, yet practiced the old ways in small notions.

You can still see it in the horseshoe at the door or the salt over your shoulder, or the wariness that came with toadstool circles and the things that go bump in the night. There were also pockets of German and Dutch immigrants, with charms and red threads tied at the wrist or used in embroidery for Godly protection. Indentured servants and freed slaves were here, too, as well as the Indigenous tribes that knew this land and revered it. All of these people, as neighbors and then communities, had to rely on one another to survive. They borrowed and learned from one another, with the Bible as a focal point and common spell book. But as time passed, seasons turned into lessons for these families, and something that is unique to Appalachia was born.

The amalgamation of Hillsfolk magic, Yarb Women and Grannies, and the elusive Cunning Folk's mysteries were left in whispers of our past; it was bred out of survival, through magic and miracles that we would call medicine. While it may be known under names like Hillsfolk magic, Granny magic or Granny Witchin', the spirit of magic and traditions that permeate our homes and lives truly has no name. Like Memaw's biscuit recipe or secret ingredient to make the perfect cold remedy, these things have been handed down orally throughout the generations. But as with the sacred recipes and Bibles given from mother to daughter and father to son, we the children have come to keep the tradition and also let it grow into something our people need in this new day and age. And while, in those days, magic was considered something bad, their workings and worshiping as a way to serve God and "use the gifts He gave" (and by that they mean, the psychic or uncanny abilities people sometimes had were seen as spiritual gifts, from the green thumbs to the dreamers and all the in between). A lot of times, the workings were done without pay, or bartered for something later, as it was seen to be work done for the Lord; they took care of one another out there, and all for the sake of community.

Northern Appalachia boasts Catholic and German folk magic as well, and could be seen in the same light; after all, doing the work of God was an honorable task, and just because you used props like candles and incense doesn't mean your faith and intention for inter- cession wasn't valid. A couple of examples of the folk magic I grew up with range from superstition to why something existed in its way in this world. Take the Dogwood Tree: Dogwood was cursed with weak structure and flowers that share stigmata after the dogwood was (supposedly) used to crucify Christ. A more common practice for mid- wifery would be when Grannies would lay an axe head under the bed of a laboring woman to "cut" the pain of childbirth. Spitting on babies was said to bring luck, too. Sewing in prayers to your quilts to protect your family was common here as well since many quilt patterns had different meanings. A broom upside down meant company needed to leave (and bad spirits weren't welcome), while when a broom fell, company would be on its way.

Something that's definitely more magical that doesn't get a second glance is using the *Farmer's Almanac*. Farming and living by moon phases, astrological signs, and seasonal patterns was a huge part to surviving on the mountain; making sure you don't do any planting when the moon is in Leo or ensuring you plant your root crops during a waning moon is incredibly witchy to folks now, but back then, it's just how things were done. There were rules for when to cut your hair, when to wean and potty train babies, and for when to butcher and harvest. I had been told that using the signs of God's creation was the best way to live in God's creation. But now I see it as just another tool to use to keep me in tune with the rhythm of the world and be mindful of my intentions and tasks ahead. As far as using the Bible, Psalm 91 is the most well known biblical magical text; I remember when the women in my family would gather up their bibles and pray a 'hedge of protection' over someone, usually before surgery or if they suspected something more nefarious, by reciting this psalm before turning to their prayer books and corner spaces. Its use in protection and curse breaking is renowned, even if they never outright say that's what they're doing. Another that I was taught was to write out Psalm 101 and keep it in a locket or in my purse to protect me when I left the house. There were times you had to combine it with other Psalms to get what you needed done. And, as always, the paper or item was prayed over and anointed with oil or holy water while wailing the words out loud lifted the intention to the rafters for God to hear.

One thing I will say, though, is that in this part of America, the occasional tool or way of doing a spell in Granny witching will cross over with many different mystic paths, including ones like hoodoo, in a more modern Appalachian syncretism. Mind you, this does not mean that hoodoo is an open practice. While "hoodoo" is not specific to any religion, its concept of using what's at hand is seen in multiple cultures around the world. The part that ties into Appalachian magic also holds ties with African magic and conjure, mostly through means of protection and healing. It is noted that many root workers and hoodoo practitioners have used the stamp of Christianity and its tools to practice under the guise of safety in this culture, and it has become something of its own through growth and repetition. Things like holy oil and water, or having altars, or seven day candles for workings, are not uniquely hoodoo on their own, but they show that Christianity lends convenience in magical ways. Not discounting the blended generations of families and Melungeon descendants, I believe that healing generational traumas can also be done through the scope of practice by giving back the parts that are unique to their own respective cultures. (White Sage use and honey jars come to mind here.)

And I couldn't close all this out without mentioning a little something of the Ozarks. The Ozarks are a mountain range in the beautiful Midwestern United States, scrawling their way through the terrain of Missouri, Arkansas, Kansas, and Oklahoma. The wild hearts of families in Appalachia settled through here, bringing their practices and patience as they honed skills and spells in a new place. That doesn't mean it's a copycat! To the contrary, the Ozarks birthed their own kind of American folk magic. Water witchin', using the native plants, and watching the ways the weather and seasons changed, the craft hewn here has its own flavor and its own imprint on American history as well as American folk magic practices. Once again, we see the growth of healers and folk practices rise up to suit the changing needs. From hag stones to how they used their berries, and even settling fevers and STDs, the Ozark faith healers and folk magic grew into its own thing over the years. From one generation to another, the whispers and hints of magic still cling to modernized life.

The Culture of an Immigrant's Child with One Foot in Each World

Sara says:

However, if you're an American whose family has been in the country for at least a couple generations, and all the wonderful Appalachian and Ozark and other such folk practices have nothing to do with you by virtue of your being born somewhere *other* than those American mountains and valleys, chances are that you'll do a DNA test and find a myriad of different cultures and peoples within. How do you know which culture speaks to you? Do you have to find a way to honor all aspects of your family line? Are you allowed to start practicing any kind of magic from those cultures, regardless of what it is or where it comes from or what living practitioners have to say about it?

These questions can overwhelm the new practitioner trying to find their way through an already endless sea of information online, and I'm here to tell you that you don't have to use every piece of your ancestry in your practice. In my case, I actually only have a little under half of Slovenian DNA according to an ancestry kit, and yet it's the central focus of my practice, cultural expression, and understanding of my roots since my mother was born in Slovenia. When I look into Scottish, French, or Italian sides of my ancestry, I find it simply doesn't click in the same way as the Slovene piece does. When reading Mary Grace Fahrun's *Italian Folk Magic* (a wonderful introductory guide to Italian Americans looking to reconnect to their ancestry), I found that I may as well have been reading a book on Japanese or Latvian or Turkish folk magic; it didn't feel like it was for me, or that I had any inherent connection to it. Given I've grown up listening to Slovenian music, eating Slovenian food, hearing the Slovene language spoken in between bits of German when my oma came to visit, have learned that language myself, have been to the country of Slovenia, and have obtained dual citizenship there, my connection with this part of my ancestry will of course be stronger than all the others. This can happen, and that's okay; it doesn't mean you're betraying your ancestors or anything of the sort. What it does mean is that certain things make more sense to people than other things. That's all.

And let me be clear: if you're from a country that's made up pre-dominantly of immigrants, such as Canada, the United States, or Australia, that doesn't mean that your sense of roots and ancestry can only come from the country your ancestors originated in. Despite my deep love for my family's home country, I also have a great fondness for the state I've lived in my whole life: Rhode Island. The tiniest state in the country, known once as "the Armpit State"—a place full of rabble rousers and troublemakers, of exiles and hooligans—is one that has such a fascinating blend of cultures within its tiny borders. Its maritime charm, being the Ocean State, and its specific treasures, like coffee milk and Del's lemonade and the Big Blue Bug, make it a place that few Rhode Islanders ever manage to fully leave behind. Growing up here has impacted my lifestyle and personality—because where else in the country can you be in the absolute middle-of-nowhere *boonies*, nothing but farmlands for miles, and then thirty minutes later, be in the heart of a bustling and fun-filled city (while also being within thirty minutes of the ocean either way)?

While it's important that we recognize our place as diaspora—that this land we stand on isn't truly ours, and that colonizing forces have done and continue to do terrible things to the rightful inhabitants of these lands (in Rhode Island's case, the Narragansetts, Wampanoags, Pequots, and more)—it would be wrong to deny the distinct cultural differences that exist between each state or province and that have made their mark on you and your lifestyle. As such, when you think of ancestry, remember it's not only about where your family came from; it's also about where you are now, and how you connect with the land, how you make associations with native plants and the many spirits that inhabit the forests and marshes and cities. All of it works together to create the ecosystem that supports and sustains you as you continue building your connection with God and working your magic with Him.

So when it comes to incorporating your background into your witchcraft, get sentimental. Go to the things you know. If you really love the Atlantic coast because you've grown up around it your whole life, collect a couple rocks and shells from those beaches and keep them close. If the misty mountains of Appalachia are your calmest, quietest place, then keep that in your mind—along with all the memories of your Memaw's cooking (and her helpful tips that, by all standards today, were witchy as hell). And if you feel your roots stretching far, *far* away, someplace across oceans and rivers and mountains that feels seven worlds away, then honor that feeling. Look into it; research where your roots are trying to tether you to, and find the family history obscured by the sore realities of immigration and diaspora. Even the most mundane of traditions, from the certain type of music your mother put on each Christmas, can become a part of a meditative, magical experience when you practice them with the intention of *connection, grounding,* and *tying the old to the new.*

And there's no better way to do this—tying old family traditions into your new, witchy life—than incorporating them into your own *new* holiday traditions. As a Christian Witch, you have much more than Easter and Christmas you can draw inspiration, spiritual connection, and mindfulness from, and that's exactly what we'll explore next.

Chapter Fifteen

The (Syncretized) Wheel of the Year

M AKING YOUR OWN TRADITIONS is a way to help you feel part of
something bigger than just yourself, and in a world as isolated
and secular and *cold* as this overly corporate, productivity-obsessed
world can be, it's so important to be able to harness a bit of that holiday
magic (in the witchy sense and the metaphorical sense). No matter how
headache inducing the office lights are after eight hours, no matter
how tired you might be after a long day of school, no matter how hard
it is to look at a sink full of dishes after a day of cooking for your family,
it's the magic of the holidays that perks us back up.

Think about December's feel (if you live in a culturally Christian
area). The Christmas lights. The smell of fresh cookies and bread.
The cheerful decor and the way the moonlight shines off the snow
(if you still get snow this time of year). The hot coco and the classic
Christmas movies. These traditions are different from those of our
ancestors a thousand years ago, and yet at the same time, they're not;
these feelings, these sights, they preserve themselves over the ages,
tying us all together as we observe the Life, Death, and Rebirth rhythm
of the four seasons. It's a part of what makes us human, all witchcraft
aside; it's a part of what keeps humanity connected in one large story
rather than struggling along in individual, isolated fragments.

But of course, in more typical witchy spaces, the common idea
you'll see resurface every Christmas and Easter season is that Chris-
tianity *stole* all these components from the pagans. In fact, even some
Christian denominations will look down on those putting up a "pagan"
Christmas tree. However, it's pretty easy to chart what happened as
Christianity developed throughout the ages. It doesn't take a lot to see

that Roman influence over its far-reaching city states simply combined solar practices with Christian celebratory days through the ideas of syncretism. Moreover, bonfires, prayers, and feasts were all still a big part of the celebration.

Why do we talk about Roman influence? Because they had the biggest part to play in what shaped our current practice, Pagan and Christian alike. And because of the way Christianity was forced upon many of the kingdoms and countries across all of Europe, the focus of conversion was to educate people about the new religion—though by doing so, it also taught the locals to just slap the face of Jesus onto their old traditions in order to keep them safe from the Church's overbearing pressure and influence. If you don't know this, though, it'll just look like Christianity "stole" all these holidays rather than pagan converts *syncretizing* said holidays. Something that often eludes people is that concept, *syncretism*: the sharing of concepts between two cultures (be they religious, artistic, linguistic, etc.) until they blend the boundaries between them and come to be appreciated by both cultures.

Without syncretism, we actually lose a lot of our culture across the globe. Especially now, as families move around and away due to jobs, finances, and conflicts, being able to tie down a tradition and carry it on for future generations brings us full circle into the way traditions evolve—from the way we wear masks on Halloween (a Celtic and Slavic tradition for scaring away evil spirits) to the way we celebrate our harvests with bread and sweets. And even with Christmas, the lights hung to give it all a cozy glow, reflecting the traditions of Yule and Saturnalia by carrying the light through the darkness of winter.

Now, we would never tell you that evergreen and mistletoe and winter demons like Krampus were a part of the original Christian faith—because of course Bethlehem didn't have pine trees and deep, dark, snowy winters. Their cultural traditions wouldn't have evolved the same way as many European ones did because of the differences in culture, environment, and tradition already in the area of Jesus's birth. There absolutely *is* a pagan element to Christian holidays that would be wrong to dismiss; no one can, or should, deny the origins of many of these traditions. Knowing this, you may be wondering how it's possible to incorporate such cultural pieces into Christianity when people tell you that all things not explicitly church-flavored have been *stolen* from so many different peoples. So before we go any further into how to find and incorporate new traditions, let's take a more in-depth look at Rome, syncretism, and cultural preservation of pagan ways in Christian life.

Syncretism and its Transformative Powers for Pagans-Turned-Christian

Knowing what syncretism is, you might guess how it would be a natural consequence of two separate cultures, faiths, or even languages being in close proximity to each other. There's no exception with the case of Christianity and pagan faiths. The clearest signs we can see are in cases like Christmas, where the Scandinavian cultures (like Sweden or Norway) still call the holiday *Jul* (Yule) and where the Yule log tradition still holds fast.

There were many reasons a group would engage in syncretism, especially with the rise of Christianity: firstly, because it's the culture they've always known and they want to keep doing their traditions. Secondly, to continue pagan ways—even under the cloak of Christian religion—is an act of resistance in a time where missionaries won't leave you alone and foreign kings want to use religion to justify taking your lands. For example, Ruth Mazo Karras, in her discussion of the conversion of Saxony (modern day Germany), she notes that "the most common way in which pagan ideas survived the coming of Christianity to Saxony...was by clothing the new religion in terms of the old."[1] It worked the other way around, too, though: in order to relate to these people, who resisted the erasure of their culture by, say, stubbornly holding onto funeral practices like cremation even when banned from doing so by Christian officials, missionaries had to also try and put Christianity in pagan terms—which inevitably led to Saxony's Christianity taking on a more pagan flavor.[2]

All this considered, it was simply easy for what Karras calls "poorly instructed converts" to reconcile all matters of "superstitious" and pagan ideas—from magic to predicting the future to weather and garden spirits—into a new religion.[3] All you had to do was think of these creatures and occurrences as existing within the same ecosystem as God and His angels. Or, rather, one might have even watched Christianity, a monotheistic religion, "[adapt] itself to a polytheistic religion of many local deities through the development of the veneration of Saints."[4] This, especially, holds an important piece of the puzzle for especially Catholic-based folk magic and folk culture, as many Saints have since replaced the native gods of an area for the yearly festivals and celebrations.

One good example is Green George in Slovenia. What was originally a holiday for the spring god, a heroic figure known as Vesnik (the male counterpart of Vesna), to defeat the throes of winter and liberate the people from the icy cold, became instead a holiday for St. George defeating a great dragon that had kidnapped St. Margaret.[5] St. George's feast day being in spring meant that he ended up being *synchronized* with Vesnik, creating the folk figure known as Green George. Each

---

1. Ruth Mazo Karras, "Pagan Survivals and Syncretism in the Conversion of Saxony," *The Catholic Historical Review* 72, no. 4 (1986): 566, https://www.jstor.org/stable/25022405.

2. Ibid. 560, 566.

3. Ibid., 561.

4. Ibid., 570.

5. Mlakar, *Ethnobotany of Slovenia*, 125-126.

April 23rd during the festival of *Jurjevo*, St. George's Day, a young man would be dressed in all kinds of greenery and parade through the streets, where people would give him gifts of food and wine as he went door to door and then break off bits of his costume to hang over their door as protection against evil, among other traditions of the day.[6] It's a custom still alive today, as are many other interesting Slovenian festivals, and it shows the way in which new names were slapped on top of old festivals in order to continue the cultural customs without being outright accused of being pagans.

But don't think that this syncretism was only limited to Christians interacting with pagans. Pagan cultures frequently engaged in syncretism with each other, too—especially where imperialism was involved. Take the Roman empire, for instance; its standard pantheon of gods we might think of today, like Jupiter, Juno, Venus, Mercury, or any other such gods, are often considered the same as their Greek counterparts: Zeus, Hera, Aphrodite, or Hermes. However, they're not the same; they're *syncretized*, often combining the attributes of native Roman deities with the Greek versions. This was something Rome did across various cultures, including among the people of modern day England. According to Jane Webster, there is evidence to suggest a sort of syncretic pairing between the Roman god Mercury and a Celtic goddess whose name is unclear (though the best guess is that this goddess is "Rosmerta ('the great provider')."[7] This pairing wasn't just an accident; the Roman empire would purposely do these things in order to suggest a unification of their culture and the cultures of the lands they came to conquer, as it was easier to rule over lands that had some kind of unifying element (in this case, religion).

With all this information, you can better understand how something so obviously *not* Christian, like Krampus, could still make his way into Alpine Christmas season celebrations, or how eggs and bunnies could find Christian reasons for being incorporated into the iconography of a holiday about God's Son rising from the dead. Christianity is interesting in that its holidays follow a narrative pattern, with holy days marking parts of the Gospels and the stories afterwards that are significant in Christian lore. However, mixed in with them are those elements of pagan festivals that, as most cultures did throughout time, mark the seasons and the rhythms of the earth—and that's where we might discuss how you can incorporate *both* ideas into your yearly traditions and celebrations without overloading yourself. After all, it's hard enough to keep track of just a couple holidays, never mind *all* the Christian ones *and* the more typical neopagan seasonal festivals.

So let us show you a combined Wheel of the Year that you might follow as a Christian Witch.

---

6. Ibid., 127.

7. Jane Webster, "Necessary Comparisons: A Post-Colonial Approach to Religious Syncretism in the Roman Provinces,"*World Archaeology* 28, no. 3 (1997): 326, https://www.jstor.org/stable/125022.

The Christian Witch's Wheel of the Year

The Wheel of the Year is a calendar of six week intervals to cele-brate the solstices, equinoxes, and cross quarter holidays of the year. Examples have been seen in ancient history, such as the Celtic solar festivals and suggested in Germanic Paganism through Jacob Grimm's *Teutonic Mythology*. However, even though it was all loosely related, the Wheel of the Year wasn't solidified in new age practices until Wicca introduced it in its completed form in the 1960s. (This does not discount the astrological and lunar cycles that many practices and cultures held, however; in fact, they have also been syncretized into the Wheel of the Year and multiple seasonal practices.)

When you examine the Wheel of the Year, you may notice each holiday has a distinct correlating holiday in the Christian liturgical calendar. This lends insight to the why and how of Christian holiday dates, especially as they're presented in today's world: they're intend-ed to correlate with pagan holidays for the sake of making conversion easier and helping people syncretize holidays that already existed. These holidays, as a result, are largely Catholic, so it's important to note that you do not have to be a Catholic to observe these traditional holidays, just so long as you're alright with angels and Saints. These days, while they may not always have a full Mass, are still days to get items and blessings for your practice, like praying over a familiar or getting holy water. They're also a way to help keep you in the proverbial broom closet, should safety be an issue—though you should ask yourself: *is it worse if people in my community know I'm a witch, or if they know I'm Catholic?* In many especially Protestant areas, it seems both can be equally looked at with suspicion.

The most basic of practices, naturally, start with the equinoxes and solstices. Across all cultures and religions, the rhythmic changing of the world from Light (Spring/Summer) to Dark (Autumn/Winter) dictated how people lived their lives, like an inhale and exhale of time. Let's start there, then move to the cross quarter holidays.

Syncretized Seasonal Festivities: The Eight Holidays of the Year

For even more details, a fantastic resource is Anna Franklin's A Hearth Witch's Year *(2020), from which we drew a good deal of this compar-ative overview from alongside Vlasta Mlakar's* Sacred Plants in Folk Medicine & Ritual: Ethnobotany of Slovenia *(2020).*

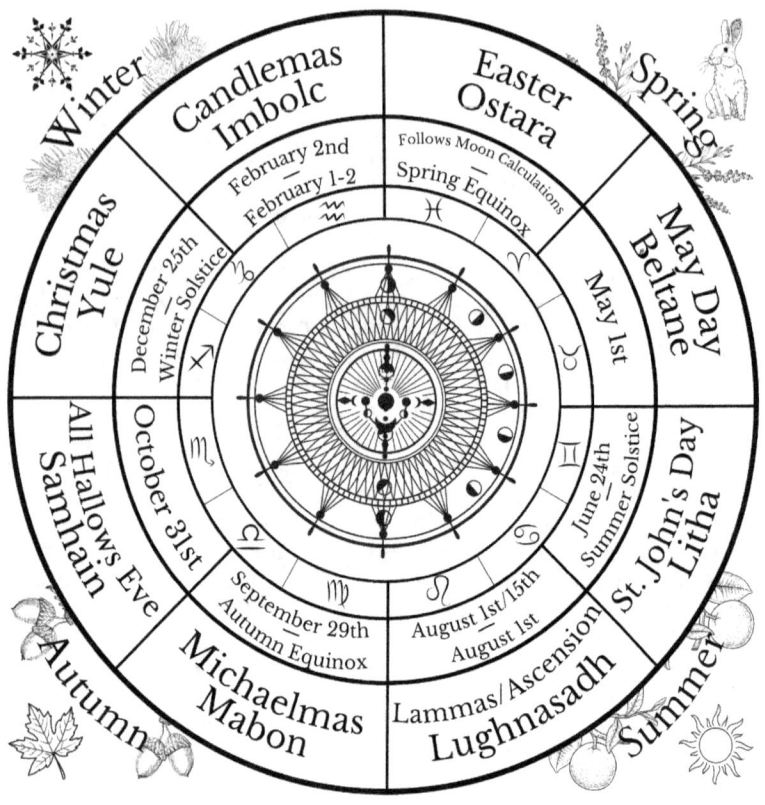

A Space for Notes on the Wheel of the Year:

Christmas †
December 25th

- Light in the Darkness (birth of Christ)
- Evergreens and candles (enduring the hard season of winter)
- Carols, an oral tradition of telling the story of the birth of Christ (became more popular in the Victorian era)
- Celebrations lasting to Epiphany Day (January 6th)

Common Family Traditions:

- Christmas church services
- Baking cookies or other sweets, caroling, and giving to charities
- Hosting big family feasts
- (America) Gifts from Santa Claus

Yule ⊕
Winter Solstice
(December 21st-22nd)

- Light in the darkness (birth of the Sun)
- Evergreens, holly, mistletoe
- Warm spices in mulled wine and cider brought protection, warmth, and vitality
- Feasting on animals culled for winter and preserved or baked foods
- The Wild Hunt made this time of year full of dangerous and harsh spirits

Light in the darkness is the theme here. With the pagans, it was the rebirth of the Sun on the equinox; the Christians brought about a celebration of Jesus' birth as their way of declaring the Light of the World in the darkness. The similarities between how things were celebrated—through laurels and wreaths, putting evergreens in homes, and burning candles—are just a few of the examples of pagan/Christian crossover. The intention behind them is what makes them so special and indicative of which traditions you choose to incorporate into your holiday season.

St. John's Day †
June 24th

- Big bonfires for the first harvest
- Commemorating the birth of St. John the Baptist (traditionally six months before Christ)
- Bringing herbs to church to bless
- Divination games for future lovers (like tossing flower rings onto roofs)

Common Family Traditions:

- Bonfires, fireworks, and feasting
- Attending church and praying
- Many towns have processions, parades, or other traditions
- Bringing things to church (candles, water, etc.) for blessings

Litha ⊕
Summer Solstice
(June 21st-22nd)

- Celebrating vitality, love, prosperity
- Herbs harvested on this day and thought to be extra powerful
- Feast of the first harvest
- The Sun (and related sun/fertility gods) reach highest power, spirits roam

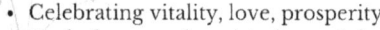

The roaring fires of summer herald the land's peak fertility and celebrate the soon-to-be first fruits in the summer solstice. So too does it lend itself to the power of the herald of Christ, St. John the Baptist. Just as the Oak King's power begins to wane and the Holly King wins his throne, the power of St. John's birth begins to wane to give it to Jesus for his birth. The parallels in stories help to push the narrative that the holidays really hold power, whether pagan or part of the church. And in between these major moments of the yearly rhythm, we have the equinoxes to help us along.

St. Michael's Day †
September 29th

- A day to celebrate the angels of heaven (with Michael leading)
- Feasts with goose, sweet bread, and blackberry pie (it's said when Lucifer fell, he fell into a blackberry bush)
- Food donated to the poor, prayer and thanksgiving for the harvest

Common Family Traditions:

- Setting an empty table seat for Michael with wine, bread, and goose
- Praying a novena to Archangel Michael for protection and help
- Celebrating and relaxing

Mabon ⊕
Autumn Equinox
(September 21st – 22nd)

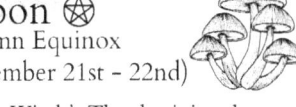

- The Witch's Thanksgiving, house blessing, and main harvest feasts
- Autumn fruits and vegetables as symbols
- Foraging, baking, and building harvest altars
- Expressing gratitude to guardian spirits and gods for the harvest

As the harvest season comes in, it's a time of thankful celebration for all who experience autumn. The underlying themes of defeating inner dragons and baking bread with your family to usher in good wishes and prosperity also make the Christian counterpart, Michaelmas, a great holiday to observe.

This is the Sabbat of thankful harvest for witchy folk, but many farming communities also celebrate with blessings over harvests and a good meal with friends after all the hard work is done. The main difference here is that Mabon is on the equinox itself, while Michaelmas is on the 29th. One of Mimi's favorite things is to celebrate the Sabbat for the whole week while weaving in themes of Michaelmas.

Easter †
First Sunday after the Paschal Moon
(Paschal Moon: the Full Moon after the Spring Equinox)

- Re-birth in Christ's resurrection, renewal and rejoicing the victory over death
- One of two major Christian holidays
- Symbols include flowers, eggs, the crown of thorns, the cross, and even rabbits because of Mary

Common Family Traditions:
- Coloring eggs (example: *pysanky/pirhi*)
- Bringing food to church to be blessed on Saturday (especially Slavic cultures)
- Easter Mass followed by family lunch
    - Ham, eggs, rich foods like *potica*
- Feasting, merry-making, *joy!*

Ostara ⊕
Spring Equinox (March 20th - 22nd)

- Celebration of spring birth and renewal in symbolism of sprouts, buds, baby animals, early spring veggies
- Cleansing away the dark of winter
- Fertility and protection rites for people and livestock, blessings for good planting

Aside from Christmas, no holiday is so deeply doused in misinformation and accusations of pagan-holiday-theft as Easter. So, how do fertility rites and symbols work with Christianity? Can these two ideals co-exist? Yes, actually, thanks to that recurring word, *syncretism*. Nowadays, we know that rabbits were super conceivers, as in they can get pregnant again while already pregnant with a litter. Centuries ago, however, that would've appeared to be a miracle in the eyes of the church, that an animal could get pregnant *without* doing the deed (again). That's why the rabbit, and its seemingly miraculous fertility, were conflated with the Virgin Mary and became a symbol of her. There's some very old Christian artwork depicting the Holy Mother with white hares either in hand or lap, which explains why these animals are still such a big part of celebrations like Easter, too: those themes of fertility are big around springtime no matter the religion.

As for eggs and how we color them for Easter celebrations, of course there were old pagan reasons for coloring them, too (such as the way Ukrainian eggs, *pysanky*, were once dedicated to Slavic god of the sun Dazhbog). However, they're also included in old Christian myth and tradition through Mary Magdalene. As we explained before, Mary approached Emperor Tiberius to declare that Christ had risen. He mocked her, saying that Christ had no more risen than an egg on the table was red. And in an instant, it turned a brilliant shade of red, which convinced the Emperor she was telling the truth.

And so, with these two stories here, we see that the eggs and bunnies so many folks like to poke fun at do, indeed, have their place in Easter via specifically Christian lore. The same can be said of those minor in-between celebrations—the four holidays that hold us over between solstices and equinoxes. Next, let's take a look at what are called the *cross quarter holidays:* the ones that come in between each solstice and equinox. We'll start with Imbolc and Candlemas.

Candlemas †
February 2nd

- Mary's re-introduction to society forty days after Jesus's birth (a tradition in Judaism commemorated as part of the story of Jesus's birth)
  - Sorrowful mystery: Gideon's prophecy to Mary in the temple
- Signifies a purification of the body and mind and a refresh for daily life

Common Family Traditions:

- Praying the rosary
- Bringing candles to church to have blessed for the upcoming year
- Eating pancakes or corn dishes

Imbolc ⊕
February 1st – 2nd

- Purification, the beginning of winter's end
- Dairy, honey, "stirring of the seeds in candles," all important to celebration.
- Centers around Brigid (as goddess for pagans, later synchronized to St. Brigid of Kildare)
- The time farm animals became pregnant

Once again, the Light is the big theme here with this holiday. As the midpoint between winter and spring appears, the Light returns to the Earth, and life can begin. The Irish goddess Brigid was so beloved by her people that her legacy lived on in Sainthood (St. Brigid of

Kildare) as the Christian conversions slowly replaced many of the old gods' feast days. Brigid is thought of as the patron saint of midwives, birth, dairymaids, cattle, chicken farmers... and the list goes on! Her presence is that of an almost all-encompassing spring Goddess, and her remembrance as one of the most important female Saints is proof of the devotion to her even after all these centuries.

Liturgically speaking, Candlemas has the same feeling with fire and Light. This is when you can take your candles to be blessed at the church to bring in the Light through to spring. The Feast of Presentation, like St. Brigid's Feast, is tied into the same cluster of days; each have their own meaning, but they all have similar themes. With Mother Mary having observed Jewish tradition to stay away from temple and society until the 40th day after giving birth, this date marks a celebration of both Jesus' dedication to the Temple, as well as their reintroduction into society; thus we, too, celebrate our own rebirth and reintroduction to the hustle and bustle of spring life. Either way, whether through Mary's honor or St. Brigid's feast, we have a way to celebrate this holiday within our Wheel of the Year.

May Day †
May 1st

- Celebrating the start of the month of May, especially dedicated to Mary
- Parades and processions for Mary to crown her the May Queen
- Religious rites to ask her to intercede for a town or church's protection

Common Family Traditions:

- Churches have more Mary-focused sermons and venerations
- May Crowning for Mary, picking flowers and decorating the church
- Singing Marian hymns and starting a garden of flowers and herbs

Beltane ⊕
May 1st

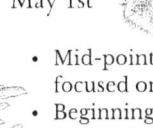

- Mid-point festival on the way to summer focused on increasing energy and warmth
- Beginning of planting season for many areas
- A time for decorating with flowers, engaging in fertility rites, dancing around the maypole

As the day marking the midway point between spring and summer, the night before May 1st was traditionally used as a time to light the bonfires and welcome in summer in full. These fires were meant to encourage crop growth and protect herds of animals. May Day itself was thought to be a time of celebrating fertility and praying for a good harvest. As these cultures became Christianized, May was dedicated to Mother Mary. In this time, it was custom to show devotion to Mary by praying the rosary or asking for intercession. Moreover, the emphasis on her being the Holy Mother naturally tied the holiday to the fertility of the land as well.

Lammas / Feast of the Assumption †
August 1st / August 15th

- Marks the day that Jesus took Mary's body up to heaven after her death.
- Holy Day of Obligation
- Signals the beginning of the end of the harvest season: this is the first big harvest festival of the year

Common Family Traditions:
- Great feasts and celebrations thanking God for the harvest
- Parades and processions for Mary
- A popular day for weddings
- Bringing loaves of bread made with freshly harvested grains to church to have blessed

Lughnasadh⊛
August 1st

- A festival named for the Celtic god Lugh
- Offerings of First Fruits to Lugh as thanks for a bountiful year
- Large focus on grains, fruits, and other late-season crops

Between the Summer Solstice and the Autumn Equinox is a feast celebrating the turning point from the growing season to the harvest season, especially with wheat, generally recognized to be on August 1st. With the first crop of wheat cut, the first loaves of the season would be brought to the church to be blessed in honor of the year's abundance. This would be known as Loaf Mass, shortened later to Lammas. The syncretism here is that the wheat and early fruit harvest were once presented as a feast for Lugh, a Celtic god (though giving thanks with a feast of first fruits is a custom many cultures share across the world!).

Another day for celebration is the day of Assumption. August 15th is recognized on the liturgical calendar as the day that Mary ascended to heaven. This has about the same function as Lammas, though it seems to be more popular for Southern and Eastern European Catholics.

All Hallow's Eve †
October 31st

- Final harvest
- Begins the three holy days: All Hallow's Eve, All Saints Day (Nov 1), and All Souls Day (Nov. 2)
- Recognizes all Saints and our ancestors
- Nov. 1 is a Holy Day of Obligation

Common Family Traditions:
- Visiting the graves of ancestors and leaving candles and flowers
- Reflecting on stories of patron Saints
- Church and praying for the dead

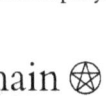

Samhain ⊗
October 31st

- Final harvest
- The veil between worlds thins for ancestors to come through (dumb suppers)
- Nasty spirits need to be tricked or scared away with bonfires, masks, etc.
- People go door to door for treats and drink

The Witch's New Year. Devil's Night. Spooks Night. Whatever you've heard it called, it all ties together with veneration to ancestors long past. Whether Saints or sinners, this time of year calls for humanity as a collective to pause and reflect on those who came before. As the glimmers of fall sink into the darkness of the impending winter, we see the acts of death and decay all around; as the cycle begins in Light, so too does it descend back into darkness.

Thanks again in part to Pope Gregory I, who suggested that the Celts be converted instead of all their traditions destroyed, the remnants of the Celts' celebrations remained for centuries and were carried over by Irish immigrants into America. What we hold now is far more commercialized, but behind every spooky mask and Jack-o-lantern smile is the whispers of tradition from those long-past ancestors.

Specialty Holidays in the Church and Across Cultures

Shrovetide

This festival is better known as Mardi Gras (as well as Fat Tuesday, Pust, Fasching, or Maslenitsa) and is seen as the one last hurrah before Ash Wednesday and Lent begins. Other cultural traditions and pagan carry-overs, such as those seen in Slovenian Kurenti, are a way to say good-bye to winter and prepare for the spring. People eat, drink, and make merry here, filling streets with the costumes and cheer of the carnival spirit; they go all out with the celebrations before forty days of solemn reflection on the end of Christ's story.

Lent

This forty-day liturgical season lasts from Ash Wednesday through Easter Sunday. Traditionally, folks go to church on Ash Wednesday to get blessed and marked with ashes on their head, symbolizing how we are all made of dust, and to dust we'll all return. The main tradition is the idea of giving up something important or picking up a spiritual practice to dedicate oneself to for these forty days. Most people give up things like chocolate or soda, but you might also consider adding something, like committing to being more charitable with your time or money during the season. The biggest custom, however, is to give up eating red meat on Fridays and Ash Wednesday as a way to honor Jesus's sacrifice of His own flesh, with people typically opting for fish or vegetarian meals instead. (Orthodox folks, on the other hand, will avoid all animal products all throughout Lent—purely vegan for forty days.)

A great way to reflect on this somber event comes on Good Friday, the Friday directly before before Easter celebrations. Consider lighting a candle that day and having a moment of silence to reflect on the story of Christ in full: His message, His imprisonment, and His death at the hands of a cruel and callous empire. Three o'clock in the afternoon is generally recognized as the hour He died on the cross, and that's when the candle is lit.[8]

---

8. Matthew 27:45-46

Other Notable Saint Feast Days:

- St. Martin's Day (November 13): when grapes are made into wine, celebrated with goose roast, in Slovenia considered an "Autumn Pust" (Shrovetide).

- St. Valentine's Day (February 14): absorbed some of the customs of Roman Lupercalia &, because of time of year, became associated with love & fertility.

- National Saint Days (St. Joseph's Day, March 19, for Italy, St. Patrick's Day, March 17, for Ireland) would be good for connecting with ancestors as well.

Other things include those like Lazarus Day, celebrating the raising of Lazarus, the day before Palm Sunday (the Sunday before Easter). If there is another lesser known Saint that resonates with you, whether personally or because of your cultural ties, by all means, celebrate their day as part of your yearly traditions!

Celebrating the Monthly Rhythms of the Moon

A favorite rhythm of many witches is the monthly cycle of the moon. Moon cycles and the astrological seasons can hold just as much importance for your practice and meaning to your every day as liturgical dates and pagan celebrations. (In fact, a lot of Appalachian folk practice revolves around moon cycles and astrological sign movement.) Start with the Full and New Moon, and see where it takes you! Feel free to also download our printable templates for crafting your own full and new moon rituals, which you can find at the QR code in the back of the book.

Full moon magic:

- For harvesting your efforts

- Psychic power, love, money

- Releasing unnecessary things

- Supercharging intent

New moon magic:

- Planting seeds for new goals

- Resetting & reflection

- Planning, starting fresh

- Manifesting desires

Celebrate Even the Little Things

One of the hardest things when you first begin questioning and de-constructing habits and practices from the church is continuing old traditions, or even picking up new ones. What if you're not ready? What if you just can't wrap your head or heart around celebrating when you have doubts or worries? It's ok. No, really! You can follow other cycles to find a connection and meaning in your world, and you can create traditions that are special and meaningful to you, no matter what's considered "traditional" or "correct."

All of this can be overwhelming, especially for those who are just starting out or trying to incorporate a more stable tradition in their practice. And it may even seem like too much expectation for a neuro-divergent practitioner or a spoonie witch. This is where you can make it as simple or as elaborate as you need. The best place to start is where you are, so look at birthdays, cultural holidays you celebrate, and New Year's Eve/Day plans. Even just lighting a candle, saying a prayer, doing an extra tarot spread, or meditating on the meaning of the day for you can be just enough. Remember that there is no exact way to celebrate!

Ask yourself: what days, ideas, or anniversaries are important to *you?* Build your list of important and sacred moments, and from there, decide yourself how you want to honor the flow of time and space: of memory recall and creation, of seasonal rhythm and religious narrative. Do so with the aim of creating grounding, centering, and cozy traditions, and your calendar will be brimming with wonderful things—gratitude and grief, love and loss, excitement and peace. It will be a calendar that lets you sink into Life in its purest, most honest form, giving you room to flourish within it.

And there's nothing more magical than that.

Section 4

Encountering the World
Beyond the Veil

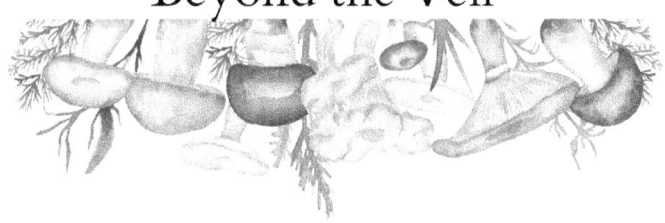

Chapter Sixteen

The Christian Witch and Angels

F OR CHRISTIANS OF ANY kind, there are some concepts that bring us a sense of comfort, and there are others that fill us with an overwhelming sense of dread, especially if they're concepts we're not very familiar with. Even Christian Witches might find themselves still radically uncomfortable with certain things that other witches seem just fine with (and, in fact, vice versa)! For instance, the chubby little Hallmark angels we see in stores, the statues of beautiful women with big bird wings, the statues and paintings and icons in our deepest Christian traditions of angels like Michael, Gabriel, and Raphael—these are things that still fill most Christians with a sense of comfort and peace (even the more anti-icon and anti-statue and anti-fun denominations). But for the Christian Witches who know better than to think angels are rolling around all sweet and playing harps and wearing shapeless bedsheets for robes, we know that these are agents of God that are here to teach, help, and protect us from the wackiest things in the Unseen Realm and the waking world. But other witches, who may not have realized how angels can really be and have since distanced themselves from Christianity, might find those angels... *difficult* to deal with.

The second a horror movie flashes the sigil of an unsuspecting and, frankly, scapegoated demon of the *Ars Goetia*, however, people are suddenly much more uncomfortable with the idea of these supernatural, conscious entities. Whereas our friends walking the Left Hand Path (LHP) are familiar with these entities to the point of working with, venerating, and worshipping them, those of us on the Right Hand Path (RHP), such as a majority of Christian Witches, may find this a step *too* far into the witchy world. After all, it's difficult even for people who grew up agnostic to shake the fear of demons and demonic possession that has been hammered into us with every scary movie—whether they be as old and classic as *The Exorcist* (1973) to ones as new and cutting edge in their effects as *The Pope's Exorcist* (2023). Demons are just *terrifying* and *scary*, no?

Sara says:

Well, when you learn that Christian and Jewish mystics quite literally invented the game of demonolatry—including how to harness their power for our own purposes in a safe(ish) manner—it becomes a little easier to peel back yet another layer of fear mongering, inaccuracies, and misconceptions we've all inherited from mainstream western Christianity. Even I, who hasn't grown up with any real religious trauma to speak of, had stretches of time where I deeply feared demons, to the point that I thought even looking at the sigil of one or speaking their name aloud would call them to me and offer an opportunity for them to torment me.

With enough research and stubbornness to push past those fears, I realized how this is not the case whatsoever. Imagine how silly I felt when I learned just how *little* the many Kings and Presidents and Princes of the *Ars Goetia* actually care about us, and how many other, more important things they have to do outside causing us trouble just for fun.

But as someone who considers herself an All Hands or Both Hands Path occultist and witch, I'm here to give you a brief overview of the two sides of the Divine coin: the Celestial Divine, with God and His angels, and the Infernal Divine, with Lucifer and his demons. This won't be a deep dive into either of these topics, as both of them are so extensive that entire books can (and have been) written on them alone. However, there are certainly places to look for more information on them, and after the brief overview I offer you here, it'll be much easier to know exactly what it is you're trying to learn about them in the first place as you continue your search for Truth.

So without further ado, let us tell you a little something about angels and demons, starting with the one you'll most likely want to investigate first as a Christian Witch.

The Function and Power of Angels in Christian Witchery

One of the most unfortunate things to ever happen to our understanding and perception of angels was not their Hallmark card depictions. We'll say it clearly: the worst thing to ever happen was actually the *New Age* interpretation and seizing of them. For those of you who have had the good fortune to have never heard of Doreen Virtue, we hate to bring that fortune to an end, because if there's anything we need to get out of the way before we start talking about angels, it's talking about what they are *not*.

In the New Age spaces, Doreen Virtue is only one of the many gurus, witches, spiritual leaders, or whatever else these individuals might call themselves who worked with angels. She has an impressive string of books, online resources, and even tarot and oracle decks about angels (which Sara still owns and, at this point, enjoys using out of spite). However, Doreen Virtue—like many an "ex-witch turned Born Again Christian™"—decided one day that everything she was doing was wrong, and that she needed to turn to God and the "inerrant, authoritative, and sufficient Word" that she claims the Bible is.[1] If you are at this point of the book, though, you likely know very well that the Bible is... *not* any of those things. Nonetheless, her impressive list of publications—which included books with titles such as *How to Hear Your Angels* and *Angels 101: An Introduction to Connecting, Working, and Healing with the Angels* and *Realms of the Earth Angels: More Information on Angels, Elementals, Wizards, and Other Lightworkers*, and so very many more—are essentially moot, as Virtue has recanted everything she's ever done before hearing a radio broadcasting about "false prophets" and deciding to take it personally enough to derail her entire brand.

Honestly, we're not complaining. A lot of her work pushes some harmful ideas, like the idea that people can be incarnated angels or Indigo Children (an older term for the ableist and racist concept of Star Seeds, which are "individuals who believe they have come to Earth from other dimensions to help heal the planet and guide humanity into the 'golden age,'" largely started with Brad Steiger's 1976 book *Gods of Aquarius*).[2] The obvious problem with this theory is that it opens people up to *spiritual psychosis*, which, if you remember, we explained already as a psychological condition in which people experience delusions, hallucinations, and other adverse affects in relation to spiritual concepts, entities, or experiences. An example of what this can look like when it comes to these New Age and other spiritual practices comes to us from Routledge's collection of essays in *Insanity and Divinity: Studies in Psychosis and Spirituality:*

> There is an illuminating account where the author tells us that, in a vision, Jesus appeared to [a patient]. Later she felt as though she had to kill the devil. And, in another first-hand account of a psychotic breakdown, the author describes an experience of what was felt to

1. Doreen Virtue, https://doreenvirtue.com/2020/11/06/why-we-should-never-call-upon -angels/

2. Ken Drinkwater, Andrew Denovan, and Neil Dagnall, "Starseeds: Psychologists on Why Some People Think They're Aliens Living on Earth" (The Conversation, 2023), https://theconversation.com/starseeds-psychologists-on-why-some-people-thi nk-theyre-aliens-living-on-earth-197291.

be revelatory visions that led her to think that she might indeed be the next messiah. These accounts might feel familiar to many who have worked in acute psychiatry.[3]

As you can see, there's a fine line to walk between having a spiritual experience or awakening, and having an actual mental health crisis. But when you're *in* that situation, it's hard to see the forest for the trees. Bloated senses of self importance, as well as othering oneself or trying to explain why one feels "different," are a hallmark of spiritual psychosis, and it's something irresponsible New Agers like to push onto vulnerable populations, like neurodivergent children, who they tell are not, in fact, neurodivergent, but instead a "Starseed" or "Indigo Child" here to save the planet, cause a religious revival, or some other nonsense.

But what we will complain about is the fact that, for the most part, New Age sentiments have watered angels down into this "love and light" concept that has not, and will never, accurately translate to angels. Even in modern Christian thought completely divorced from New Age ideologies, there's an idea that angels are so pure, always looking out for us, so comforting and loving and shining with bright light that cleanses and refreshes us... that they forget that ha-Shatan, or *Satan*, is himself an angel and active agent of God (that righteously screws people up *with God's permission*, like in the Book of Job). They also forget that angels do not work for *us*, but solely for God, and that there are many stories in the Bible that demonstrate that *thoroughly.*

Like the story of Balaam and the donkey, for instance.

The only "love and light" you're going to get from angels is extremely *tough* and unyielding love that takes no excuses, and light so bright and agonizing that you may as well be staring directly into the sun. That's not to scare you off of them, of course, but it is to warn you that whatever those goofy New Age websites tell you about angels is *not* the most accurate stuff out there, and if you go looking to engage with angels based on it, you will not have as great of a time as you'd like. In fact, you may even encounter a trickster spirit that wants you to believe it's an angel so it can take you for a ride and steal your energy. Generally, trickster spirits won't answer your questions in a way that makes sense and will demand offerings from you before you even get started petitioning them like some greedy businessman, which tips you off that they aren't angels.

However, if you want to talk about things that *are* angels, it's important to take a look at sources that are not exclusively Christian, because obviously, Christianity didn't invent the concept of angels to begin with. In Judaism alone, we see angels taking shape as auspicious and ominous figures (like with Balaam and the donkey), mouthpieces for God (like in Genesis, when the angels visit Abraham and Sarah),

---

3. John Gale, Michael Robson, and Georgia Rapsomatioti, *Insanity and Divinity: Studies in Psychosis and Spirituality* (Routledge, 2013), xvii.

active (and sometimes even mischievous) forces in Biblical stories (like Raphael with young Tobias in the Book of Tobit), unwilling participants in the stories being told (like the angel Jacob wrestles to the ground for a blessing), expository figures that explain deep mysteries to human prophets (like Uriel with the prophet Ezra), and yes, even antagonists to Biblical characters (like Satan with Job and, in Christianity, Jesus). We see these entities being multifaceted, knowledgeable, helpful, and sometimes harmful. This is because there is no one way in which an angel does their job.

Were Abrahamic Angels Created in a Vacuum?

But let's step back a bit further. Did you know that angels aren't exclusive even to the Abrahamic religions (the most well known of which are Judaism, Christianity, and Islam)? It'd be a massive oversight if we didn't mention that, in other religions, such as Zoroastrianism and Yezidism, angels likewise play a massive role in the organization of their divine beings and understanding of the cosmos. Zoroastrianism, which George Foot Moore describes as "the only monotheistic religion of Indo-European origin" (as it's the pre-Islamic faith of the Iranians), is one that figures the supreme god Ahura Mazda at its head.[4] However, working under Ahura Mazda are three great archangels, and then yet more angels below them, which Moore explains are there helping mankind against the evil spirits that are responsible for all wickedness in the world. In fact, it's in Zoroastrianism that we find a dualism between a benevolent God and a wicked Devil that, had we described before saying anything about the prophet Zoroaster and his religion, people would think is Christianity. It's this religion, which was the official faith of the Persion empire as of 650 BCE[5] and which came to dominate Babylon after the death of Nebuchadnezzar and the later fall of the Babylonian empire in 550 BCE[6], that some scholars believe had an impact on some development of the concept of the afterlife in Judaism and, later, Christianity. One scholar, N.F. Gier, in the twelfth chapter of his book *Theology Bluebook*, for example, notes that:

> The Babylonian captivity was a great blow to many Jews, because they were taken out of Yahweh's divine jurisdiction. Early Hebrews believed that their prayers could not be answered in a foreign land. The sophisticated angelology of late books like Daniel has its source in

---

4. George Foot Moore, *Zoroastrianism* (Cambridge University Press: 2011), 180.

5. "A Thousand Years of the Persian Book," Library of Congress, accessed November 30, 2023, https://www.loc.gov/exhibits/thousand-years-of-the-persian-book/religion.

6. Peter Davidson, "Achaemenid Empire," World History Encyclopedia (2011), https://www.worldhistory.org/Achaemenid_Empire/.

Zoroastrianism. The angels of the early Hebrew books were disguises of Yahweh or one of his subordinate deities. The idea of separate angels appears only after contact with Zoroastrianism.

And to drive home the point about even heaven and hell not being defined the way we know them now, Gier also explains:

> The central ideas of heaven and a fiery hell appear to come directly from the Israelite contact with Iranian religion. Pre-exilic books are explicit in their notions of the afterlife: there is none to speak of. The early Hebrew concept is that all of us are made from the dust and all of us return to the dust. There is a shadowy existence in Sheol, but the beings there are so insignificant that Yahweh does not know them.[7]

It may very well be the case that these angels of Zoroastrianism helped influence an understanding of these beings as separate from God, as no doubt, we see often how these angels will speak as if they *are* God in the ancient, pre-exilic texts like Genesis. But Zoroastrianism's three major archangels protect people from the "assaults of demons," with "Mithra, Sraosha, and Rashnu [sitting] in judgement" of mankind.[8] Other angels work to help humans escape the evil influences of the devil, a character conjured to "to clear God of the responsibility of evil" in the divine narrative.[9] The God vs. Devil, and Reward vs. Punishment, is made pretty distinct in the development of Zoroastrian cosmology.

Likewise, the Yezidis have a fascinating take on angels in their ethno-religion, thanks to syncretic elements from neighboring Abrahamic religions (notably Judaism and Islam). According to Victoria Arakelova:

> In both cases, they are the seven great angels; particularly visible is the position of the four angels governing the four elements: fire, water, earth, and wind. The concept of the seven angels penetrated to Yezidism from the Biblical-Muslim tradition; in a very similar form and functional meaning it occurs in the religious beliefs of

---

7. Excerpt of N.F. Gier's *Theology Bluebook*, Chapter 12, as sourced from the University of Idaho, https://www.webpages.uidaho.edu/ngier/309/zorojud.htm.

8. Moore, *Zoroastrianism*, 219, 180.

9. Ibid., 180.

the Extreme Shi'a sects in general. In Gnostic tradition, too, there is an idea of the Seven Creator Angels, though associated with the Seven Days of Creation, the latter being a matter of interpretation only.[10]

One of the leading figures that makes up the Yezidi Holy Triad—a three-part culmination of what Yezidis understand to be their One God, or Xwadē, that doesn't seem far off from a concept of the Christian Trinity—includes "Malak-Tāwūs, the Peacock-Angel."[11] It's believed that this angel is also syncretized with the Islamic Azrail, "the messenger of death, one of the four archangels nearest to God"—but unfortunately, many other people of the region Yezidis reside in consider this angel to be the "embodiment of the lord of darkness," instead, causing "travellers entering the Yezidi environment at different times to describe them as worshippers of Satan" and leading to brutal persecution at the hands of other religious groups in the area.[12] It's led to an ongoing and systematic erasure of this group's culture, religion, and identity, which still poses a massive risk to the Yezidis today.

But the function of these angels is unique and parallels with many other cultures, in that the overall concept is that Yezidis believe one God created the world and handed it to these seven angels to govern for the rest of time. In fact, these angels parallel those in Judaism. If we take a look at the names of these seven angels, we see that some names are strikingly similar to ones we're familiar with: Mikail (Michael) and Jabrail (Gabriel). Jabrail and Israfil are "known in the Muslim tradition," too.[13] We find even parallels of the Adam and Eve story in Yezidism, in which it's Malak-Tāwūs that has Adam eat the apple and expels him from heaven, and it's Jabrail that takes Adam's rib to make Eve.[14] As we can see, within this region of the Near and Middle East, between religions like Yezidism and Zoroastrianism and Judaism, a lot of angelology seems to be shared and syncretized—as makes sense, since most culture and religion doesn't have the opportunity to develop in a vacuum.

---

10. Victoria Arakelova, "Notes on the Yezidi Religious Syncretism," *Iran & the Caucasus* 8, no.1 (2004), 20. https://www.jstor.org/stable/4030889.

11. Garnik Asatria and Victoria Arakelova, "Malak-Tāwūs, the Peacock Angel of the Yezidis," *Iran & the Caucasus* 7, no. 1, 4. https://www.jstor.org/stable/4030968.

12. Ibid., 9.

13. Ibid., 14.

14. Ibid., 15-16.

Angels in Christian Occult History and Philosophy

So knowing the background of angels, and how they've come to take on such personalized, deeply intricate forms in Judaism with the help of differentiating syncretic elements and developing understanding of God's agents in the world, it brings us to two important questions: what exactly *are* angels to God and to us as Chrisitans, and how do we work with them? Well, frankly, there are a lot of places we can go to answer the first question. While as Christians, we are barred from directly participating in Jewish mysticism (Kabbalah), as it's a closed practice, we can still learn something about angelology and theory from many occult resources and proponents, especially those of the medieval era. In regards to angels, two names of medieval philosophers come to mind: Dr. John Dee and Henry Cornelius Agrippa von Netterheim (known by many practitioners simply as Agrippa).

The latter, a German man who went on to become a "famous spiritualist and alchemist,"[15] penned several works, including the *Three Books of Occult Philosophy*, that describe what magic is, how magicians can use it, and how certain figures, like angels, may come to aid the magician in their work.[16] It also includes the *Ars Notoria*, a Latin text Agrippa compiled (but did not write) that has only ever been translated into English by one dedicated Robert Turner, "a student of magical and astrological texts," in 1656.[17] A deeply Christian man with a love of exploring the hidden world of spiritual understanding, Agrippa gives us an inkling of the nature of angels in his works. He mentions that some angels "are fiery, as *Seraphim...* and authorities, and powers," while others are "earthy as *Cherubum*" or "watery as Thrones, and Archangels; airy as Dominions, and Principalites."[18] Despite some of his predictable misgivings around "Witches" and women who partake in such witchcraft, as one would expect of someone alive in the 1500s, he does offer us insights like these:

> Light also is a quality that partakes much of form, and is a simple act, and a representation of the understanding: it is first diffused from the Mind of God into all things, but in God the Father, the Father of Light, it is the first true light; then in the Son a beautiful overflowing brightness, and in the Holy Ghost a burning brightness, exceeding all Intelligences; yea, as Dyonisius saith, of Seraphins, In Angels therefore it is a shining intelligence

15. Walter I Trattner, "God and Expansion in Elizabethan England: John Dee, 1527-1583," *Journal on the History of Ideas* 25, no. 1 (1964), 19. https://www.jstor.org/stable/2708083.

16. Agrippa, *Three Books of Occult Philosophy*, 1-2.

17. Benjamin Rowe, *Ars Notoria*, 1.

18. Agrippa, 13.

diffused, an abundant joy beyond all bounds of reason
yet received in divers degrees, according to the Nature
of the intelligence that receives it.[19]

If you notice Agrippa's mention of the different types of angels—which he calls "Triplicities" or "intelligible hierarchies"—you'll
notice that yes, there are different types of angels, and no, they do
not all do the same thing.[20] He describes these angels as existing in
the Intellectual world, along with Triplicities of the Tribes of Israel,
the Apostles, and the Angels ruling the corners of the world: Michael,
Raphael, Gabriel, and Uriel.[21] If we go further back from Agrippa, to
the massive text *Summa Theologiae* written by St. Thomas Aquinas
between 1265 and 1273 CE, we find quite a few musings on angels
and their hierarchies. He even gives us the exact Scriptural references
of which we can find mentions of Seraphim, Cherubim, Thrones,
Dominations (Dominions), Virtues, Powers, Principalities, Archangels,
and Angels, and he also notes that "it is necessary to observe that the
proper name of each order expresses its property" as "in the angelic
orders all spiritual perfections are common to all the angels," going
on to explain exactly what each of these names mean.[22] No doubt
Agrippa grabbed onto these ideas, these designations of angels, and
more from writers like St. Thomas Aquinas to craft his own alchemical
and occult based ideas—but it's difficult to piece together a distinct
idea of what angels exactly are from this ardent student of occultism
and Jewish mysticism.

If we try Dr. John Dee, we may find a very different understanding of
angels. After all, Dr. John Dee—the court mathematician, astrologer,
and *magician* working under Queen Elizabeth I—did the work of
actually *channeling* the angels and creating what is now known as the
Enochian alphabet and language, allegedly the language of the angels
themselves. He was a student at the university Louvain in France,
which was apparently "still under the spell of" the works of Agrippa,
and while Dee was in Paris, he "already had acquired international
fame as a mathematician," being "offered an appointment as a Royal
Mathematician with an annual salary of 200 (French) crowns"—but
rather than take the job, Dee returned to his native England.[23] However, as his pursuits in natural sciences (and occult knowledge) continued, people came to see him as "no mere scientist, but a conjur-

---

19. Agrippa, 57.

20. Ibid., 104.

21. Ibid., 104.

22. Aquinas, *Summa Theologiae*, q108 a5

23. Walter I. Trattner, "God and Expansion in Elizabethan England: John Dee,
1527-1583," *Journal on the History of Ideas* 25, no. 1 (1964), 19, 21, https://www.jstor.o
rg/stable/2708083.

er and magician of doubtful reputation"; he was even charged with "treason—using magic against the Queen's life—and heresy" when he read Elizabeth's fortune while Queen Mary still ruled.[24] But when Elizabeth came to power, she remembered him, and gave him plenty of work to do in exchange for the luxury of studying his many interests in peace, even making him her "court astrologer, magus and philosopher," which were apparently "perfectly respectable posts" at the time.[25]

Those interests, of course, included angels and the world beyond. Partnering with Edward Kelley, "who, in Dee's mind, had marked mediumistic powers," Dee was able to record the results of channeling angels.[26] Following the Hermetic Philosophers that "regarded the stars and planets as channels through which God transmitted his powers," Dee, himself something of a natural magician, dove into a world of trying to summon these powers, with Kelly as his partner so that he might remember what happened and what the angels said.[27] Though in our opinion, one of the shadiest things to ever happen was when Kelly told Dee that the angel Madimi "had counseled that [the two magicians] should 'share all things in common, including their wives,'" and when Dee initially refused, Madimi apparently insisted on it, until they did, in fact, all live together and share each other's things (and... each other).[28] Didn't last long, but it did happen. (Honestly, it's more believable that Kelly made a lot of this up just to see how far he could take Dee's confidence and trust.)

You'll notice some of the angel names that Dee and Kelly found (like Madimi) aren't really related to any angel names we know of in the Bible. Even still, for those who work Enochian magic (a style of magic named after the prophet Enoch, who had his own adventures with the angels in the Book of Enoch), there's a heavy emphasis on the language and letters that Dee and Kelly channeled together, as well as several "calls" or "keys" with which a magician might bring these beings forth for whatever purposes. This magic became one of the many moving pieces that would inform groups like the Hermetic Order of the Golden Dawn, whose magicians and magical systems would go on to support Gerald Gardener in his organization of the ritual practice of Wicca.

Now, while these sources are integral for understanding the development of modern angelology, they still aren't very helpful in terms of practicality: that is, they don't give us a solid understanding of exactly what angels are in an Abrahamic context or help us figure out how we might include them in our practice. (They are fun to know about, though, and so you can read more about other religions' angels and

---

24. Ibid., 19-21.

25. Ibid., 22.

26. Leo Vinci, *Gmicalzoma! An Enochian Dictionary* (Regency Press, 2006), 28.

27. Ibid., 30.

small notes on Dr. John Dee and Agrippa through relevant resources listed in the References section.) But in terms of angelology for the *magician*, we can look past the works of these medieval philosophers to one of the pieces of an anonymous 17th century grimoire, the *Lesser Key of Solomon*. As you already know, King Solomon is a legendary figure who Jewish historians like Flavius Josephus have written about in terms of his great magical feats, and who features prominently in Jewish apocryphal texts like the Testament of Solomon. As a result of his legendary status, several grimoires have been written in his name (as well as written in the names of other great Saints, religious figures, and more; one example is the Book of Cyprian, a Portuguese grimoire attributed to the pagan-sorcerer-turned-Saint, Cyprian of Antioch). One grimoire attributed to King Solomon is the *Lesser Key of Solomon*, also known as *Lemegeton Clavicula Salomonis* or *Clavicula Salomonis Regis* (Key of King Solomon). Within the five books that make up the Lemegeton—the *Ars Goetia, Ars Theurgia Goetia, Ars Paulina, Ars Almadel,* and *Ars Notoria*—two are especially of value to modern occult practitioners, and those are the first and last books.

In the *Ars Notoria*, we discover some extrapolations of Kabbalistic elements. Again, Kabbalah is Jewish mysticism, which means it is off limits to Christians (and even a fair amount of Jewish people, depending on which sect you ask). However, the reason we see it being so prolific in medieval Christian philosophy and in later grimoires derived from them, and the reason we see such differences in spelling ("Kabbalah" vs. "Cabala" vs. "Qabalah") is because many Christian philosophers and occultists sought to use it to connect to God *and* to convert Jewish people to Christianity. As noted by Don Karr in his work, "The Study of Christian Cabala in English," Cabala spelled with a "C" specifically "refers to Christian developments," drawing out of Jewish Kabbalah in order to use it as "dogmatic weapon to turn back against the Jews to compel their conversion."[29] It then evolved again into Hermetic Qabalah, which Jacobi describes as a "Frankenstein-like tradition."[30] She goes on to explain how this branch became something of an everything-but-the-kitchen-sink occultism like we see in the Hermetic Order of the Golden Dawn, where ancient Egyptian, Greek, and Jewish mysticism all gets blended together into some manner of mystical practice with no regard for the actual context and source material of said mystic systems.[31] But nonetheless, this proliferation of Kabbalah into Cabala and Hermetic Qabalah gave rise to the development of this *Ars Notoria* towards the 17th century, which draws on the Kabbalistic concepts of the 72 angels of the *Shem HaMephorash*, or the Explicit Name [of God]. These concepts were later outlined for Christian Cabalists in *De Arte Cabalistica* by German

---

29. Don Karr, "The Study of Christian Cabala in English" (Don Karr, 2007), 1.

30. Zo Jacobi, "Kabbalah vs. Cabala vs. Qabalah," Jewitches (blog), accessed November 30, 2023, https://jewitches.com/blogs/blog/kabbalah-vs-cabala-vs-qabalah.

31. Ibid.

scholar Johann Reuchlin in 1517. Knowing what we know about Cabala and Qabalah, it is imperative that we recognize the sources of this occult knowledge, and the insidious nature of the sources' intent (in this case, trying to convert Jewish people away from their religion using a warped version of their own mysticism and tools).

However, in these grimoires and Cabalistic texts, therefore, we do get some semblance of what angels might be from a Christian standpoint. According to Jan Veenstra and Jan Bremmer, it is through Reuchlin's work that we might understand angels to be "products of the will of God" that are "substantially based on the tetragrammaton," or four of the seventy-two letters/sounds that make up God's name (hence the *Explicit Name* is much longer than the Tetragrammaton, and is something Reuchlin pulled out of the verses of Exodus 14 to get an idea of this name).[32] It's also something Kabbalists already knew how to operate to display the seventy-two names of God.[33] Thus, you may notice if you ever see the corresponding seventy-two angel names, that they have a suffix like -El or -Ah put at the end of them to signify some aspect of God that they're referring to (for example: *Michael* means *He Who is Like God*, and *Hakamiah* means *The Raising God*).[34] It is this information that medieval Christian occultists like Agrippa grabbed onto and later anonymous writers ascribed to figures like Solomon for occult purposes and explorations.

Therefore, while much can be said about the anti-semitic origins of these "Cabalistic/Qabalistic" practices, and much respect can be paid to original Jewish Kabbalah in which this concept of God's Explicit Name comes from (as well as the respect to *leave alone the specific practices of a closed religion*), there is one shaky gray area that comes into play here. The simple fact that *these angels exist in Christianity, too*, because the God of Jesus, a *Jewish* Man, is the God of the Israelites, and as such, while Kabbalah is overall closed, there are pieces of it that bleed into our religion as well, just by nature of how the religion even came about. There is no avoiding every sliver of Kabbalah as a result. After all, the very same Archangel Gabriel that exists in Judaism is a defining figure in the narrative of Jesus's birth, and so too does Archangel Michael—the Advocate of Israel—have profound impact on especially Catholic culture, both in the existence of the autumn holiday Michaelmas and in the prayer to St. Michael the Archangel created by Pope Leo XIII in 1886, which is commonly truncated as follows:

---

32. Jan N. Bremmer and Jan R. Veenstra, "The Metamorphosis of Magic from Late Antiquity to the Early Modern Period," University of Gronigen (2002), 261. https://research.rug.nl/en/publications/the-metamorphosis-of-magic-from-late-antiquity-to-the-early-moder.

33. Moshe Yakov Wisnefsky, "72 'Names' of G-d," Chabad, accessed November 30, 2023, https://www.chabad.org/kabbalah/article_cdo/aid/1388270/jewish/72-Names-of-G-d.htm.

34. Travis McHenry, *Angel Tarot* (USA: Rockpool Publishing, 2020), 25, 47.

St. Michael the Archangel, defend us in battle. Be our defense against the wickedness
and snares of the Devil. May
God rebuke him, we humbly
pray, and do thou, O Prince of
the heavenly hosts, by the power of God, thrust into hell Satan, and all the evil spirits, who
prowl about the world seeking
the ruin of souls. Amen.

O glorious prince St. Michael,
chief and commander of the
heavenly hosts, guardian of
souls, vanquisher of rebel spirits, servant in the house of
the Divine King and our ad-
mirable conductor, you who
shine with excellence and su-
perhuman virtue deliver us from
all evil, who turn to you with
confidence and enable us by
your gracious protection to
serve God more and more faithfully every day.

While it can become something of a difficult dance to give all due
respect to Jewish people and their holy Kabbalistic practices and
knowledge, the fact remains that God is God, and if these angels
exist in one understanding of Him, then they simply *exist*. As such,
these angels can be called on for help even *without* knowing their
names—but by knowing their names, we might also come closer to
understanding what these angels are and how they operate.

Sara says:

Truthfully, I find it fascinating that Reuchlin describes these angels
as "products of the will of God," because that is exactly how I have
come to understand them in my own work and meditations with them.
These are genderless beings that visit humanity in ways that humans
can best appreciate them, though of course, they take on different
forms and physical appearances depending on how you'll best receive
them. According to Echols, "like the other anthropomorphic details to
follow, gender is just another tool to assist [a magician's] visualization

work," and he notes that the practitioner should "feel free to envision the angels and archangels in whatever way works best for [them]."[35] But even then, there's a reason the angels' catch phrase is "Do not be afraid," like in Luke 2:10 and many other places of the Bible: they can still appear obviously *Other*, and that *Other* appearance is terrifying. Occultist Travis McHenry, in his guidebook to the *Angel Tarot*, notes that the Grand Pentacle of Solomon, an old occult tool used to evoke these entities for questioning or for requesting favors, is one that helps manage the fear we might experience in the presence of angels as magicians:

> This pentacle serves to reconcile the benevolence of good spirits, and to granulise and destroy our fear so that we will be able to protect ourselves from the fury that may occur with [angels'] arrival. When the spirits gaze upon the beauty of this pentacle, it is so great that it restrains the spirits and compels them to appear under forms that will not cause fear or trembling.[36]

However, truth be told, I've never used these kinds of occult tools to encounter angels, and you certainly don't need to, either, unless for some reason you are *overbearingly* terrified—in which case, I would recommend working through that with God first before beginning to approach angels. Still, McHenry's *Angel Tarot* does serve as a brilliant tool, not so much for divination but as a means of invoking or evoking entities.

What's the Difference Between Invocation and Evocation?

Invocation is when you call on an entity to bring it close to you, in your space and with the permission to affect your mind, your countenance, and your very life. You may think of invocation as putting on the mask of the entity you're calling for protection, or speaking to them face to face with no barrier between you.

Evocation is when you call on an entity in a limited and separated fashion, usually with a magic circle separating you from the entity, or some kind of metal vessel or other binding circle keeping the entity contained, for the sake of safely questioning or demanding things of them. You might think of it like speaking to a prisoner via the prison phones as you watch them through a pane of thick, protective glass.

But it seems that the angel itself is, as a sentient intelligence and conscious creature, *defined* by the aspect or facet of God that it wears.

---

35. Echols, *Angels and Archangels*, 20-21.

36. McHenry, *Angel Tarot*, 9.

This facet tells you what you can expect of the angel, as well as what it can help you with. For example, Raphael, whose name means *God Heals* or *God Has Healed*, is an angel often invoked and prayed to for intercession among nursing students, doctors, and other medical workers, with occultist Damien Echols noting that one might invoke him "for assistance with meditation and mental clarity" (for example, to ace an exam) or "for healing of any sort."[37] Michael, on the other hand, is known as the patron of law enforcement professionals and soldiers, according to many Catholic sources. It's also important to note that the angels are divided into nine categories as we talked about before with St. Thomas Aquinas's list. This is known as the hierarchy of angels, which are as follows (and whose brief descriptions here we might thank McHenry for, though you can find more about them generally anywhere in Catholic resources as well):

- Seraphim

  - "The highest rank of angels... six-winged beings that fly around the throne of God." Spoken about in Isaiah 6:1-3.

- Cherubim

  - Angels that "guard the Garden of Eden and escort the throne of God." Mentioned in Ezekiel 1:5-6.

- Ophanim (Thrones)

  - The wheels covered in eyes everyone thinks of when they think of "Biblically accurate" angels. They "deliver divine justice and hold up God and remain forever in His presence." They're mentioned in Daniel 7:9.

- Dominions

  - These angels "appear as humans of perfect beauty with wings" and "are responsible for regulating the duties of the lowe ranks of angels." Mentioned in Colossians 1:16.

- Virtues

  - These ones are "responsible for making miracles occur on earth. They possess an unshakeable energy welling forth from their god-like abilities." Also mentioned in Colossians 1:16.

- Powers

  - These are the angels that "ensure the cosmos remains in

---

37. Echols, *Angels and Archangels*, 27.

order. They are warrior angels, prepared to destroy evil spirits or cast them down to prisons." Also mentioned in Colossians 1:16.

- Principalities

  ○ Principalities "guard and protect nations, races, and institutions. They are educators and guardians of the realm of mortals." Once again, mentioned in Colossians 1:16.

- Archangels

  ○ Despite being so low in the listing, these are actually "the chief leaders of the angels that appear among mortals. Their power is great and they serve God directly." Mentioned in 1 Thessalonians 4:16.

- Angels

  ○ Your regular everyday angels zipping around doing angel things. They're "messengers of divine light who descend from the heavens to minister to mortals. They have diverse powers and roles, and some are given specific tasks." Can do "great miracles" or "tremendous destruction." An example is the earthquake mentioned in Matthew 28.[38]

According to St. Thomas Aquinas in his *Summa Theologica*, the higher rank angels seem to have more knowledge of universal secrets, knowing more the closer they are to God.[39] However, we also know that they have a complete knowledge of good and evil regardless, which they exercise as they watch over us, per Aquinas again.[40] As beings with complete knowledge, angels have an advanced view of the world, the way you might be able to see everything on the field when watching a football game on T.V. In this comparison, us humans are the football players, trying to navigate the chaos of the game from deep within the throng. Angels are the ones yelling at the T.V. and wondering why we didn't make this *obvious play* (that's really only obvious if you're, you know, watching from outside the game rather than being in the thick of it). They can be brutal to work with because of this, as the lack of empathy or understanding of what you're experiencing as a human can create some gaps in expectations and reality for both you and the angel you're trying to work with. However, they generally have your best interests at heart as per God's will, and they are incredible allies. While we won't go through the entire list of angels and their

---

38. McHenry, *Angel Tarot*, 3-6.

39. *Summa Theologiae* I-I q55, a3.

40. *Summa Theologiae* I-I q58, a3.

functions here, as this in and of itself is an entire book (Damien Echols' *Angels and Archangels*, to be specific), we will tell you a little bit about the four archangels of the cardinal directions from our experience, McHenry's tarot booklet, and Echols' book, as well as how you might come to know of your own guardian angel.

The Angels of the Four Cardinal Directions[41]

MICHAEL

Angel Name Meaning: *He Who is Like God*
   Element: Fire
   Direction: South
   Season: Summer
   Invoke For: Protection, ambition, motivation in physical tasks (like building your physique or training for sports), "ferocity in competition," and fire-based spells.
   Visualize With: the color red, swords, anything summer-related

GABRIEL

Angel Name Meaning: *God is My Strength*
   Element: Water
   Direction: West
   Season: Autumn
   Invoke For: Emotional growth and healing, creative writing, intuition building, inner healing
   Visualize With: the color blue, chalices, autumn-related things, writing tools

RAPHAEL

Angel Name Meaning: *The Healing of God*
   Element: Air
   Direction: East
   Season: Spring
   Invoke For: Mental tasks, exam success, safe travels, healing, understanding philosophical secrets
   Visualize With: Yellow or green robes, the caduceus (medical staff with two snakes), herbal medicine, anything springtime-related

---

41. Echols, 27-33, McHenry, 25-30.

URIEL

Angel Name Meaning: *The Fire of God*
   Element: Earth
   Direction: North
   Season: Winter
   Invoke For: Assistance with divination, money and financial
matters, material wealth and fortune, and wisdom.
   Visualize With: Ruby red or deep green robes, a pentacle (the
five-point star in a circle), anything winter-related, a wizard staff.

Sara says:

When it comes to finding your guardian angel, there are a lot of
mixed sources. Some, like Agrippa, will insist "every mortal born
on earth has three guardian angels," one of "divine rank and order,"
one "from the astrological world," and one "from the physical
world," with different functions that help humans do different
things at the soul, moral order, and physical level.[42] If I followed
this function and went by McHenry's angel guide, my guardian
angels would look like this:

- First (Soul) Guide: Ielahiah (*God the Eternal, Everlasting*)

- Second (Moral) Guide: Omael (*The Patient God*)

- Third (Physical) Guide: Chauakiah (*The God of Joy*)

However, I find that, as with all things, nothing is so neatly cut
and dry. There are so many angels, and so many *people*, and so
many different systems of going about this, that you can easily find
a completely different angel that actually follows you around.
   What I did so many years ago was ask my guardian angel its name.
I read about this trick from some New Age website or another, and
I decided to try it. Granted, as a young scup of a witch, I didn't
really know how to meditate yet. I just looked for anything that even
remotely resembled a sign as I laid in bed. What I got, after asking the
same question over and over like a mantra—*Guardian Angel, what is
your name?*—I saw a letter flash bright in my mind's eye: Z. In nice
Times New Roman font and everything. I didn't know what that meant,
but I couldn't get anything other than that. As a result, I tucked the clue
away for years, *years*, until one day, I decided to try again to get the
full name and see if I couldn't finagle some way of finding out via my
own astrological chart (which you can easily find for yourself if you use
Astrolabe, Cafe Astrology, or any other sites, and enter your date, time,
and location of birth). After all, an astrological chart is something like

a cosmic fingerprint, in my view, and so I figured it must've had some secret to unlocking my angel name.

My rising sign is Sagittarius. Knowing this, I decided to Google what angels were associated with Sagittarius, and lo and behold when *Zadkiel* came up—the archangel of mercy. However, I thought to myself that it wouldn't make sense for an *archangel* to be my guardian, given how these angels are basically the creme de la creme, the top rank, the ones who work with God directly and make all kinds of ruckus on His behalf among the mortals on Earth. Still, it confirmed for me that my search for angels that had to do with Sagittarius was correct, and so with Echols' *Angels and Archangels* in hand, I decided to flip to his section on the angels of the zodiac. Then I asked my guardian angel forward and went one by one down the list of angels of Sagittarius, asking *this one? that one?* until I felt the tell-tale *yes* signal on one specific name:

Omemiah (or Imamiah). *God Hidden in Darkness.* One that, according to Echols, helps one gain "patience and strength while undergoing adversities" and "weakens the power of those who would seek to victimize" me.[43] One that, according to McHenry, "destroys the power of enemies and humbles them, governs voyages and protects prisoners and gives them the means of obtaining their freedom."[44] One who, according to occultist Henry Archer, rules over the demon Alloces (more on angel/demon connections in the next chapter), and who, with Alloces and three attending angels, can accomplish these things:

> To bind an enemy, so they become ineffectual and harmless. *To gain energy from the verbal or written attacks of a person or a group of people.* To research with greater perception and efficiency. To understand the better option when faced with a difficult choice. To cause somebody to make a series of foolish decisions. To know the true emotions of somebody who appears to be hiding something. (Emphasis mine.)[45]

Anyone who knows me, and knows how much I love to argue, will find as much humor in that second line of Omemiah's and Alloces' collective gifts as I do. That was yet another confirmation that *yes*, this is my guardian, and *yes*, he does his job damn well.

But as you continue your journey into Christian Witchcraft, and communicating with the many angels that make up God's army and oversee all things on Heaven and earth, you'll get used to these ener-

---

43. Echols, *Angels and Archangels*, 90.

44. McHenry, *Angel Tarot*, 83.

45. Henry Archer, *The Magick of Angels and Demons: Practical Rituals for The Union of Power* (London: The Power of Magick Publishing, 2019), 128.

getically intense creatures. It may take a long time, but you'll get there. Keep in mind, though, that angels work for *God* first, not you, which means the angels that protect you one day may put you to quite the test the next. Nobody said working with them would be easy, but I can say that it is rewarding—if you can handle it.

Chapter Seventeen

The Christian Witch and Demons

Y OU KNOW THAT IF we were to talk about angels in Christian magic, we would have to talk about demons, too. After all, one cannot be without the other, and this is a theme we'll find often when dealing with the concepts of God and the Devil (however you understand this Devil): the theme of *duality*. Where there is light, there is shadow—and when you know how to make use of both, there is nothing in this world that can shake your foundation.

Sara says:

This is by no means a perfect or full overview of the entire concept or history of working with demons, but it will help you get a foundation. To begin, though, I'll be perfectly transparent: much of what is revealed here in the sense of practical application is my own experience working with demons, along with the knowledge I've collected from a few books that helped me get started. As such, I'll be taking you through this entire chapter on demons from start to finish. The parts not born of my own experience—the brief dip into demonolatry's history and the voices that made this path what it is—give you some context for how this even came to be a part of Christian workings and magical philosophy. And lastly, this section will tell you something about protecting yourself from the shadowy entities that do genuinely mean to cause you some trouble. Don't worry, though: whatever trouble these entities could give you is still *nothing* like what silly horror stories most of mainstream Christianity would like to fill your head with.

So to get started, let's talk just a little about how demonolatry as we know it today came about.

Demonolatry's Development Throughout the Ages

By this point, we've already talked quite a bit about King Solomon and the many things God showed him how to do—including using a special ring to perform exorcisms, thanks to Josephus's description of the tool. However, did you know that King Solomon also actively harnessed and used the power of demons? That he even built a temple of God with the power of demons, binding and commanding them to work, and even invoking angels to pressure them into progress if they tried to refuse? All of that is made clear in the apocryphal text, the Testament of Solomon, where we get the names of several demons—including Asmodeus, Ornias, and Beelzeboul. It's a wild text that's freely available to read online, and in just this text alone, you can learn things about some of these more popular demons, like the fact that Asmodeus seems to be one of the Nephilim ("But how shall I answer thee, for thou art a son of man; whereas I was born an angel's seed by a daughter of man...") and that Ornias's associated zodiac sign is the "water-pourer" (or Aquarius).[1] More of these stories come from the Babylonian Talmud, where Solomon loses his magical ring and throne to the clever Asmodeus and is exiled for years before getting his exorcism ring back.[2]

All this being said, we can see by Solomon's legendary exploits where the term *Solomonic magic* came from. For centuries, Solomonic magic was the style of magic that magicians would use to bind, control, and command the demons they came across; it's also why so many anonymous grimoires, like ones we've already talked about in our section on angels, are attributed to Solomon. Jewish Kabbalists and Christian occultists, over these centuries, would come to create quite a complex system for ensuring that a demon would stay contained within a specific vessel (usually made of precious metals) while an elaborate magical circle would be set up to further contain the demon and provide the practitioner with a solid buffer zone for protection. While this style of dealing with demons is now out of fashion among modern demonolaters, largely because of how it appropriates Hebrew letters and Jewish Kabbalah in general like no tomorrow *and* is incredibly coercive, aggressive, and plainly rude towards the entities

---

1. *Testament of Solomon*, 21, 10.

2. Joseph M. Davis, "The Demons Inside Ashmedai," Herbert D. Katz Center for Advanced Judaic Studies (2021), https://katz.sas.upenn.edu/resources/blog/demons-inside-ashmedai.

evoked, it is one that would explain a lot about the how and why of demonic appearances as cataloged occult texts like the *Ars Goetia.*

However, the *Ars Goetia* is far from the first attempt at listing any of the demons you may be familiar with now. The seventy-two spirits cataloged there can be traced to the works of several earlier Christian Cabalists and occultists, such as Johann Weyer, whose work *Pseudomonarchia Daemonum* (The False Kingdom of Demons) poured dozens and dozens of names, functions, and descriptions of demons out into the world. Given Weyer was speaking at the height of the witch burnings in Germany (during the 1500s-1600s), and was also speaking *out* against the fact that so many women were being accused while the men doing similar things as "philosophers" got little to no attention, his works on demons were actually somewhat satirical. He wrote *Pseudomonarchia*, and his other work *De Praestigiis Daemonum* (On the Deceptions of Demons), to strike out at those who were so concerned with women, witchcraft, and demons, insisting instead that these women accused of witchcraft should've been treated for mental illness and seen as victims of demons' illusions.[3] He likely never imagined his mocking works would be then used to create the *Ars Goetia* later, or inspire others like Jacques Collin de Plancy to write his *Dictionaire Infernale* (1818), but they did.

Of course, with so many people making so many lists of demons, it's a fool's errand to try and sift through every single demon name that could ever be out there. According to demonolatress S. Connolly, "It is almost impossible to find all of these hierarchies [of demons] in one publication. They are compiled from numerous sources including literature."[4] What it does mean, however, is that the list of seventy-two you'll find in any standard copy of the *Ars Goetia* is a great place to begin dabbling with these demons, who have only continued to become more and more ingrained in the occult world with (however unsavory) figures like Alesteir Crowley. Crowley wrote a translation of this old grimoire with S.L. Mathers in the mid-20th century and worked extensively with these demons for all matters of things, including even curing Crowley's teacher Allan Bennett of asthma (of which they claimed the demon Buer helped them do so).[5] The long and short of demonolatry history, however, is that centuries of magicians toying with demons for all kinds of things—knowledge, treasure, love, and bringing misfortune on others—has led to many different compendiums, opinions, ideas, and methods in working with them.

---

3. Sledge, "How Witchcraft Skepticism Produced the Lesser Key of Solomon, Modern Demonology & Psychiatry."

4. S. Connolly, *The Complete Book of Demonolatry* (USA: DB Publishing, 2015), 31.

5. Karlsson, *Qabalah, Qliphoth, and Goetic Magic*, 162.

What Exactly Are Demons?

This is a question worth exploring, and one that, frankly, depends on who you ask. According to Connolly, who describes demonolatry as its own religion separate of Christianity or any other established faith, "each of the Demons is the embodiment of an emotion, an element, or an idea"—and she specifically draws on the original Greek term, *daimon*, to insist that these entities, and all they embody, are, in fact, *"Divine Intelligences Replete with Wisdom,"* noting that these beings "represent misunderstood or clandestine parts of the world around us."[6] However, it's important to point out that these seventy-two demons we know today—like Ba'al, Beelzebub, Astaroth, and more—can be bastardizations of gods from pagan cultures surrounding the Jewish people. Others, such as Azazel, Prince Vassago, Prince Stolas, and more, were also in their lore once described as angels before the fall. Some come from concepts described in the Bible, like King Belial, whose name means "worthless" or "lawless" and appears in 2 Corinthians 6:15. There are then those outside the traditional seventy-two, that resources such as Rosemary Guiley's *Encyclopedia of Demons and Demonology* are especially helpful with. One example is Belphegor, who was apparently a "Moabite god absorbed into Hebrew lore and then Christianity as a major demon."[7] Others, like Lucifer, are tricky, as Lucifer is simply a title that means *light bringer*, and it's also the name of the Roman god of the morning star. What fallen angel or demon wears this title depends entirely on your practice, but in my practice, I've come to understand the angel Samael as the one who wears this name. Still, like God, the concept of Lucifer (or Satan, more accurately *Ha-Shatan*, the Adversary), is one so massive that it can take on as many qualities as you can dream for it.

Now, this next part might be confusing, but something important you may have noticed in my description of these seventy-two demons is that... they're not actually demons. Fallen angels are not demons. Warped versions of pagan deities are not demons. Concepts personified are not demons. The Kings, Princes, Dukes, Presidents, and so on of Hell are simply... *not* actually demons. No, rather, the *demons* are the things they manage, or "command"; when you read the *Ars Goetia*, you may note how many times one of the listed spirits is mentioned to command some number of legions of demons (one legion being about 3,000 to 6,000 beings, if we're going by the Roman military unit). Duke Focalor, for example, commands thirty such legions, while Prince Stolas commands twenty-six. If we do some math, that's... quite a few demons just under those two alone. And there are seventy more of the Infernal Divine who may have some number of legions under their command. According to Guiley:

---

6. Connolly, *Demonolatry*, 17.

7. Rosemary Ellen Guiley, *The Encyclopedia of Demons and Demonology* (New York: Checkmark Books, 2009), 27.

There are 6,666 demons per legion. JOHANN WEYER
cataloged demons, listing 72 princes who commanded
legions totaling 7,405,926 underlings. The legions are
organized in military fashion, with ranks and specific
duties assigned to each demon. The legions attend their
princes when summoned by a magician. They are dispatched by SATAN to infest, oppress, and possess victims.[8]

It might be uncomfortable to see that idea there—*infest, oppress,
and possess victims*—but there's something you need to know about
Satan, and God, and that's that they work together. If you're familiar
at all with the story of Job, and how Satan proposes a plan to test Job's
faith that God agrees to and lets Satan manage, then you'll know just
one of the many examples in the Bible where God is the one actually
behind the many trials and tests humanity goes through. It's not talked
about often enough, but that doesn't mean it stopped being true: Satan
is an angel of the *Lord*, sent to test us and see if we trip, much the way
a prosecutor presses a defendant to catch them in a lie or make them
stumble in court. It instills a level of vigilance in a person that, since
we know about the *real* threat that is the shadowy husk of God trying
to steal His face, is absolutely necessary to achieve by any means.

However, knowing that Weyer's works were mostly sarcastic jabs,
and knowing that the Infernal Divine are considered gods and divine consciousnesses and all that by the people that work with them,
you might imagine that there's a disconnect here. If these beings
are apparently good and helpful and wise and ancient, and a lot of
them don't even have anything to *do* with God since they're from
completely separate religions, what the hell are they doing sending
these little demons to infest, oppress, and possess us? Well, we *could*
call it propaganda, I suppose—but I think I'd rather tell you what many
of these spirits have told me directly, or at least implied, which is that
they don't necessarily *command* these demons.

They *corral* them. Like a farmer corrals their livestock. And it's
apparently pretty aggravating work for the members of the *Ars Goetia*,
who, being scholars with expensive tastes, would much rather enjoy
their books and finery in peace. They can't, of course, because these
demons they're charged with leading are wily and chaotic and difficult
to keep under control.

Think of it this way: the *actual* things we might call demons are
something more like minor fairies. They're the tiny little spirits that
cause mayhem and create a bit of Hollywood-esque drama for their
victims—but unlike fairies, which are neutral and can help or harm
you, and certainly unlike minor angels, which are always trying to

---

8. Ibid., 145.

help, these demons are always trying to cause problems just for sport. They're not all that powerful by themselves, and they can't really do much to you that you don't let them do, but that's exactly how they work: the more afraid of them you are, the more powerful they become, and the better they can terrorize you. And it's the goal of teaching us these lessons—to master our fears, to contain darker forces, to identify when they're causing havoc in our or our loved ones' lives, to overcome bad luck and other trials in life, and to make use of their chaos—that they might get sent to us in the first place by the Infernal Divine, *per the will of God*.

Personally, I'd rather deal with a minor demon being a pain in my back end than deal with an angel staring me down with a sword in hand, like with Balaam on that donkey.

But all in all, the many named "demons" we know, like Gusion and Gepar and Furfur and Fornas, aren't really demons; they're the bosses of demons, the top brass. And when it comes to Solomonic magic, in fact, the seventy-two angels of the Shem HaMephorash are *their* bosses, allegedly: not only could a magician trap a demon into a brass or other metal vessel and contain them outside the magic circle, but they could also invoke the name of the corresponding angel (for instance, Omemiah if one were speaking to Alloces), and essentially browbeat the demons into submission. Solomon does this in the Testament of Solomon when Ornias doesn't want to cut stones, invoking Archangel Uriel to force Ornias to work, for example. This is why there are seventy-two demons and seventy-two angels: they come in pairs, and should a demon not want to do what a practitioner asks, then the corresponding angel can be invoked to force them to behave.

This style of working with demons is, as I said, out of fashion, and for *good reason.*

Why Work With Demons at All?

Which brings us to the question: why *would* you want to work with a demon in the first place, especially if they can do some really nasty stuff (like any of the stuff Asmodeus caused to befall Solomon, or admitted to doing when first bound)? Honestly, there are as many reasons as there are practitioners. It's Swedish occultist and esoteric writer Thomas Karlsson that provides one way of looking at them in his book, *Qabalah, Qliphoth, and Goetic Magic*, noting that:

> If one is to believe the *Goetia*, the invocation or evoca-
> tion of a spirit is good for many things. The demons can
> awaken love and destroy enemies; they grant power and
> honor, but above all they are good teachers and tutors.
> They can communicate what has occurred in the past,
> what happens in the world of the present and what will

take place in the future. The demons can provide famil-
iars, which is a form of lesser spirit that can assist with
all possible matters, such as cleaning or milking cows...
One of the main characteristics of demons has been
the dispensation of knowledge and science, something
that can be traced back to the time of Socrates when
the word 'Daimon' was associated with reason and the
higher self.[9]

In fact, I'd even say getting started with demons is something that,
when you're ready, will help you break off the last few links of the
chains that mainstream Christianity have put on your understanding
of the world. When you come to realize what is possible through the
work of demons, then you begin to learn just how balanced God's
creation really is. You learn that for every problem, there is an angel *or*
demon that can help you, and that they can help you in very different
ways depending on your learning style, personality, and specific goals.
As God said to my father in a dream one night, nearly a decade ago:

> You see two sides; I see one
> coin.

That dream—where my father stood in a courtroom, Jesus as a
defense attorney, Satan as the prosecutor, and God as judge—remains
a cornerstone of how I understand this situation. God, with a coin
spinning above His hand, made it clear then: there would be no God
without Devil, no Light without Dark, and it all worked *together*,
not against each other. God and Satan (or Lucifer, or the "Devil," or
whatever else) are not enemies. Rather, they're coworkers in on the
joke, playing roles to see if we can peer past the theater to recognize
all of this for what it is: a test.

Because there is something wicked out there in the shreds of Creation, and it is *not* some "devil." You already know what it is, based on
our conversation in Chapter 7.

But What About Evil Spirits? Possession? How Do We Ex-
plain This?

With all this said and done, let me be clear: just because one might
vouch for these creatures we call demons today and explain their many
values, their true nature, and their helpfulness to humanity, doesn't
mean that no dangerous spirits exist—nor does it mean that being

---

9. Karlsson, *Qabalah, Qliphoth, and Goetic Magic*, 171-172.

harmed by a spirit is out of the question. In fact, this is where we might look a little closer at the creatures that make up those legions that these powerful entities have to manage (and back again at the concept of egregores, this time thinking of spirits born of our fears and angers and woes). Those fairy-like creatures that make up those many legions, they are born *of us.* To that point, some Jewish stories insist that after the Nephilim (the children of humans and angels) died, be it by killing each other or in the flood of Genesis, it was their spirits that became some of the evil spirits that roam the world.[10] But even at its most basic, when we look at egregore theory, we see that there are two forces which can create artificial entities or breathe life into these new spirits: *love* and *fear.* When we fear things like scorpions, for example, we suddenly find ourselves facing off with scorpion *demons*, as we can see early Christians did by some of the amulets and charms against them that have been discovered.[11] As such, we get these spirits running around causing chaos. These spirits of disease and misfortune and deadly animals and whatever else absolutely exist, and these are the things that might be unleashed on the world at any time with *God's* signal. One of the consequences of true monotheism, it turns out, is that God has to be responsible for everything, good and bad, as we see put forward in Isaiah 45:7:

> I form the light and create darkness, I bring prosperi-
> ty and create disaster; I, the Lord, do all these things.

While many demonolaters might vehemently disagree—and under-standably so—the Jewish viewpoint, at least, is that God is in control of the evil spirits of the world. They do His work for Him. If that means giving them permission to mess up Job's life, if that means giving them permission to tempt humanity to evil, if that means giving them permission to spread plague and disaster and what-have-you, then so be it. The Christian viewpoint, while emphasizing the idea of the "Devil" wanting to drag souls to hell by any means necessary and the idea of fallen angels in rebellion of God, still does acknowl-edge that there's nothing this Devil can do without the permission of God—which makes you wonder why all the exorcists in horror movies have such a hard time getting rid of them at first. Maybe the power of Christ doesn't compel them to leave because the power of Christ

---

10. "Nephilim." The Jewish Virtual Library, accessed November 30, 2023. https://www.jewishvirtuallibrary.org/nephilim.

11. Andrew Mark Henry, "Early Christian Exorcism: Theory & Practice" (webinar, Dr. Andrew Mark Henry, Zoom, October 26, 2023), https://www.eventbrite.com/e/early-christian-exorcism-theory-and-practice-tickets-736338928557.

has already compelled them to stay, and now we're trying to pull these spirits in two directions. Food for thought.

By our discussion of Geburah earlier, however, we can say that, at the very least, God (Him and His angels and Saints) and the "Devil" (Lucifer and the rest of the Infernal Divine) do work together to keep things in check. The Judge, the Prosecutor, and the Defense are all part of the same court system and can't achieve true justice without each other, after all. And so we might imagine that these leaders of the *Ars Goetia* tut their tongues and heave big sighs at the idea of managing these little spirits precisely because they know how troublesome the little spirits are—and that they have to carefully manage when and where these things get the opportunity to roam free and cause havoc. Those little spirits are the things most often causing problems for people and getting everyone worried about demonic activity or even possession.

On the subject of possession, I want to make something abundantly clear: in pretty much any case we see a so-called "example" of demonic possession, what we're *really* seeing is typically a case of mental illness or stress response blamed on some outside spirit or *other* to absolve the apparently "afflicted" person of all responsibility for their actions during a breakdown or episode.[12] While some folks, like Mark Crooks, might insist on " a great logical and empirical rigor that may be attached to the traditional conception of demonology," the reality is that much of his data throughout his eighty-nine page work is anecdotal, which is not the kind of research or study that would be able to concretely differentiate between a mental breakdown and a "real" demonic possession.[13] While stories of items floating in people's houses and creatures threatening to kill a possessed person if they're removed are fascinating, as are the many different stories across time, culture, and religion, the scientific method requires studies that can be replicated and results that can potentially be reproduced, with full transparency as to possible factors that would affect the outcome of the study. One can have faith that these spirits exist and also acknowledge the need for proper scientific method to be applied to start talking about whether or not something is *proven* to be true.

The more plausible explanation of demonic possession is along the lines of what Colleen A. Ward and Michael H. Beaubrun discuss in their article, "The Psychodynamics of Demon Possession." Within this article, Ward and Beaubrun discuss multiple case studies of people reporting being possessed by demons in Trinidad—though in each and every one, there is a plethora of information that might explain exactly what would cause one to claim to be possessed by demons in the first place. These *stress factors*, including sexual violence, do-

---

12. Colleen A. Ward and Michael H. Beaubrun, "Psychodynamics of Demon Possession," Journal for the Scientific Study of Religion 19, no. 2 (1980), 201. https://www.jstor.org/stable/1386254.

13. Mark Crooks, "On the Psychology of Demon Possession: The Occult Personality," *The Journal of Mind and Behavior* 39, no. 4 (2018), 1. https://www.jstor.org/stable/26614369.

mestic violence, familial discord, and a wide array of emotional pains resulting from them, are present before any such claims or cases of demonic possession.[14] Ward and Beaubrun go on to offer a connection between these stressors and the concept of possession, therefore, noting that "possession, unlike any other psychological defense, is ideally suited to coping with their conflicts"; in fact, this specific concept we call *demonic possession* "affords two positive advantages: escape from unpleasant reality, and diminution of guilt by projecting blame onto an intruding agent."[15] After all, how much easier is it to blame our dwindling health, our pain, and our difficult behavior on some *other* that the more intimate institutions in our life—like the churches or our own families—will actually take seriously? How many times have people seeking help for mental health issues like depression been waved off? And how many people, before the advent of modern psychology, simply had no other way to explain the symptoms of such mental health crises they witnessed in their loved ones?

Therefore, no, demons—especially the ones of the *Ars Goetia*, these Kings and Presidents and Princes—are not out there possessing people. Even the smaller ones aren't, as they don't really have the power to (though damn if they won't trick you into thinking they do, acting big and scary to make you cower to their little games of terror). What possesses people are the *metaphorical* demons people battle everyday: depression, anxiety, bipolar disorder, OCD, schizophrenia, or any of the other many mental health concerns that the average person grapples with in a world that seems built on nothing but the deepest, darkest suffering. To call these things demons can be a poetic way to understand it for some, certainly, and a way to externalize them to better deal with them in everyday life, but for others, calling these things demons has caused untold amounts of abuse and inadequate care.

However, with all this said, that doesn't mean that there aren't other spirits out there that will cause problems. While little demons can't possess you, as I said, they can cause a ruckus. They can cause ill fortune or try and whisper lies to you; they can hold up a funhouse mirror that distorts your understanding of yourself and try to trick you into forfeiting your power, your agency, and your sense of self. Just because their keepers, the seventy-two members of the *Ars Goetia*, don't do that—and just because God's angels can banish them—doesn't mean that God Himself didn't allow them to be here for the sole purpose of seeing if you can conquer such lies and tricks to recognize your own power and worth.

It also doesn't mean that demons are the only spirits out there that would trouble you. We'll talk more about this in the next chapter, but in essence, just as you don't readily trust any stranger on the street, you also shouldn't readily trust any spirits you meet—*especially* human

---

14. Ward and Beaubrun, "Psychodynamics of Demon Possession," 206.

15. Ibid., 201.

spirits. Some human spirits that still roam the earth are not friendly. Some, like some people, have one hell of a chip on their shoulder, and they'll take it out on you if you let them. Maybe they're ghosts who refuse to leave the house they build with their own two hands and hate that you're living in it. Maybe they were mean "pranksters" in life and stayed that way in death. Maybe there's just something about you, specifically, that they decided they really do not appreciate, and they want you to know. There are as many reasons for a spirit to not like you as there are for a person still breathing to not like you, and while that *shouldn't* be your problem, spirits have an extra advantage in being able to float through walls and *make* it your problem. If you're encountering that kind of problem, what you can do is perform an exorcism—or, as most witches would call it, a ritual of banishment.

How to Banish or Exorcize Unwanted Spirits

Within Christian exorcism, there are many forms and ways of banishing spirits. And while the Catholic church would want to try and tell people that there's nothing superstitious or magical about the rite of exorcism, by this point, we all know that at its very basic, a spell is simply a way to channel one's spiritual energy and make petitions to a person's God or gods—which is exactly what most exorcisms we see post-Jesus do. Jesus even calls it in Mark 16:17, where He says of those that come after Him: "And these signs will accompany those who believe: in my name they will cast out demons; they will speak in new tongues..." demonstrating how the name of Jesus becomes a powerful exorcistic tool, His holy authority alone enough to drive spirits away. We also see Paul put it into action with the girl with a spirit capable of telling fortunes following after his group in Acts 16:18: "And Paul, having been greatly-annoyed, and having turned to the spirit, said, 'I command you in the name of Jesus Christ to depart from her!' And it went out at the very hour." That's pretty comforting, isn't it? If you have nothing else, as a Christian Witch, you'll always have the help of Jesus.

However, more than commanding spirits in the name of Christ, another common form of banishment or exorcism among witches and mystics alike is the use of items that smell bad. In most modern magical resources, such as Scott Cunningham's *Encyclopedia of Magical Herbs*, you might notice that some of the most common items in the average person's household, like garlic and onions, aren't just protective; they specifically list *exorcism* as one of their talents and uses.[16] Likewise, in apocryphal works like the Book of Tobit, we see King Asmodeus being kept at bay with the smoke of old fish guts that Tobias throws into the fire—and what's more, he throws these guts into the fire on the recommendation of none other than Archangel

---

16. Cunningham, *Encyclopedia of Magical Herbs*, 277

Raphael himself.[17] Other items, like rosemary, are thought to have the smell of their smoke hated by evil spirits—which means rather than cleansing a space with white sage, which is both sacred to many Native American tribes and *endangered* from overharvesting for New Age spiritual practices, you might bundle up some dried rosemary and burn that instead.

The tools I commonly use to cleanse my house of any negative spirits *or* negative energy (as negative energy, too, can gather like cobwebs in your house) are *holy water, dried rosemary,* and *prayer.* Psalms or stories from the Gospel are fantastic to use as inspiration and to begin your prayers, but you can also ask God to send His spirit through the place to chase a spirit out, as well as wield the name of Christ in full authority to command something to leave your space and your loved ones. In an exorcism, your confidence is a large part of your magic; use that magic first and foremost to connect to God, invoking the Father, Son, and Spirit, and use it to channel His might forth to rid the space of these annoying spirits. Use it also to build yourself up and root yourself in your home, imagining it flourishing outward and pushing all unwanted things out until only the things you allow past your magic remain. When it comes to negative energy specifically, I like to fill the corners of my house with the rosemary smoke or circle my head with the burning rosemary three times, as well as sprinkle holy water around. If for whatever reason you aren't able to tolerate or have smoke in your home, I would consider investing in a silver bell: *sound cleansing* is another viable way to rid yourself of negative energy or troublesome spirits, as the pure tones of the silver bell will help to irritate them and drive them out or help to dissipate the energy entirely.

However, one tip: *keep a window open* as you perform this cleansing, as it's commonly believed that if there's no opening to your home, that the spirit or energy in question will restlessly bounce around looking for a way to escape you and your banish-ment weapons of choice. Once the spirit settles down after that, if there is one, it'll only be more upset—and any energy still in the house will be scattered around even worse. Imagine if you took the trash out, but instead of opening your door and going outside, you just threw the trash bag at the door until it burst and exploded all over your foyer? That's what cleansing energy without giving it a place to go will do. So keep in mind to give negative spirits or energy a place to go, be it an open window or door to travel out of, a container to trap it in permanently, or an object like in our adaptation of Leviticus 14 that we talked about earlier.

---

17. Book of Tobit 6:8

Don't Be Afraid of Demons (Whether You Work With Them or Not)

With all this said about demons, I do hope that this helps you understand these creatures—and the magicians that love and work with them—a little bit more. From old gods to fallen angels, the demons people most often talk about aren't here to hurt us or torture us, but to show us a way forward. It may be harsh. It may be uncomfortable. But with great challenge to our comfort and sense of self comes great change, and for some people, that kind of push is exactly what they need to begin a healing process they didn't think was possible.

Here with demons is where we begin exploring that side of Creation that is more closely connected to the chaos everything spawned out of. Here is where the things humanity would rather not acknowledge lurk, and where we can learn to master ourselves by mastering that which we fear, hate, and find so vile. When we are willing to confront our darkness with curiosity rather than judgement, with grace rather than scorn, we can find ourselves fostering deeper compassion, mercy, and empathy for others than ever before, because we *understand* what it is to be in the dark. We develop the courage to look at our most hidden parts head on rather than pretend they don't exist, and we learn to accept ourselves for what and who we are, rather than try and force ourselves to be some picture of perfection that mainstream churches wrongly demand we be. When we master not only our territory and our magic, but also ourselves and all of our darkness, we set boundaries and borders within ourselves that allow our light to shine that much brighter. And wouldn't you know that of all creatures that could help you with such a thing on your path, that could help you become fearless and ironclad, it could very well be the demons that people fear the most?

God creates light and darkness alike, remember. God makes use of *all* His resources in His efforts to teach us, His children, how to walk with a head held high and the power to move mountains with the smallest scrap of faith.

What about you? Do you, can you, *will* you use all the resources available to you?

Chapter Eighteen
Other Spirits a Christian Witch May Encounter

B *UT WAIT, ANGELS AND* **demons and ghosts can't be the only spirits out there,** you may be thinking. *Is anything else out there? Can they hurt me? Can they help me?*

Yes, yes, and yes again.

In the world of spirits, it's important to understand that binaries don't really exist—that *neutrality* is an option. There are some spirits so indifferent to you that it may *seem* like they're attacking you when in reality, they just don't care to protect you from harm. Likewise, there are other spirits that may *seem* friendly, but in reality just have no care or reason to mess with you. Much like spotting a lone coyote in the wild during a nature walk, these spirits can be unpredictable, fickle, and downright dangerous—and they are *everywhere.* So how do you know which spirits are worth trying to approach, and which spirits are better left alone? Well, while each spirit is very much a case-by-case situation, we can tell you this much: you can get a lot of help, kinship, and learning from *nature spirits* and *house spirits*, both of which we'll be exploring in this chapter.

Before we get into that, we want to make one thing extremely clear: while some of these spirits don't consider themselves affiliated with the Christian God (especially creatures like fairies), they are *not* demonic. Think of these creatures exactly as you would think of people: even if we believe God created humanity and therefore all human beings, there are countless people who don't worship God, who don't align themselves with Him or His teachings and wishes for humanity, and who don't care to follow His rules or His orders. Likewise, some spirits would rather just live their lives and mind their business, unbothered by the hoopla that surrounds angels and the baggage attached to demons. Demonic entities are entirely different from these creatures, despite what mainstream Christianity will tell you, and frankly, *treating* these other spirits like they're demonic will only get you into even more hot water with them, because you'll gravely offend them. (And these... are *not* spirits you want to offend.)

So let's dive into this—starting with nature spirits. **Sara** will once again be taking you through this chapter, sharing her knowledge on these specific types of spirits.

Nature Spirits in a Christian Witch's Path

When we say *nature spirits*, we mean exactly what it sounds like: the spirits of the waters, the trees, the animals, the winds, the mountains, and so on and so forth. This concept, known as *animism*, is one that argues that *all* things are alive in some way, and that we might engage with them as directly as we would any other conscious or sentient entity. It's also perfectly compatible with Christianity to view these creatures as not just biologically alive, but spiritually sentient and capable of engaging with us, especially if we take a look at key Bible passages, such as in 1 Kings, Psalms, and Job.

Starting with 1 Kings, I'll tell you a little story. It was actually during a trip to the Wild Goose Festival in North Carolina that I first encountered the idea of Christian animism, thanks to the presentation led by a Christian Druid named Joseph Michael. As an ordained minister in the Christian Church (Disciples of Christ) and a Druid Ovate member of the Order of Bards, Ovates, and Druids (OBOD), with a Master in Divinity, PhD in sociology, and extensive clinical training in pastoral care, Joseph was there to speak about the spirit of the Raven, and how it connects to Biblical stories like that of the prophet Elijah in 1 Kings:

> Now Elijah the Tishbite, from Tishbe in Gilead, said to Ahab, "As the Lord, the God of Israel, lives, whom I serve, there will be neither dew nor rain in the next few years except at my word." Then the word of the Lord came to Elijah: "Leave here, turn eastward and hide in the Kerith Ravine, east of the Jordan. You will drink from the brook, and *I have directed the ravens to supply you with food there.*" So he did what the Lord had told him. He went to the Kerith Ravine, east of the Jordan, and stayed

there. *The ravens brought him bread and meat in the morning and bread and meat in the evening,* and he drank from the brook. (Emphasis mine.)[1]

Throughout Joseph's presentation, we were invited to meditate on the Raven and understand the spirit of this creature, which put forward a fascinating opportunity to understand and connect with God's creation on a spiritual level. More than just beasts, the birds of the sky and all other animals are God's works, just as you are, and they hold their own traits, significance, and lessons that you might learn from. If you'd like to learn more about Joseph or see more of his work, he leads Church as Folk, "a Christ centered ministry that incorporates the wisdom of Druidry, as he has "a passion for integrating these traditions in service of healing, justice, and liberation," according to the Wild Goose Festival's website.

Next comes the Psalms, which says quite plainly all we've already said. In Psalms 66:4, the writer proclaims to God: "All the earth worships you and sings praises to You; they sing praises to Your name." Now, is this just poetry, as some say? Maybe. But for those who think this is just metaphorical and symbolic, let's go beyond that, to Job where we discover that the animals and plants can give testimony on God's actions and works. As we see here:

But ask the beasts, and they will teach you; the birds of the heavens, and they will tell you; or the bushes of the earth, and they will teach you; and the fish of the sea will declare to you. Who among all these does not know that the hand of the Lord has done this? In his hand is the life of every living thing and the breath of all mankind.[2]

Others might also translate *bushes* as *earth*. And while some very well may call this *only* metaphor again, just as they might call Psalms nothing more than poetry, I'll tell you a secret: in the mystic view, metaphors are exactly that which conceal the truths that plain speech gives away too freely. I've said it once, I'll say it again: Jesus spoke

---

1. 1 Kings 17:1-6

2. Job 12:7-10

in parables for a reason. Nonetheless, look here: the beasts, like the fish and birds, have the capacity to teach us something about God and His works, yes, but so too do the plants and other non-moving things. If these creatures are alive, then they have *spirits*, which you can meditate with and come to understand. You might call forward the raw concept of the Raven or the Salmon or the Cypress or the Rose Quartz forward, and see what things it can whisper to you—what secrets you might learn that most people don't stop to discover. These spirits, *nature* spirits, exist all around you, and they always have, even if you haven't been aware of them. Now that you understand the basics of communication and divination, you might figure out how to connect with and communicate your questions and requests to these spirits.

Keep in mind, though, that nature spirits don't really care about human issues like getting to work on time or getting lucky on dating apps or earning lots of money. They're nature spirits. They care about living and being alive; they care about the *rhythm* of life and the flow of all things, the cycles of death and rebirth in the seasons and the growth after a period of destruction and calamity. If you're going to ask them about things and seek their wisdom, seek it on topics they're actually wise on. Likewise, if you're going to ask them to do things for you, ask them to do things that actually make sense for them to do and that are within their *interests* to do.

For example, the concept of using house plants (or outdoor plants) as wards is a pretty common magical tip. If you'd like home protection wards, one of the go-to plants to bring into your home and ask to be one of your mighty spiritual defenders is a cactus. Spiky, resilient, compact, and very easy to take care of, these cacti can be little ones, like Easter Lilies (which make *the* most beautiful white flowers during their blooming season), or they can grow to be massive towers of spikes, like the Organ Pipe Cactus. Either way, you know that you can take them in, ask them to be your guides, and in return, promise to take good care of them and give them all the water, food, sunlight, and attention they deserve. Just be mindful of any animals you may have that might get hurt brushing around these plants or trying to chew on them.

Likewise, if you go outside on your property and have a tree or a bush you gravitate towards, you might also ask that tree or bush to be a *house guardian.* With all the spooky things that prowl around at night, physical or spiritual, a house guardian like a big tree or bush, and especially one you planted yourself (like a rosemary bush), can keep your outside zone a bit safer from all kinds of issues. I have a massive pine tree in my front yard that I've asked to be a house guardian, and as he's right outside my big window, I get to watch the birds sit in his branches, the new green pine needles and sticky pine cones grow in, all that—and I get something to do with my kitchen scraps, which I throw to the base of his trunk as gifts for his good work. That's something you need to know about nature spirits: they are *very* motivated by gifts. After all, who wants to work for free? And they don't have to be very expensive or anything; as I said, I throw out kitchen scraps, because the tree is a *tree*. Organic matter that composts down into more fertilizer for his roots? Very good. Anything that isn't biodegradable, though, like plastic or other trash, will make all of the nature spirits upset, because that's not a gift; that's just littering! If you wanted to do an *act of service* as an offering, you'd want to be picking that litter up, not adding more to the environment.

However, let me give you a stern word of warning when it comes to nature spirits: they are not automatically benevolent or malevolent. Like anything wild, if they don't know you, they can get defensive. You might guess their disposition by the energy that clings to them, and that they've been fed with, though. For example, if people have been particularly afraid of a patch of dark forest, chances are that the trees there have soaked up that fear and angst and use it to their spiritual advantage to keep people out of the woods. (Either that or there's actually another spirit in there—maybe a forest guardian, such as the Slavic Leshy, or a powerful fairy—that is keeping people away with their menacing energy.) These nature spirits, and the other entities that live among them and hide from people, will make it very clear whether you're wanted there or not, and if you're not welcome, you best *keep it moving*. Especially if it's something like a fairy or the Leshy. Some of those will kill first and ask questions later. Some of them will kill just for sport.

And yes, you read that right: I said *kill*. Do not think that just because you're a Christian Witch, you're automatically protected from all harm. You wouldn't think this and start acting brave if you encountered a bear in the woods. Or a wolf. Or any other creature capable of tearing your face off. So do not get cocky and go thinking it of the spirits of the forest, either, because that's an awesome way to die. Remember the warning you've already gotten from Deuteronomy 6:16 and Luke 4:12 and don't go putting God to the test. Respect the forest, respect the ocean, respect the rivers. Respect the rocks, respect the mountains, the valleys and the fields and the cities—yes, even the cities—and respect their spirits. In short: don't put yourself in stupid situations to begin with, and you'll have nothing to worry about, but should you find yourself in a stupid situation, don't make it worse with arrogance.

Most importantly, don't be afraid of the natural spirits. Even if they can be dangerous, so long as you ask God if it's a good idea beforehand, and then meet a spirit where you know you've been safe before (like, again, your yard), you'll likely be fine. Just be cautious. Even housecats can do some damage to you, and so too can spirits that otherwise seem benign. (After all, if you notice you and other people *always* trip on a root or somehow get hurt every time you pass a tree, maybe that tree just isn't very fond of people for whatever reason.) And any plants you plant yourself, like flowers and vegetables and herbs—especially ones you raise from seeds—will be born into your hands and come to know you as you pour your love and attention into caring for them.

Just be safe, be *smart*, and you'll be alright.

House Spirits in a Christian Witch's Path

Alright, so if nature spirits are like the wild animals outside—varying in danger levels from *ducks at the park* to *bears in the mountains*—then how about house spirits? Surely those must be comparable to domestic pets, right? Soft and cuddly and easy to handle?

Well, I don't know about you, but I've seen common house pets like dogs and cats do some real damage to people. I've seen parrots do damage; I've seen hamsters do damage. Having an animal is never a foolproof, safe situation (save with *maybe* fish, I guess), and neither is having a house spirit. While they can be really helpful to you and your family in all kinds of ways, they can also be quite dangerous if you ever offend them. However, they have their place in the magical ecosystem you're creating if you so choose, and what's more, they're a great avenue for some more cultural connections with wherever you hail from.

But before we think of any separate spirits, it's important to build on our conversations about animism. Not only are the rocks and the trees and the waters and the winds alive, you see: the very house you live in, being made of these materials, can also be thought of as alive, as it carries the spiritual energy of the materials it was built with, and that energy takes on its own form as it mixes with the energy and attention of the people that built it.

From a more ceremonial magician perspective, I might also consider the house to be like a centurion or Skyrim-style atronach: it's alive, but given it's an amalgamation of all these energies, it can be considered an artificial creature. Still, whether you think your house is its own spiritual entity or something more like energetic AI, what matters is that you can interact with it if you so choose: pouring your love and attention into it, asking it to keep you and yours safe and warm and protected. In return, you might commit to decorating it in ways that the house appreciates, keeping it clean and warm, and making sure its inner structures are well maintained. The more care you show to it, the more it shows to you. So when it comes to your house spirits, the first place available to find one is the spirit of the house.

However, there are many other spirits that you might look into depending on your ancestry or your needs. Arin Murphy-Hiscock in her book, *The House Witch*, discusses quite a few of the potential spirits you could invite into your home, as well as their talents and their requirements for sticking around your house. While I won't get into the details of every single one of them, I will tell you that you might recognize some of these creatures from other popular works of fantasy—such as the brownie of the *Spiderwick Chronicles*.

These little fairies are real creatures of English and Scottish folklore, and while they can protect the house, they're also very good at cleaning a house. While they're often depicted as a little person "dressed in tattered clothes or in nothing at all," they are, remember, *spirits*, and they can take many different forms; they're great with helping in "every domestic activity" (unlike their English cousin, the hob, which focuses more on the hearth specifically), but they do *not* like to be directly thanked for their work; doing so will make them leave.[3] Silently giving them a snack of some honey-slathered bread and cream in an out-of-the-way spot of the kitchen is more than enough thanks for them.

Likewise, the Swedish tomte is one you may be used to seeing in general decor nowadays. The gnomes (or gonks for the Scottish) that seem to appear in every possible iteration in modern home goods stores, with their hats that cover their eyes, their long white beards, and their big, round noses, are actually a picture-perfect folk representation of the tomte. This male house spirit really likes "porridge, often with a pat of butter on top, served to him on Christmas morning"—and he's a tricky one, as he can help a family be prosperous and efficient, "sometimes at the expense of neighbors who lose grain or supplies to the *tomte*" (which makes me wonder now about the Slovenian witches accused for stealing milk and such from their neighbors' animals).[4] Analogous with the Finnish *tonttu* and the Norwegian and Danish *nisse*, however, this is another fairy-like house spirit that can be helpful (or dangerous, depending on your treatment of him) in your home.

And of course, there are many more after that described in Murphy-Hiscock's work that you may want to look into. For instance, she mentions the Roman house spirits known as the *lares*, who once found themselves being celebrated on the fourth of January, on the festival known as Compitalia. She also mentions their pantry-habitating counterparts, the *penates*, would help a family keep their storerooms full—and for Germans, it was the little kobold that would protect a home, finish uneaten food, drive off pests and threats, and keep a family abundant. All of them have more or less the same function, as you can see: protect the family, bring fortune, and maybe help tidy up here and there.[5]

To give you a more concrete example of a house spirit, now, let me focus on the one I have in my home. As a Slavic person, the type of house spirit my people most often came in contact with was known as the *domovik* (or, for Eastern Europeans, the *domovoy*). *Dom* means home, and *vik* implies a person or creature; it literally means *house creature*. If you've ever read fantasy books like Katherine Arden's *Winternight Trilogy*, you may remember that the main character, Vasya, had such a spirit in her home, living in the house oven and eating scraps of bread whenever they were offered; this creature was fiery, stout, and it kept the big evil of the first book out of the house with all its strength. But there are rules to the domovik, as well as his

3. Arin Murphy-Hiscock, *The House Witch: Your Complete Guide to Creating a Magical Space With Rituals and Spells for Hearth and Home* (Stoughton: Adams Media, 2018), 96-97.

4. Ibid., 97-98.

5. Ibid., 94-99.

wife, the kikimora; there are preferences and protocols that should be observed to guarantee a good relationship with these creatures.

It was through Madame Pamita's *Baba Yaga's Book of Slavic Witchcraft* that I found any procedure for inviting my own domovik inside. In this book, she confirms the version of the fantasy domovik in the *Winternight Trilogy*:

> The fire in the pich is the spirit of our ancestors, and the Domovyk is the guardian spirit of the hearth. Nowadays, he might house himself in an out of the way place: a fireplace, of course, or an attic, or a cellar—someplace he can stay safely hidden when people are about.[6]

She also notes that this creature may appear as many different things: frogs and snakes, rats and birds, even a mini version of male ancestral figures you've been particularly attached to in life.[7] It's at this point I'll warn you: when you invite a spirit such as the domovik into your home, you absolutely should *expect* to hear things go bump in the night, because those "things" are, in fact, your domovik running about. I've seen and heard mine from time to time: the sudden cracks of sound in the house, even a shadow of a little figure running to the kitchen from the corner of my eye.

But as I was saying: if you disrespect or anger the domovik, you'll be in trouble. Pamita notes that such an angry fellow can cause a real ruckus, as he'll potentially go "hiding items, spilling salt, slamming doors, howling, moaning, or knocking over furniture"—and if you don't do anything about it, the domovik will up and leave your home entirely, taking any benefits of keeping the house safe and alerting you to danger well away from you and your family.[8] The most important things to do are to keep your house tidy (which I often fail to do because life happens) and keep the peace in the home, but also to feed your domovik with offerings.[9] For me, I notice my domovik (who I call *dedek*, Slovenian for grandpa) is happiest with savory things, and I'll give him a good piece of bread whenever I bake a fresh loaf, as well as a small glass of water, making sure to return his dishes into the cabinet with our dishes as a sign that he's part of our home. The sweets I've given him were appreciated, but not a favorite. The domovik is a simple creature who likes good, hearty, quality items, not icky things. If you don't make bread, though, you might give your domovik a spoonful of what you cooked for dinner. Whenever I give him something, I tell

---

6. Pamita, *Baba Yaga's Book of Slavic Witchcraft*, 34.

7. Ibid., 33.

8. Ibid., 34.

9. Ibid., 41.

him the same Slovenian phrases, ones that have become words of offering:

> *Evo, dedek, zate: mal' sveži kruh in tud' pa mal' svežo vodo. Uživaj.*

In English:

> There you go, grandpa, for you: a little fresh bread and some fresh water, too. Enjoy.

Likewise, Zuza Zak in her book, *Slavic Kitchen Alchemy*, discusses such protective spirits from a more Polish and western Ukrainian and Belarusian lens. Once again known as *dziadek* (grandad), or *domowik* (pronounced the same as *domovik*), these spirits—along with other ones like the *krasnoludki*, or *beautiful little people*, which seem to be a type of fairy—would protect and bring fortune to a home, as well as potentially bring mischief. However, as one might expect, Christianity changed things for Slavic people. Zak illustrates what happened with these spirits, as well as how these new Christians kept holding fast to the general idea of them in their new religious context:

> In time came Christianity, and many of the smaller deities, such as the house spirits, were sadly (and literally) demonized. However, they were so ingrained in the Slavic psyche that their protective role needed to be filled with something, which is where the Angel Gabriel came in. While I was growing up, and for centuries prior, many children would have a picture of the angel looking after children, hanging near their bed at home—even when, like my family, theirs wasn't a particularly religious household. Even now, when my daughter is scared, I say the prayer to Angel Gabriel that I was taught by my Babcias. While I am not a practicing Catholic, this protective prayer holds power for me, as it calls forth the protective energy that I know is there and always has been.[10]

As we've already talked about angels, I'll tell you this: if you don't feel ready for a house spirit or engaging with your ancestors, the angels

---

10. Zuza Zak, *Slavic Kitchen Alchemy: Nourishing Herbal Remedies, Magical Recipes & Folk Wisdom* (London: Watkins Media Limited, 2023), 136.

are always there for you, and *yes*, their magic works, their *power* works, whether someone is particularly religious or not. One thing people need to understand about God and His angels is that, unlike fairies or egregores, belief is not required for them to act—and contrary to popular belief, God doesn't choose favorites, nor does He abandon those who, for whatever reason, don't walk with Him in their journey. As goes the old saying, *God causes His sun to rise on the evil and the good, and sends rain on the righteous and the unrighteous.*[11] And even then, that's talking about one's character, the constitution of their soul, not whether or not they believe. God oversees all people and sends His angels to ward off evil, always, no matter what—even when that protection and blessing and closeness actually looks like letting people go to be on the path they need to walk in this lifetime.

But if you find yourself longing to get more deeply connected to your roots, then just as the trees and wind and rocks can tell you some of the wisdom of God's creation, so too can a house spirit your ancestors once honored—which, yes, does itself count as an ancestral spirit—teach you something about the traditions and customs of your family from generations back. As with nature spirits, you need to be mindful and attentive, but when you accept the responsibility of having a house spirit and put your all into them, just as they put their all into your home and family, the relationship you get and the things you learn can be incredible. Just remember that there are always options for your home protections and domestic assistance, and there are also many different ways of exploring your cultural background. Do so with love and enjoy the process, and it'll only ever add to your budding practice.

---

11. Matthew 5:45

Chapter Nineteen

Ancestor Work as a Christian Witch

B EFORE YOU GET TOO worried, *no*, it is not a pre-requisite of Christian witchcraft, or witchcraft in general, to know your ancestry or do ancestor work. In fact, many traditional Christians will tell you that ancestor work is off the table because we "can't speak to the dead" and "the dead can't hear us." However, we would mightily invite these folks to spend some time at a Dia de los Muertos celebration, where largely Catholic families still take the time to honor their ancestors and leave food and drink for them to enjoy during a time where spirits are believed to more easily come back from beyond the veil. We're just saying: there's a *lot* more to the idea of spirits and ghosts in Christian psyche than a lot of mainstream Christianity wants us to believe.

For now, the point stands: ancestor work isn't necessary to be a witch, but it *does* help quite a bit if you at least know where your family hails from. By knowing this, you know what kind of magic your family was more likely to do way back centuries ago, and you're able to find a deeper connection with your own roots, culture, and history. As Mimi works more with her ancestors than Sara, she'll walk you through this part of the chapter.

Venerating (and Working With) Your Ancestors

Veneration is important, and you're already doing it when you make a family recipe or share the same stories. No one wants to be forgotten; even through dirty picture frames and stories filled with holes, the memories of our loved ones remain. Every time you make that biscuit recipe or cake that Granny always brought to potlucks and church suppers, you're honoring her memory. Papaw had a favorite author or show, so you keep one book tucked away to leaf through or find an episode to have on in the background while your heart calls out to 'em. Anytime you feel like they're near, their image or voice flickers in your mind, or even something reminds you of them, let them know. Say their name out loud, tell them you remember them, share the moment with someone.

Moreover, if you're not living out of touch with modern day society, you know that there have been a few popular movies that depict Latin and Spanish traditions for ancestor veneration. These movies *Coco* (2017) and *The Book of Life* (2014) brought a light to a beautiful tradition and lifestyle that includes honoring our ancestors. Culture plays a huge part in how people venerate their ancestors, and you can see that across Europe, the Americas, and a lot more.

For example, Dia de los Muertos and All Soul's Day have feasts, altars, and celebrations wrapped up into them. Samhain has the Dumb Supper, where you set a place for your dearly departed for the grand meal. Totensonntag in Germany is a day of remembrance and silence. Many eastern European countries have the Day of the Dead on Nov. 2nd for remembrance. Common practices that anyone can do include having a piece of jewelry, clothing, or an item they commonly used, placed with pictures of them, and setting a candle in a safe and/or sacred space to honor them.

Is it Something Mundane, or Has Grandma Come to Visit?

But how do you know there's a loved one near? Having a Clair- ability helps, sure, but there's plenty of ways to discern a visit from the dearly departed. Most of them are old wive's tales or little notions passed down. An example of this would be seeing and hearing a cardinal, seemingly out of nowhere. Cardinals have been said to be the mes- sengers of the divine, reminding us of loved ones passed on. Some stories say that when you see one shortly after their death, it means they've come to visit. Others say it means a lost soul has found you. The *Farmer's Almanac* speaks on birds and their meanings, and quite a few have been passed down through my family; however, there is no one origin story for the cardinal and its spiritual meaning. They appear in a wide range of myths across many cultures, including many indigenous and European stories.

Sometimes, it's in something so innocuous to others but holds grand significance to you. A common thing said around my Kentucky family was when a penny would appear out of nowhere, it was a message from your loved ones from heaven. When my Papa Harold was set to pass, he told my Mama he'd send dimes so she'd know it was him. And every so often, when her heart is pining, she'll find one and save it in a jar.

Other notions include finding white feathers on the ground, or hearing them calling your name when you're alone or when you're almost asleep. Even seeing them in a dream could be a way for them to reach out. I've even heard that seeing certain numbers associated with the loved one is a sign they're saying hi. The best thing to do is acknowledge that feeling and keep watch for more signs while also not obsessing over every moment. When you've started to see a pattern, you can more easily identify who you're speaking with or the times they come around.

Once you've established that pattern, using your favorite divination device can help you communicate and glean any messages of hope, wisdom, etc. they may have for you.

Decolonizing and Cycle-Breaking

Sometimes, you'll find that your ancestors were not the best kind of people. A lot of us from the South probably have a lot of muddy backgrounds, "lost" information, and stories spread around to cover up scandals until no one knows the truth anymore. So how do we go about healing that? How do we move forward? Firstly, *acknowledgement* is key. Accepting that these things may be part of the spiritual baggage you've been handed down is the first step. Second, look back at the language that was used around you, or that you've used yourself. Are there any racial slurs that might've slipped in, like *g*psy*? Or maybe you notice there's a lot of division between white magic and black magic in what you've read or learned? (As we mentioned earlier in this book: magic is magic, but the implications of these terms, *black magic* and *white magic*, have racial undertones that discredit BIPOC practitioners.) Third, look into creators and practitioners from the BIPOC community and listen to what they have to say.

Even those who have the best intentions at heart can slip into using things outside of the culturative norm, like using spirit animals (a Native American term co-opted by New Age folks) and chakras (a part of Hinduism that's been watered down and bastardized in New Age spaces). While these concepts are amazing in their proper context and practice, there is rampant erasure and indigenous silencing over their use. The best ways to start doing the hard work is by taking a few steps back, listening to those in the circles, and having a healthy conversation. Why are you drawn to these things? Have you taken the time to learn the meaning behind why and what they are? Are you infringing on closed practices? Were these practices handed down without acknowledgement? I am *not* saying to ignore any part of your background. But social media has convinced many people that nothing is sacred to those cultures and it's all a free-for-all in the spiritual community when that isn't so. Instead, part of healing the wounds in the past is in the acknowledgement and moving forward, perhaps even letting go of certain things you'd done that would've been appropriative or damaging.

Doing ancestor work can be emotionally grueling and feel as if you're chained to a past you had no control over. And many, many of us have trauma from families and their religions and rules, to the point that we might ask ourselves what we're even trying to contact those ancestors for in the first place. But truth be told, grief and generational trauma can be a heavy thing to work through, and ancestor work can be a boon to help you heal those wounds and move forward with blessings in your life. If you're really worried about the nastier ancestors coming through, though, then when you're first starting out in veneration and work, set up your protections—the SATOR square, a sigil, a candle, a crystal—and set your intention. Just as you would cleanse your space of negative energies, you pour that same feeling into dismissing the ancestors whose heart and mind do not align with yours. This can help you find your way when you take your first steps.

For the rest of this chapter, however, we'll be going into a different topic: Saint work. As Sara is the one coming from the Catholic background, she'll tell you all about it.

Sara's Tip: Saint Work as Ancestor Work

Now, say you want to work with more human spirits—because angels, demons, and nature spirits are simply too much right now—but you also don't have any ancestors you want to try talking to. That's okay! Working with your own kin is not a requirement for Christian Witchcraft. While decolonizing and cycle-breaking are fantastic ways to use ancestor work, there are some ancestors with stories too painful, or too strange, for us to feel comfortable engaging with—and sometimes, the concept of working with our ancestors just doesn't click or make sense to begin with. But if you're looking for that human touch somewhere in your practice, then aside from Jesus Himself, this is where *Saints* come in.

You don't have to be Catholic to enjoy the connection and help you can get from the Saints. Since Saints were once human, they have a perspective on life that angels don't (aside from the two that were once human: Metatron, originally the prophet Enoch, and Sandalphon, originally the prophet Elijah). They can also be patrons of all kinds of different things, with really cool prayers on many Catholic blogs asking for their intercession. For instance, St. Cyprian of Antioch is officially considered the Saint of Northern Africa, but because of his background as a pagan magician before conversion, he's also considered the de facto Saint of sorcery and necromancy. A part of a chaplet prayer (a prayer for a set of beads smaller than a rosary) from the Order of St. Cyprian shows this:

> St. Cyprian, patron of Sorcerers and Magicians, I beseech you that you preserve me from all evil intents, arts, and perfidies. May they be full of confu-

sion, those who attempt against
my life. May my enemies be
confused and scattered to the
winds. Guard my vision and my
thoughts that I may understand
the secret doctrines without er-
ror. Assist me to grow in power
and wisdom that I may serve the
good of mankind. Grant me the
power to intervene on behalf of
those that come to me for help.
Assist me in serving those who
are bound by hexes, bewitching,
and possessed of evil, so that the
rabid wolf shall have dominion
over them no longer.[1]

While the OSC is geared towards magic (theurgy and thaumaturgy,
esoteric practices that acknowledge "traditional forms of magic and
prayer" according to their website), their chaplet prayer definitely isn't
unique in its nod to St. Cyprian's past as a mage. Other organizations,
and even just other prayer blogs, acknowledge his history and include
it in prayers. It's important to point out that a lot of these prayers are
essentially homebrewed, though, meaning that they were made up by
members of the church for their own needs. That means it's perfectly
okay to write your own prayers for your own situations—and honestly,
it's encouraged, because it means you're building a deeper connection
with the Saint by including personal elements rather than repeating
the same general prayers all the time. There's nothing wrong with the
Lord's Prayer or the Glory Be or any other repetitive prayer, of course,
but adding a personal touch to another prayer afterwards will help you
feel closer to your practice.

Just like with angels, there are Saints of all kinds of different things:
love, marriage, vengeance, widows, farming, animals, and more. A
couple of the most famous ones include St. Francis of Assisi, who was
said to give sermons even to the birds and is a go-to for pet owners
praying for intercession, and St. Anthony of Padua, who is said to be a
Saint of lost things. St. Anthony has his own folk jingle for finding lost
things that goes like this:

> "Tony, Tony look around, some-
> thing is lost and must be found."

---

1. "Chaplet of St. Cyprian," Cyprian Orisons, accessed November 30, 2023, https://prayer
s.cypriani.org/chaplet/.

Super short, super simple, and super informal—it's basically a cantrip. Plenty of people have their own interesting stories using simple cantrips like these to find things, be they the T.V. remote or an engagement ring that slipped off someone's finger. Granted, of course, any Catholic will tell you that when they pray to Saints, they're not praying to the *Saint* for a miracle, but for that Saint to then pray to *God* for a miracle. Folks of other denominations insist that the Bible says we should only pray to God, but Catholics will point out the fact that people ask other people still living to pray for them, too, and that asking someone in Heaven to pray for you is no different than asking someone on Earth to do so. Then opens up another separate debate about whether or not the people in Heaven are awake and can hear you—a question that once bothered me a lot, too.

How Can the Dead Hear Us in Heaven?

This was a question that bothered me mostly because I'd heard misinformation about the story of the Witch of En Dor in 1 Samuel. Another interpretation I'd read before suggested that Samuel's spirit was actually the *first* real human spirit the Witch had ever summoned, and everything before then had been just a charlatan's trick, meaning it was *impossible* to actually get a ghost to come up. However, this is patently not the case, as the Jewish Study Bible's footnotes makes it clear that this magic was real—and *effective*.[2] It wasn't a case of the Witch playing tricks; her magic worked. The reason that Samuel's ghost was upset with being disturbed from his sleep was because pre-Resurrection, that was how the underworld was conceived of: as a *resting place*, with Sheol more of a typical underworld like Hades or anything else, where the dead waited for the coming of the Messiah.

While Judaism doesn't believe the Messiah has come yet, Christianity does, and Jesus is the religion's Messiah. We might start with the theory of *Christus Victor*, an alternative to the Protestant-popularized *Ransom Theory* (now called Penal Substitutionary Atonement: the idea that Jesus died as a payment for all the sins of the world). Unlike Ransom Theory, the Christus Victor theory doesn't say Jesus paid for the sins of the world with His death; it says that His death *and resurrection* was a decisive victory *against* the "powers of evil, including sin, *death*, and the devil" (emphasis mine).[3] It might not seem like a big difference, but it is: the latter suggests that these evils aren't debts to be paid off, but enemies to overcome, which Jesus did—meaning through Him, all of these things can be avoided and denied. Even death!

---

2. Berline and Brettler, *Jewish Study Bible*, 388.

3. Steve Schramm, "What Actually Happened on the Cross? Exploring Atonement Theories." Premier UnBelievable. March 29, 2023. https://www.premierunbelievable.com/articles/what-actually-happened-on-the -cross-exploring-atonement-theories/15233.article

This is the reason that St. Paul, in his many letters, doesn't describe the dead as being *dead*, but rather just having "fallen asleep." While modern Christian theology dictates that people will return and awaken, body and all, in the final days (hence why most Christian sects are staunchly anti-cremation), there's nothing to suggest that those who fall asleep stay that way permanently in Heaven, especially given the other times that the dead have made an appearance in the New Testament. In fact, you'll find that Catholics point to the fact that Jesus talks to two *dead* prophets—Moses and Elijah—in Matthew 17, as the biggest and most obvious clue that the dead still live. Another clue, according to the writers of Catholic Answers, is in Revelation 5:8:

> And when he had taken it, the four living creatures and the twenty-four elders fell down before the Lamb. Each one had a harp and they were holding golden bowls full of incense, *which are the prayers of God's people.* (Emphasis mine.)

This verse is insinuating that it's the Saints who offer those prayers to God, and also the Saints who carry them up to God.[4] In both of these examples, though, we can see how there are *people* in Heaven who are pretty active for those who are supposed to be so very "asleep."

But Why Pray to Saints When We Can Just Pray to Jesus?

That's a good question, and it's one that, of course, Catholics have an answer for as well. As we discussed before, the concept of asking a Saint to pray for you is no different than the concept of asking your friends and family still on Earth to pray for you. Moreover, there's Scriptural reference to the fact that God gives the prayers of the righteous some serious firepower (James 5:16-18) and that Christians who have died and gone to Heaven are in the "city of the living God" (Heb. 12:22-23)—meaning they're, according to the writers of Catholic Answers, apparently righteous enough to earn that privilege of living there.[5] Therefore, if you pray to them and ask them for a boost, then they can carry your concerns to God with perks.

---

4. "Praying to the Saints," Catholic Answers, accessed November 30, 2023, https://www.catholic.com/tract/praying-to-the-saints.

5. Ibid.

Think of it this way: when applying for a job, there are a couple ways to go about it. One is to apply cold, just shooting your resume to the company and hoping that it works out. Another way is to network, getting to know someone within the company you're trying to work for, and then putting them down as a reference and asking them to put in a good word for you to the hiring manager. Either way, it's the boss that has the final say—but having an extra vote of confidence from an employee that already works there is always a plus. It's the same with Saints: your single prayer is, of course, very powerful on its own, just as a strong resume is for a job application. But having someone on the other side to add that extra bit of goodwill, a Saint to vouch for you, can only ever help your case. And these Saints are putting these prayers forward to God—who, if you follow the idea of the Trinity, is Jesus. In fact, a lot of folks pray to Mother Mary precisely because she is Jesus's Mother, and therefore she has direct access to Him at all times, making her the best to ask for intercession to Him.

But of course, us Christian Witches will take this idea of praying to Saints a step further from the Catholic church. Catholicism insists that there *is* a separation between the bans on soothsaying and necromancy in the Old Testament (namely Deuteronomy and Leviticus) and the practice of praying to Saints to put in a good word for us. The writer of Catholic Answers specifically put it in such a way:

> God thus indicates that one is not to conjure the dead for purposes of gaining information; one is to look to God's prophets instead. Thus, one is not to hold a seance. But anyone with an ounce of common sense can discern the vast qualitative difference between holding a seance to have the dead speak through you and a son humbly saying at his mother's grave, "Mom, please pray to Jesus for me; I'm having a real problem right now."[6]

We apparently have *more* than an ounce of common sense, though, don't we? We know, based on our conversations in Chapter 2, that the bans against these necromantic practices were from a different covenant of interacting with God (a pre-Messianic one), that they were referring to specific pagan practices (like *ov* and *yide'oni*), and that the things people were asking about was typically the future. Beyond that, if one follows the idea of Christus Victor and follows the Catholics' own logic that these Saints are *alive*, then it's hardly a seance to speak to them, is it? If a Saint like St. Maria Faustina Kowalska of Poland (1905 - 1938) can allegedly perform miracles *post-humously*, that is, *after she died*—if the receiver of the miracle can be at her tomb and hear an "innerly voice" that says that she'll help with her intercession so long as she's called on—then we know Saints can not only hear our prayers,

---

6. Ibid.

but respond to us.[7] We know they can interact with us. And if they can do all that, then we know they can share a little of their wisdom they've learned throughout their lives in meditation, too. The Catholic Church tries again and again to cut itself off at the knees theologically with its fears of going too far out of bounds, or of not crediting God properly. It refuses to call a spade a spade; it doesn't want to acknowledge what it means for these stories to hold true and these possibilities to exist.

The possibilities being, of course, that we can learn to see a world beyond our own and gather wisdom from those far removed from an institutions' two-millenia old corruption.

So when it comes to working with spirits outside the typical Christian confines of angels and demons, know that there *are* options available to you. Whether it's the grandmother you miss everyday and have fond memories of, the spirit of your favorite tree in your yard, a house spirit you invite inside, or a Saint you find particularly fascinating, there are so many options for mentors and allies in your spiritual practice. We understand the idea that all power comes from God, including our own. But that doesn't mean there isn't value to be had in asking the Saints for a good word or the angels and demons to help you out in a similar way. In the end, the inclusion of these spirits, as well as the spirits of any of your tools or anything and anyone else you might encounter, are all connected—and by involving other bits of God's creation, you become something of an organizer, and orchestrator, bringing the trees and rocks and angels and demons and dead and alive *together* to look up to God. That in and of itself is a powerful thought, and I hope it serves you well in your journey ahead.

---

7. "St. Maria Faustina Kowalska," The Divine Mercy, https://www.thedivinemercy.org/message/stfaustina/graces.

Section 5
Parting Words and Works
Involved in Creating This Book

Going Forth with Confidence and Courage

Sara says:

One thing that I find pretty dishonest in the more witchy spaces, be they online or in books or anywhere else, is the idea that witchcraft—of *any* kind—is for everyone. Truth is that it's no more for everyone than being a doctor, engineer, writer, teacher, poet, or anything else is. Some people can live just fine lives in the structure and routine of organized religion, and that's great. But others—like you, if you're likely holding this book—might find themselves withering in such a thing instead. Still, it's worth saying that the path of a Christian Witch is one that is full of just as many sorrows as it is joys, and it's one that does have a prerequisite: a need for something *more* than the modes of spirituality organized religion offers us, and a determination to forge our way through a complex, historied, and rich world of spirituality.

However, for those who can read through this book and feel called to a path like this one, you are now equipped with the necessities to begin your own self-directed journey to, and with, God. There is no right way to encounter Divinity and experience its wonders as they work their way into your soul. There's hardly even a wrong way, really. Outside of the most obvious prohibitions, like hurting and abusing others, there's no one who can tell you what to do, or how, except God.

In the words of Sister Karol on page two of her book, *Sister Karol's Book of Spells, Blessings, and Folk Magic:* "There are as many paths to God as people who walk this earth, and not all of them lead to church."

So we hope that, above all, you find peace in your path. Peace, as well as wisdom, love, and acceptance of all the world's wild mysteries. May you go forward unafraid, unburdened, and undaunted by the world, and may the soul God gave you forever shine bright enough to cut through even the deepest darkness.

Mimi says:

Most people start out in folk magic to reconnect, whether it's to their family's direct past, the land they came from, or long-lost ancestors. There is something real and raw in the way our grandparents and great-grandparents held onto hope and practiced their faith. God, Jesus, and the Holy Spirit were in everything. My biggest dream is that we can all sit down and share again, with the respect that is deserved of those who came before, both indigenous and immigrant. Even as you read and re-read this book, I ask that you remember your own reasons for coming to Christian Witchcraft. Know that deconstruction is not just important, but imperative, as the church itself is not always right, especially when it comes to how we treat the world and people around us. We were called to be stewards of nature and keepers of our neighbor, to take care of it and one another with love, as everything is imbued with the Holy Spirit—with God's life.

If you're coming from the outside looking in, the folk ways might not seem too appealing. You have to disregard the stereotypes of hillbillies and rednecks, of peasant and rural folk, to look at what we truly stand for. In the words of our loving Aunt Jet Owens from *Practical Magic*: "You can't practice magic while looking down your nose at it." Granny magic needs more people to learn and share its wonder without being demeaned and disregarded because of those assumed backwater ways. My encouragement for you, moving forward, is to continue in your prayers and studying. Read often, ask questions of scholars *and* God, and take the time to pour love and honor into what you do every day. May you be blessed in all ways.

Love,

Sara & Mimi

Acknowledgements

T HERE WOULD BE NO way for us to end this book without recognizing our greatest supporters: our family, our friends, and our mentors. To be specific, it's the Christian Witch leadership—namely Lina (@linathejesuswitch) and Hannah (@spirituali.tea)—that have cheered us on the whole way through writing this, as well as incredibly knowledgeable and steadfast folks like Reverend Kyle Mackey who have pointed us in the right direction for resources and been there to answer our theological questions. All deserve recognition for their work in teaching, guiding, and supporting others, and for showing us yet more examples of liberation theology and justice-minded Jesus-lovers that already exist in a loud and busy world.

And of course, we have all of you to thank: the Christian Witches (or soon-to-be Christian Witches) who believe in this mission and want to see a type of Christianity that comes back to its roots of *love*, *justice*, and *hope*. It's for you we wrote this book, and it's because of you that we had the inspiration and dedication to see it through to the end.

So thank you a million times for being here with us in this great journey of faith and magic.

About the Authors

Sara Raztresen is twelve years a Christian Witch, as well as an online educator, faith leader and ordained minister of the Universal Life Church. As a Slovene-American, she also has a strong grasp of Catholic folk tradition, especially in Slavic lore, with many of her mother's stories and tips to share. Her lived experience as a witch and extensive Biblical scholarship and community with other progressive Christian leaders gives her the practical and academic lens to discuss the way Christian and witchy worlds collide.

Sara is also a part of a vibrant online Christian Witch community on Tiktok, with other social media channels dedicated to education on a variety of Christian witchcraft topics. Find her online via her social media:

- @srazzie97 (Tiktok, Twitter)
- @sararaztresen (Instagram)
- www.sararaztresen.com

Emyle (Mimi) D. Prata is what many would consider a hereditary witch. Her work of over 20 years to maintain the familial practice as well as lean further into apologetics and gnostic theology has helped shape her path from childhood. Immigrant grandparents and great-grands that settled in Appalachia and the Ozarks have given her a beautiful blended tapestry of magic found in God's nature. She studied at WISE Academy under Belladonna LaVeau in 2006,  and took what she learned from there to sharpen her skills in nature. She has an A.S. in Applied Health studies, with her lifelong love of herbs and magic leading her into the naturopathic world.

Mimi is also a blossoming content creator on TikTok and blog writer, blending magic and motherhood in simple ways. Find her online via her social media:

- @feralsouthernhousewife (Tiktok, Instagram)

- www.feralsouthernhousewife.wordpress.com

References and Suggested Reading

Arakelova, Victoria. "Notes on the Yezidi Religious Syncretism." *Iran & the Caucasus* 8, no.1 (2004), 19-28. https://www.jstor.org/stable/4030889.

Archer, Henry. *The Magick of Angels and Demons: Practical Rituals for The Union of Power.* London: The Power of Magick Publishing, 2019.

Asatria, Garnik and Victoria Arakelova, "Malak-Tāwūs, the Peacock Angel of the Yezidis," *Iran & the Caucasus* 7, no. 1, 1-36. https://www.jstor.org/stable/4030968.

Auryn, Mat. *Psychic Witch: A Metaphysical Guide to Meditation, Magick & Manifestation.* Woodbury: Llewellyn, 2020.

Babič, Saša. "Charms in Slovenian Culture," *Icantatio: An International Journal on Charms, Charmers, and Charming* 3, no. 3 (2013), 67-77, DOI:10.7592/Incantatio2013_Babic.

Berline, Adele and Marc Zvi Brettler, ed. *The Jewish Study Bible.* London: Oxford University Press, 2014.

Bremmer, Jan N. and Jan R. Veenstra, "The Metamorphosis of Magic from Late Antiquity to the Early Modern Period," University of Gronigen (2002), 232-266. https://research.rug.nl/en/publications/the-metamorphosis-of-magic-from-late-antiquity-to-the-early-moder.

Bristow, John T. *What Paul Really Said About Women: An Apostle's Liberating Views on Equality in Marriage, Leadership, and Love.* New York: HarperSanFrancisco, 1988.

Camp, Claudia V. "Woman Wisdom: Bible." *Shalvi/Hyman Encyclopedia of Jewish Women.* 31 December 1999. Jewish Women's Archive. https://jwa.org/encyclopedia/article/woman-wisdom-bible.

"Chaplet of Cyprian." Cyprian Orisons. Last accessed November 22, 2023. https://prayers.cypriani.org/chaplet/.

Cleveland, Christena. *God is a Black Woman.* USA: HarperOne, 2018.

Connolly, S. *The Complete Book of Demonolatry.* USA: DB Publishing, 2015.

Copeland, F.S. "Some Aspects of Slovene Folklore." *Folklore* 60, no. 2 (1949): 277-286. https://www.jstor.org/stable/1256715.

Conner, Robert. *Magic in Christianity from Jesus to the Gnostics.* Oxford & Robert Conner: Mandrake of Oxford, 2014.

Cunningham, Scott. *Encyclopedia of Magical Herbs.* Woodbury: Llewellyn Publications, 2013.

Davies, Rev. T. Witton. "Magic, Divination, & Demonology among the Semites," *The American Journal of Semitic Languages & Literature* 14, no 4 (1898): 241-251. https://www.jstor.org/stable/527968.

Duffy, Martin. *Anathema Maranatha: Christianity and the Imprecatory Arts.* USA: Three Hands Press, 2022.

Echols, Damien. *Angels and Archangels: A Magician's Guide.* Boulder: Sounds True, 2020.

Echols, Damien. *High Magick: A Guide to the Spiritual Practices That Saved My Life on Death Row.* Boulder: Sounds True, 2022.

Ehrman, Bart. *Misquoting Jesus: The Story Behind Who Changed the Bible and Why.* New York: HarperCollins, 2005.

Fahrun, Mary-Grace. *Italian Folk Magic: Rue's Kitchen Witchery.* Newburyport: Weiser Books, 2018.

Franklin, Anna. *The Hearth Witch's Year: Rituals, Recipes & Remedies Through the Seasons.* Woodbury: Llewellyn Publications, 2021.

Fox, Matthew. *Hildegard of Bingen: A Saint for Our Times: Unleashing Her Power in the 21st Century.* Vancouver: Namaste Publishing, 2012.

Gale, John, Michael Robson, and Georgia Rapsomatioti, *Insanity and Divinity: Studies in Psychosis and Spirituality*. Routledge, 2013.

Geller, Markham J. "Defining Magic in the Ancient World" in *Between the Worlds: Magic, Miracle, & Mysticism* (eds. Maeva, M., Y. Erolova, P. Stoyanova, M. Hristova, V. Ivanova) 2. Boulder: Paradigma, 2020. 16-24.

Guiley, Rosemary Ellen. *The Encyclopedia of Demons and Demonology.* New York: Checkmark Books, 2009.

Guiley, Rosemary Ellen. *Harper's Encyclopedia of Mystical and Paranormal Experience*. USA: HarperCollins, 1991.

Jacobi, Zo."Can You Even Be a Jewish Witch?" Jewitches (blog). Last accessed November 23, 2023. https://jewitches.com/blogs/blog/can-you-even-be-a-jewish-witch

Karlsson, Thomas. *Qabalah, Qliphoth, and Goetic Magic.* Jacksonville: Ajna Bound, 2017.

Karras, Ruth Mazo. "Pagan Survivals and Syncretism in the Conversion of Saxony." *The Catholic Historical Review* 72, no. 4 (1986): 553-572. https://www.jstor.org/stable/25022405.

Kivelson, Valerie A., and Christine D. Worobec. *Witchcraft in Russia and Ukraine: 1000-1900.* Ithaca: Cornell University Press, 2020.

Kobes du Mez, Kristin. *Jesus and John Wayne: How White Evangelicals Corrupted a Faith and Fractured a Nation.* USA: Liveright, 2020.

Kugel, James L. *The God of Old: Inside the Lost World of the Bible.* New York: The Free Press, 2003.

Levine, Amy-Jill and Marc Zvi Brettler, eds. *The Jewish Annotated New Testament.* London: Oxford University Press, 2017.

Matt, Daniel C. *The Essential Kabbalah: The Heart of Jewish Mysticism.* USA: HarperOne, 2009.

McHenry, Travis. *Angel Tarot.* USA: Rockpool Publishing, 2020.

Mencej, Mirjam. *Styrian Witches in European Perspective: Ethnographic Fieldwork.* London: Springer Nature, 2017.

Mlakar, Vlasta. *Sacred Plants in Folk Medicine & Rituals: Ethnobotany of Slovenia.* Translated by Filip H. Drnovšek Zorko. Markham, Ontario, Canada: The Raymond Aaron Group, 2020.

Moltmann, Jürgen. *The Crucified God.* Minneapolis: Fortress Press, 2015.

Murphy-Hiscock, Arin. *The House Witch: Your Complete Guide to Creating a Magical Space With Rituals and Spells for Hearth and Home.* Stoughton: Adams Media, 2018.

Owens, Yvonne. "The Saturnine History of Jews and Witches." *Preternature: Critical and Historical Studies on the Preternatural* 3, no. 1 (2014): 56-84. https://www.jstor.org/stable/10.5325/preternature.3.1.0056

Pamita, Madame. *Baba Yaga's Book of Slavic Witchcraft: Slavic Magic from the Witch of the Woods.* Woodbury: Llewellyn Publications, 2022.

Picknett, Lynn, and Clive Prince. *When God Had a Wife: The Fall and Rise of the Sacred Feminine in the Judeo-Christian Tradition.* USA: Bear & Company, 2019.

"Praying to the Saints." Catholic Answers. Accessed November 22, 2023. https://www.catholic.com/tract/praying-to-the-saints

Rushton, Peter. "A Note on the Survival of Popular Christian Magic." *Folklore* 91, no. 1 (1980): 115-118. https://www.jstor.org/stable/1259824.

Schramm, Steve. "What Actually Happened on the Cross? Exploring Atonement Theories." Premier UnBelievable. March 29, 2023. https://www.premierunbelievable.com/articles/what-actually-happened-on-the-cross-exploring-atonement-theories/15233.article

Simmons, Robert. *The Pocket Book of Stones, Revised Edition: Who They Are & What They Teach.* Rochester: Destiny Books, 2015.

Simpson, Jacqueline. "Margaret Murray: Who Believed Her, and Why?" *Folklore* 105 (1994): 89-96. https://www.jstor.org/stable/1260633.

Spencer-Arsenault, Michelle. "The (Re)Construction of a Female Icon." *Sociology of Religion* 61, no. 4 (2000): 479-483. https://www.jstor.org/stable/3712533.

Stanmore, Tabitha. "The Spellbinding History of Cheese and Witch-craft," The Conversation, January 22, 2021, https://theconversatio n.com/the-spellbinding-history-of-cheese-and-witchcraft-153221.

Stavish, Mark. *Egregores: The Occult Entities that Watch Over Human Destiny.* Rochester: Inner Traditions, 2018.

"St. Maria Faustina Kowalska." The Divine Mercy. https://www.thedi vinemercy.org/message/stfaustina/graces

Throop, Prischilla (translator). *Hildegard von Bingen's Physica: The Complete English Translation of Her Classic Work on Health and Healing.* Rochester: Healing Arts Press, 1998.

Thurman, Howard. *Jesus and the Disinherited.* USA: Beacon Press, 1996.

Trattner, Walter I. "God and Expansion in Elizabethan England: John Dee, 1527-1583." *Journal on the History of Ideas* 25, no. 1 (1964), 17-34. https://www.jstor.org/stable/2708083.

Vance, Laura. *Women in New Religions.* New York: New York University Press, 2015.

van Oort, Johannes. "The Holy Spirit as feminine: Early Christian testimonies and their interpretation." *HTS Theological Studies* 72, no 1 (2016), 1-6. https://dx.doi.org/10.4102/hts.v72i1.3225.

Vermes, Geza. "Jewish Miracle Workers and Magic in the Late Second Temple Period," ed. Gideon Bohak, in *Jewish Annotated New Testament,* eds. Amy-Jill Levine and Marc Zvi Brettler. London: Oxford University Press, 2017. 680-682.

Vinci, Leo. *Gmicalzoma! An Enochian Dictionary.* Regency Press, 2006.

Ward, Colleen A. and Michael H. Beaubrun, "Psychodynamics of Demon Possession," *Journal for the Scientific Study of Religion* 19, no. 2 (1980), 206. https://www.jstor.org/stable/1386254.

Watterson, Meggan. *Mary Magdalene Revealed: The First Apostle, Her Feminist Gospel & the Christianity We Haven't Tried Yet.* USA: Hay House, Inc., 2021.

Webster, Jane. "Necessary Comparisons: A Post-Colonial Approach to Religious Syncretism in the Roman Provinces." *World Archaeology* 28, no. 3 (1997): 324-388. https://www.jstor.org/stable/125022.

Wilken, Robert Louis. *The Christians as the Romans Saw Them.* USA: Yale University Press, 2013.

Young, Francis. "The Woman who Inspired Wicca." First Things. August 25, 2020, https://www.firstthings.com/web-exclusives/2020/08/the-woman-who-inspired-wicca.

Zak, Zuza. *Slavic Kitchen Alchemy: Nourishing Herbal Remedies, Magical Recipes & Folk Wisdom.* London: Watkins Media Limited, 2023.

Suggested Further Reading:

Ballard, H. Byron. *Roots, Branches, & Spirits: The Folkways & Witchery of Appalachia.* Woodbury: Llewellyn, 2021.

Richards, Jake. *Backwoods Witchcraft: Conjure & Folk Magic from Appalachia.* USA: Weiser Books, 2019.

Weston, Brandon. *Ozark Folk Magic: Plants, Prayers & Healing.* Woodbury: Llewellyn, 2021.

Wiggiton, Eliot and the Foxfire Fund. *The Foxfire Books* (1 - 17). USA: Anchor Publishing.

Bonus Material

If you'd like to get started creating your own spells and moon rituals, we've got some extras for you! Scan this QR code to get to Sara's website, where you can download printable spell sheet templates and moon ritual templates to make your spell creation that much easier. (Or edit them on your computer and keep them for a digital grimoire!)

QR Code not working? No problem: visit us here at:
https://www.sararaztresen.com/christian-witch-bonus-content